China's Anti-monopoly Law in the Digital Era

The book aims to depict the whole picture of China's Anti-Monopoly Law (AML) in the digital sector and reveals the three key factors that shape AML enforcement.

The author introduces the legal revolution and a major enforcement campaign in the digital sector. She focuses on three typical monopolistic behaviours—abuse of dominant position, merger control, and monopoly agreements. High-profile cases—such as administrative penalties against Alibaba and Tencent and private lawsuits against Apple and Didi Chuxing—are discussed in detail. She also identifies three underlying factors that have influenced AML enforcement reform: the political factor, the legal factor, and the academic factor. Finally, the book raises open questions and challenges that are relevant not only to China but to a wide range of jurisdictions.

The book will appeal to competition law (antitrust) and Chinese law academics, practitioners, and officials, as well as general readers interested in the subject.

Jingmeng Cai is Associate Professor of Beijing University of Chemical Technology. She holds doctorate and master's degrees in law from Chicago-Kent College of Law. Her research and teaching interest is primarily in competition law. She has published dozens of articles related to competition law in renowned international and Chinese law journals, and she has translated academic articles and books from English to Chinese.

China's Anti-monopoly Law in the Digital Era

How China Tames the Digital Behemoth

Jingmeng Cai

Routledge
Taylor & Francis Group
LONDON AND NEW YORK

First published 2026
by Routledge
4 Park Square, Milton Park, Abingdon, Oxon OX14 4RN

and by Routledge
605 Third Avenue, New York, NY 10158

Routledge is an imprint of the Taylor & Francis Group, an informa business

British Library Cataloguing in Publication Data
A catalogue record for this book is available from the British Library

Library of Congress Cataloging-in-Publication Data
Names: Cai, Jingmeng, 1983– author.
Title: China's anti-monopoly law in the digital era : how China tames the digital behemoth / Jingmeng Cai.
Description: Abingdon, Oxon [UK] ; New York, NY : Routledge, 2025. | Includes bibliographical references and index.
Identifiers: LCCN 2025014569 (print) | LCCN 2025014570 (ebook) | ISBN 9781041103097 (hardback) | ISBN 9781041103158 (paperback) | ISBN 9781003654452 (ebook)
Subjects: LCSH: Antitrust law—China. | Restraint of trade—China. | Competition, Unfair—China. | Internet marketing—Law and legislation—China. | Electronic commerce—Law and legislation—China. | Information storage and retrieval systems—Antitrust law.
Classification: LCC KNQ3242 .C35 2025 (print) | LCC KNQ3242 (ebook) | DDC 343.5107/2—dc23/eng/20250331
LC record available at https://lccn.loc.gov/2025014569
LC ebook record available at https://lccn.loc.gov/2025014570

ISBN: 978-1-041-10309-7 (hbk)
ISBN: 978-1-041-10315-8 (pbk)
ISBN: 978-1-003-65445-2 (ebk)

DOI: 10.4324/ 9781003654452

Typeset in Times New Roman
by Apex CoVantage, LLC

Contents

Figures

Tables

Preface

When I was on the verge of finishing the manuscript of this book, two influential events took place just as China was ushering in the Year of the Snake.

First, a Chinese startup in artificial intelligence (AI) rocked the entire industry. DeepSeek, launched before the Chinese New Year, made a splash in the AI sector as big as the blue whale depicted in its icon. DeepSeek signals a seismic shift in the entire industry, achieving a stunning degree of efficiency with significantly fewer resources and much less investment. DeepSeek's shocking achievement has had a ripple effect, driving AI developers and cloud service producers into a frenzy, sending chipmakers' stock prices plummeting and igniting political tensions on the other side of the Pacific Ocean.

The second event was Chinese blockbuster *Ne Zha 2*, which has already become China's highest-grossing film and is now gearing up for an international rollout. Jiaozi, the director of the animated series, embodies an inspirational story of a small-town rebel creating a cinematic phenomenon. After giving up the idea of becoming a pharmacist from China's prestigious medical school, Jiaozi was unemployed and lived off his mother's meagre monthly pension of RMB 1,000 for over three years. That was a time when he could hardly have imagined his success today, not to mention the numerous box office records his film would make.

How I felt when I set out to write a book about China's anti-monopoly enforcement in the digital sector a year ago is similar to how I feel reading these two pieces of news today. We stand at a crucial cross-road that signals a major change in our era. I know everything will be different, but I am not sure when those changes will occur or what they will consist of.

The delayed and inaccurate enforcement of the anti-monopoly law in the market often leaves me frustrated and confused. I was convinced by the theory of structuralist economics developed by the Harvard School and concerned that 'super platforms' like Alibaba and JD.com were abusing their market power by forcing retailers to sell goods exclusively on their e-commerce platforms. But then small e-commerce platform Pin Duoduo (also known as Temu) slipped past the defense of its mighty rivals' and swiftly became China's second-largest e-commerce platform through a savvy strategy combining social features, gamification, and low prices for users.

When China's competition authority ordered platforms to terminate all exclusive music copyright licensing (with certain exceptions), I had no doubts about the correctness of that decision and believed the ban would help revitalise innovation in the music market since the majority of those exclusive licenses were held by a handful of super platforms, such as Tencent. However, TikTok (known as 'Douyin' in Chinese mainland), with seemingly no interest in the music copyright market, has directly changed the pattern of competition and the music landscape in an unanticipated way. The short-form videos on TikTok popularise previously unnoticed songs, thrusting them into the limelight in a very short period thanks to viral trends and user-generated content on this social media platform. The 'Doulive sofa concert', popular when people stayed at home during the COVID-19 pandemic, shifted even more data traffic away from major music platforms and significantly decreased consumers' willingness to pay for music streaming services. Since then, I have started to reconsider the rationale of the competition authority's order to terminate exclusive copyright licenses. If competition has not in fact been suffocated, did the competition authority unduly interfere in the market, considering that granting an exclusive license is a legal right enjoyed by copyright holders?

As this suggests, traditional antitrust theories have been repeatedly challenged by surprising incidents in the digital sector. Instances of David toppling Goliath abound, just as we have seen with DeepSeek. That was my initial catalyst for writing this book. China, despite being a fledgling antitrust jurisdiction, has one of the world's most energetic and rapidly developing digital markets. Thus, it can provide abundant cases and experimental data for testing and refining antitrust theories. I was inspired to record developments in China's digital sector and the response by anti-monopoly law enforcement since English literature on this topic is very limited compared to abundant research and discussion on the Western market.

The discussion in this book is centred on three major factors: policy, law, and the academics. These factors interact and constrain each other, determining the contours and peculiarities of China's anti-monopoly enforcement in the digital sector. At the same time, they jointly pose predicaments and challenges for lawmakers and regulators. It is true that anti-monopoly enforcement has never been a purely legal issue, but in this book I stress China's efforts and determination to make anti-monopoly enforcement more legalised and professional. There are some points in this book where I raise questions without providing definitive solutions, but given the cutting-edge nature of the subject matter and the constraints of length, I believe readers will nevertheless find this book valuable and engaging, particularly considering its comprehensive coverage and up-to-date information.

Certain portions are excerpted from my previous work. More specifically, Section 4.1.2.1 'Before the AML's amendment in 2022' partly draws, with revisions, on my published article 'Public Antitrust Enforcement of Resale Price Maintenance in China: A Crusade or Discrimination?' (1 Brook J. Int'l l. 2016) and 'Private Antitrust Enforcement of Resale Price Maintenance in China: What Lessons Can China Learn from the United States?' (2 Asian-Pac. L. & Pol'y J. 2017 1). Section 3.2.1.1 'Problems arising from the turnover-based threshold' is partly excerpted, with revisions, from my published article 'The Sharing Economy and China's Antimonopoly Law: from The Didi Case to Regulatory Challenges' (28 Asia Pacific Law Review 2020 159).

In the process of writing this book, I have been fortunate to receive tremendous support and assistance from many friends. First and foremost, I owe immense gratitude to my doctoral advisor, David J. Gerber, who inspired me to pursue an academic career in competition law. His unwavering encouragement and the knowledge he imparted reinforced my commitment to finishing this book. Also, I would like to express my gratitude and admiration to Xiaoye Wang. As a prestigious female scholar, she has always been my role model and inspired me to pursue my career. Her extensive academic publications have substantially informed my own writing. I am grateful to Allison Jones, who kindly invited me to King's College London to engage in a comparative study of competition law in the European Union and China. I hope a trip to London materialises in the near future. My thanks also go to Xu Liu, whose comments and insights have been enlightening. I was fortunate to have the meticulous proofreading of my postgraduate students Penghui Cui, Yixia Chen, and Yue Chen. I would like to thank David Carruth for polishing up my phrasing.

In addition, I owe thanks to my family. My husband Yang Li, an M&A lawyer, always provides insightful comments from a practical perspective as well as unconditional support, empowering me to pursue the career I love. My deepest thanks go to my mom, who has always believed her daughter can achieve anything she sets her mind to. The basement she tidied up served as a quiet place for writing when my kids were on their summer and winter breaks. I thank my two boys, Nathan and Ethan, for their complete cooperation. Had they not let me focus on my writing, I would never have been able to finish this book.

Last but not least, I would like to thank the editorial assistant Zixu Fan at Routledge Press, whose extreme patience and tireless guidance made it possible for this book to be published.

This evening, my eldest boy was drawing a picture of Ne Zha for his art homework. This figure from Chinese mythology, at least as depicted by my son, has a childlike round face with two fiery unkempt buns coiled high on either side of his head, floating barefoot in mid-air, radiating formidable power with fluttering sashes and a flame-tipped spear. I was suddenly touched. This image of Ne Zha is so much like China's digital market: highly energetic, powerful, and untamed. As an antitrust scholar, perhaps I may now fathom the struggle of Ne Zha's father to keep his son from succumbing to the demonic path and ensure he exerted his power righteously.

Suddenly, my son asked me, 'Mom, do you know which line in the film about Ne Zha I like the most?'

'The question the Dragon King asked Ne Zha?' I asked.

'Yes! The Dragon King asked Ne Zha, "Do you still want to change the world?" Ne Zhe said, "I want to give it a try." That's cool!' he replied.

February 2025
Beijing

1 China's anti-monopoly enforcement revolution in the digital economy

1.1 Anti-monopoly enforcement in the digital era: China's stance and the purpose of this book

In 2025 and the coming years, the world economy faces big challenges. Rampant regional protectionism, escalated trade sanctions, and limitations on cross-border investments present great difficulties for the global economic recovery. In this context, the digital economy becomes 'a key force for relocating global resources, restructuring the global market, and changing the global competition pattern', as China's President Xi Jinping stated in a policy paper.[1] In recent years, competition authorities in major countries have launched a series of aggressive investigations and lawsuits against giant platforms like Google, Amazon, Facebook, and Apple. A variety of leading economists, expert panels, and practitioners worldwide have expressed deep concerns about anti-monopoly enforcement in the digital sector.

China—whose digital economy was worth about USD 7.7 trillion in 2023, ranking second in the world and accounting for 42.8% of China's GDP—has also joined in this global antitrust crusade. Although China's AML[2] is still a fledgling regime, China's regulators' attitudes and actions cannot be overlooked, considering both the size of the Chinese market and the impact of the digital companies operating therein.

But despite increasing interest in China's anti-monopoly enforcement and its digital market, there is very limited English literature on the topic, especially compared to the abundance of academic research and practitioners' discussion about

1 Xinhua News Agency (新华社), "Xi Jing Ping Zai Zhonggong Zhongyang Zhengzhi Ju Di Sanshi Si Ci Jiti Xuexi Shi Qiangdiao Bawo Shuzi Jingji Fazhan Qushi He Guilv Tuidong Woguo Shuzi Jingji Jiankang Fazhan" (习近平在中共中央政治局第三十四次集体学习时强调 把握数字经济发展趋势和规律 推动我国数字经济健康发展) [Xi Jinping Emphasized the Need to Grasp the Trend and Laws of Digital Economic Development and Promote Its Healthy Development in China During the 34th Collective Study Session of the Political Bureau of the CPC Central Committee], *xinhua net*, October 19, 2021, http://www.qstheory.cn/yaowen/2021-10/19/c_1127974061.htm

2 The term that is used to refer to the area of 'anti-monopoly law' varies among different countries. In the United States, this area of law is referred to as 'antitrust law'. In China, the term used is 'anti-monopoly law'. In the European Union, the term is 'competition law'. In this book all three terms are used interchangeably to refer to a set of laws that aim to fight restraints on competition in the marketplace.

DOI: 10.4324/ 9781003654452-1

Western markets. In addition, due to major adjustments in China's competition policy toward the digital economy over the past three years and rapid updates and substantial changes in legislation and enforcement, some information in the existing literature is no longer accurate anymore.

Outsiders' misunderstanding and misrepresentation of the AML largely arise from such incomplete and inaccurate information. For instance, although China's competition authorities have reiterated that the AML applies equally to domestic and foreign companies, China has often been criticised for using the AML as a tool to protect domestic companies. Another criticism is that it is very rare for the competition authorities' decisions to be challenged. Investigated companies seldom defend themselves against the competition authorities' accusations either, even when they face a formidable penalty. That unusual level of cooperation and obedience has often surprised and even bewildered overseas observers. The elusive presence of non-legal considerations and competition authorities' vast discretionary power over digital companies have often frustrated international antitrust intellectuals and business operators. While there may be truth to these observations to some extent, they are misleading because they only tell part of the story. As the saying goes, 'Half the truth is often a whole lie'. In this book, I intend to tell the whole story about AML enforcement in the digital sector and reveal the underlying factors shaping those phenomena.

The current reform of anti-monopoly enforcement in the digital sector signals China's determination to hold enforcement within the legal framework. Major scholars and legislators on the Chinese mainland have advocated to improve AML enforcement by making it more legalised and professional. The newly amended AML and the supporting regulations and guidelines also reflect such efforts. Moreover, the inherent drive of digital platforms to expand their business across national borders became an endogenous force that requires curbing the competition authorities' discretion by law. As China's digital economy underwent exponential growth over the past years, investigations and other steps taken by China's competition authorities have attracted ever-increasing attention from the global antitrust community. Western regulators' jittery concern, international intellectuals' criticism, and the potential threat of escalated trade sanctions become an exogenous force pushing AML enforcement to be more legalised and normalised. Therefore, China's anti-monopoly enforcement is not a tool to purely achieve bureaucratic missions, and the competition authorities would not abuse their discretionary power to force foreign companies to yield to their demands or retaliate against those that decline to cooperate, which may run contrary to the image held by some observers overseas.

The much criticised and imperfect facets of anti-monopoly enforcement are due to two major reasons. First, it is widely accepted by the global antitrust community that modern antitrust analysis is firmly grounded in economics. As a fledging antitrust jurisdiction, however, China's competition authorities, especially those at local level, have not yet mastered the methods of economic analysis needed to deal with traditional antitrust issues, but have to face new problems arising from the burgeoning digital economy. Although the reasoning of administrative decisions and judgements has become more sophisticated in recent years, China's anti-monopoly enforcement still lags behind that of antitrust jurisdictions with abundant experience. Besides, anti-monopoly issues arising from the digital market have proven intractable even for advanced antitrust regimes. Thus, some of the decisions of China's competition authorities that have been criticised for lacking sufficient details, solid reasoning, and convincing analysis are largely the result of decision makers' inadequate knowledge of antitrust law and economics and their limited experience with enforcement in the digital sector, rather than their arrogance or arbitrariness.

Second, AML enforcement reform is a work in progress and may not go as smoothly and perfectly as expected. The legislative texts and supporting regulations deliberately leave room for future improvements to suit rapid changes in the digital market and global trade. But that also leaves room for competition authorities to abuse their discretionary power (whether purposefully or unintentionally). In addition, controversies about the AML's core goals and the viability of certain legal mechanisms (like 'gatekeeper' and 'safe harbour') also leave uncertainties about the ultimate effects of reform. Furthermore, it is undeniable that political factors are important in the field of anti-monopoly enforcement, especially given the critical role of the digital economy in the national development strategy.

So while multiple factors are shaping AML enforcement in the digital era, they break down into three major factors: national policy from the central leadership sets the tone for anti-monopoly enforcement (the policy factor); there is a series of legislative efforts to establish a law-based regulatory regime (the legal factor); and academic research and influential scholarship substantially shape the anti-monopoly regime (the academic factor). These three intertangled factors interact to determine the contours and peculiarities of China's AML enforcement in the digital market. At the same time, they jointly pose dilemmas and challenges to China's anti-monopoly regulators. This book's discussion will pivot on these three factors. We will see how the central government's policies drive legislation and enforcement, how various enforcers made divergent decisions that in turn ignite furious debate in academic community and push lawmakers to make clarifications and revisions, and how scholars with various educational backgrounds affect legislation and enforcement and cause problems arising from anti-monopoly law's transplantation and localisation.

This book first sketches an outline of the AML to provide readers with some background. Then it introduces the legal revolution and a major enforcement campaign in the digital field after a long period of relatively lax regulation (Chapter 1). Chapter 2 discusses AML enforcement against abuse of dominant market position. This is the area where the AML has been applied most vigorously, where high-profile cases have occurred and well-known high-tech giants have been exposed to media attention and public concern. Chapter 3 addresses merger controls in the digital sector. Merger controls are a major change in the AML 2022's amendment, reflecting lawmakers' determination to hold enforcement power within the legal framework and improve the efficiency of the digital economy. This section also addresses cases that have had a major influence. Chapter 4 discusses monopoly agreements under the AML, which is one of most controversial topics in the Chinese antitrust community. That typically reflects confusion and uncertainty due to legal transplantation. Chapter 5 addresses two unsolved issues on the future research agenda for China's lawmakers, competition authorities, and academics, covering the conflicts within the competition law regime and the core goal (or value) of the AML. Although I cannot offer satisfactory solutions for these two issues now, I do propose solutions that may help China as well as other antitrust jurisdictions explore sound solutions in future.

1.2 Background of China's AML

1.2.1 The AML's gestation

As early as 1987, the State Council proposed enacting a national law to protect competition and then drafted the *Regulations for Prohibiting Monopoly and Unfair Competition*, but that regulation was never passed or enacted. In Chinese legal system, the concept of competition law is consisted of two laws: the AML and the Anti-unfair Competition Law. Correspondingly, regulations include ones against monopoly behaviours and unfair competition behaviours. However, at that time, issuing a law perceived to be 'against' big enterprises inevitably left some people jittery, especially industrial regulators, since so-called large-scale companies were enterprises owned by the central government or local governments (collectively referred to as 'state-owned enterprises' or 'SOEs'). Dissenting voices were too loud, so the idea of promulgating an anti-monopoly law was put on hold. Nevertheless, free competition after China's reform and opening up in 1978 was accompanied by various kinds of dishonest behaviour and market chaos, creating an urgent need for a law to curb such behaviours. Therefore, the Anti-Unfair Competition Law (AUCL),[3] which faced less pressure from industrial regulators, was enacted as a spearhead. Today, Chinese scholars are accustomed to referring to the AML and the AUCL together as the 'Competition Law', even though there is no law by that name in China's legal system. That also could explain why the early AUCL covered some regulations against monopoly behaviours, such as tying, and anti-competitive behaviours that enterprises with dominant market positions require their trading partners to exclusively deal with specified business operators. The inclusion of such regulations may have been an outflanking tactic adopted by drafters who advocated making an anti-monopoly law.

In the 1990s, the market-oriented economy was the breeding ground for the emergence of the anti-monopoly law. The field of China was too barren to 'grow' such a law until the Constitution was amended in 1993, stipulating that 'the State carries out the socialist market-oriented economy'.[4] Since in 1994 drafting and enacting a law to curb monopoly and anti-competitive behaviour was put on the

3 Anti-Unfair Competition Law of the People's Republic of China (promulgated by the Standing Committee of the National People's Congress, September 2, 1993, effective December 1, 1993, amended November 4, 2017 and April 23, 2019), CLI.1.331488(EN) (Lawinfochina).

4 Constitution of the People's Republic of China (1993 Amendment) (promulgated by the National People's Congress on September 20, 1954, amended March 29, 1993), CLI.1.48115(EN) (Lawinfochina), Art. 15.

agenda, the AML's gestation took 14 years. The AML was finally promulgated on 30 August 2007 and took effect on 1 August 2008.

Both endogenous and exogenous factors together worked to push the AML's enactment. The market-oriented economy has been developing for almost 30 years in China, during which time various behaviours have arisen that restrict and injure competition. Additionally, along with China's reform and opening up, a number of international companies with advanced technology and deep pockets have gradually gained dominant market positions and abused their dominance in many markets.[5] More importantly, Chinese enterprises, and especially SOEs, urgently needed to eliminate obstacles resulting from increasingly intense competition in both domestic and global markets. Scholars who were seeking to introduce a competition mechanism in SOEs, reduce government' interference, break down local protectionism, and develop a unified, open, and competitive national market prevailed.[6] Those are the endogenous factors that inspired China to have an anti-monopoly law. After China joined the World Trade Organization (WTO) in 2001, enacting a series of laws, including the AML, was part of its commitments for trade liberalisation.[7] Moreover, major antitrust jurisdictions (especially the United States and the European Union) and international organisations such as the Organisation for Economic Co-operation and Development (OECD) exerted a great deal of pressure and provided consultant opinions to prompt China to enact an anti-monopoly law. Those are the exogenous factors.

1.2.2 Administration-led enforcement approach

In the AML drafting process, the AML enforcement authority remained contentious. Some proposed adopting a court-centred enforcement approach, following the US model.[8] Professor Xiaoye Wang, a leading Chinese anti-monopoly scholar as well as the legal expert for the AML drafting, enumerated the following reasons why an administration-led enforcement approach would be the best choice for China: (1) Traditionally, Chinese governments have shouldered the responsibility of regulating the economy; (2) before the AML's enactment, some administrative bodies (such as the State Administration of Industry and Commerce) had already investigated and regulated certain anti-competitive behaviours and obtained enforcement experience under laws like the AUCL and the Price Law; (3) the independence of

5 Zhenzhen Zhong (钟真真), "Fanlongduan Fa Caoan Chutai De Beijing" (反垄断法草案出台的背景) [Background of the Draft Anti-Monopoly Law], *npc.gov.cn*, July 7, 2006, http://www.npc.gov.cn/npc//c2/c189/c221/201905/t20190524_32399.html

6 Xiaoye Wang (王晓晔), "Rushi Yu Zhongguo Fanlongduan Fa De Zhiding" (入世与中国反垄断法的制定) [China Joining the WTO and Drafting the Antimonopoly Law], *Chinese Journal of Law* 2 (2003): 122, 132–33.

7 *Ibid.*

8 Xiaoye Wang (王晓晔), "Guanyu Woguo Fanlongduan Zhifa Jigou De Jige Wenti" (关于我国反垄断执法机构的几个问题) [Several Issues Regarding China's Anti-Monopoly Law Enforcement Agencies], *Dongyue Tribune* 28 (2007): 30, 32.

judicial review still needs to be improved; and (4) general courts cannot assume the complicated economic analysis normally required in an anti-monopoly case.[9] From my point of view, the fact that the AML regime was mainly modelled on EU competition law would be another important reason for choosing the administration-led enforcement approach. In conclusion, the supporters of administrative agencies prevailed.

However, the question of which agency would enjoy that authority became another focus of debate. The contest for enforcement authority concerned three major national administrative ministries: the Ministry of Commerce (MOFCOM), the National Development and Reform Commission (NDRC), and the State Administration for Industry and Commerce (SAIC). The earliest proposed draft of AML was submitted to the State Council for review by MOFCOM and SAIC in 1994. In 2004, MOFCOM set up an office to take charge of anti-monopoly investigations and actively launched a series of investigations against regional protections, revealing its ambition to obtain sole enforcement authority.[10] The NDRC, regarded as China's most powerful bureaucratic body, joined that contest in 2003, by issuing the *Interim Regulation for Prohibiting Price Monopoly Behaviours* to endow itself with authority in that area.[11]

Although major scholars strongly advocated the establishment of a unified and independent AML authority,[12] a tripartite approach to enforcement was inevitably adopted. Legal experts also suggested dividing enforcement power by industry,[13] but power was divided according to the three agencies' pre-existing authority. As a result, the NDRC and the SAIC were responsible for investigating monopoly agreements, abuse of dominant market positions, and abuse of administrative power.[14] The boundary between the two agencies' power was whether the conduct under

9 *Ibid.*, at 33.

10 Yiyu Li (李亦儒), "20 Nian Li Yibu Fa, 'Fanlongduan Fa' De Qianshi Jinsheng" (20年立一部法，《反垄断法》的前世今生) [Enacting a Law for 20 Years, the Past and Present Life of the Anti-Monopoly Law], *new.qq.com*, January 5, 2021, https://new.qq.com/rain/a/20210105A0F5Z300

11 Interim Provisions on Preventing the Acts of Price Monopoly (promulgated by National Development & Reform Commission, June 18, 2003, effective November 1, 2003, expired February 1, 2011), CLI.4.47253(EN) (lawinfochina).

12 Wang, note 8, at 36–39; see also Lujia Xu (许鹭嘉), "Woguo Fanlongduan Zhifa Jigou Gexin Tanxi" (我国反垄断执法机构革新探析) [China's Innovative Reform of Anti-Monopoly Enforcement Authority], *Academic Exploration* 3 (2013): 84, 84–85; see also Peizhi Zhu, Hao Chen (朱沛智，陈浩), "Guanyu Woguo Fanlongduan Zhifa Jigou Shezhi Moshi De Sikao" (关于我国反垄断执法机构设置模式的思考) [The Thinking About the Setting Mode of Anti-Monopoly Law Enforcement Agency], *Journal of Tianjin Normal University (Social Sciences)* 212 (2010): 7, 9.

13 Wang, note 8, at 36.

14 See "Guojia Gongshang Xingzheng Guangli Zongju Zhuyao Zhize Neishe Jigou He Renyuan Bianzhi Guiding" (国家工商行政管理总局主要职责内设机构和人员编制规定) [Regulations of the SAIC Major Duties, Internal Institutions and Personnel], (issued July 11, 2008), sec. II, Art. 6, CLI.2.107034 (Lawinfochina) [Hereinafter Regulations of the SAIC]; see also Notice of the General Office of the State Council on Issuing the Provisions on the Main Functions, Internal Bodies and Staffing of the National Development and Reform Commission (issued July 15, 2008), CLI.2.108511(EN) (Lawinfochina), sec. III, Art. 23 [Hereinafter Regulations of the NDRC].

investigation was price-related or not. The MOFCOM was responsible for reviewing mergers and international cooperation related to competition laws.[15] Such divisions of power unavoidably led to both conflicts or gaps in law enforcement. For example, when a dominant company abuses its market power, that usually takes various forms (such as setting prices, dividing geographic markets and consumers, and tying), representing a mixture of price and non-price-related measures. Thus, the tripartite power-sharing arrangement that resulted was a compromise due to pressure from various parties. No wonder Professor Wang once admitted in an interview that the AML drafting process was an arduous battle.[16] That tripartite system remained unchanged until 2018, when the State Council launched institutional reform to inaugurate a unified competitive authority—the State Administration for Market Regulation (SAMR).

Actually, The AML sets up a two-tiered administrative structure to ensure enforcement of the law. The top tier is the Antimonopoly Commission of the State Council ('Antimonopoly Commission'), which is responsible for formulating policies and guidelines, coordinating high-level strategies, and supervising overall enforcement; managing the three agencies' relations is especially important here. After 2018, the SAMR replaced the three agencies to exclusively enforce the AML, but the Antimonopoly Commission was also retained as the top tier to organise, coordinate, and guide nationwide anti-monopoly enforcement.[17] On November 2021, the National Antimonopoly Bureau (NAB) was inaugurated, being upgraded from a SAMR internal division to a vice-ministerial-level department.[18] That demonstrates Beijing's determination to further strengthen anti-monopoly supervision in China.

The SAMR can authorise local agencies at the provincial level (local agencies in provinces, autonomous regions, and municipalities directly under the central government, collectively referred to as 'provincial agencies') to enforce the AML within their respective administrative region.[19] Other than merger reviews, the SAMR investigates monopoly cases directly when (1) the cases are inter-provincial

15 "Shangwubu Zhuyao Zhize Neishe Jigou He Renyuan Bianzhi Guiding" (商务部主要职责内设机构和人员编制规定) [Regulations of the MOFCOM's Major Duties, Internal Institutions and Personnel], (issued July 11, 2008), CLI.2.175409 (Lawinfochina), sec. III, Art. 11.

16 Chao Chen (陈超), "'Fanlongduan Fa' Qicao Zhe: Lifa Guocheng Jiushi Yichang Douzheng" (《反垄断法》起草者：立法过程就是一场斗争) [The Drafter of the Anti-Monopoly Law: The Legislative Process is a Struggle], *huanqiu.com*, October 27, 2014, https://china.huanqiu.com/article/9CaKrnJFJEr

17 Anti-Monopoly Law of the People's Republic of China (promulgated by the Standing Committee of the Tenth National People's Congress on August 30, 2007, amended July 24, 2022), Art. 12 [Hereinafter AML (2022)].

18 "China Establishes Anti-Monopoly Bureau to Secure Fair Competition," *english.www.gov.cn*, November 19, 2021, https://english.www.gov.cn/statecouncil/wangyong/202111/19/content_WS61973e4cc6d0df57f98e52d9.html

19 SAMR, Notice of the State Administration for Market Regulation on the Empowerment of Anti-monopoly Law Enforcement (issued December 28, 2018, effective December 28, 2018), No. 265 [2018] of the SAMR, CLI.4.328320(EN) (Lawinfochina).

in nature or involve provincial governments abusing administrative power, (2) the cases are complicated or influential, or (3) the matter in question needs to be regulated by the SAMR at its own discretion.[20] As to merger reviews, in July 2022, SAMR entrusted five provincial-level local agencies as pilot agencies to review nationwide merger cases[21] to alleviate its workload. The pilot period is from 1 August 2022 to 31 July 2025.

1.2.3 Obstruction from industrial policy: a subtle and complicated relationship

When the AML was being drafted, the sharpest conflict arose between the drafters and industrial regulators over contradictions between competition policy and industrial policy. That is not uncommon in a country undergoing an economic transition.

When the Standing Committee of the National People's Congress (NPC) reviewed one draft version of the AML in 2006, Article 44 authorised industrial regulators to investigate and deal with monopoly behaviours in regulated industries.[22] For a long period of time, China had heavily relied on industrial policy to develop and regulate the economy. Industrial regulators used to hold immense authority for regulating enterprises and the market, so they were naturally defensive and disgruntled to think that the forthcoming AML would put a finger in their pie. They pushed to insert the phrase 'the State strengthens and improves macro-control of the economy' into the AML to underline the significance of industrial policy.[23]

The tug of war between the AML drafters and industrial regulators lasted throughout the drafting period, but the AML drafters obtained a transitory victory. The final version of the AML, which was issued on 30 August 2007 (effective on 1 August 2008) omitted Article 44. Thus, the authority for enforcing the AML in regulated industries belonged to the competition authorities, rather than being retained by industrial regulators. Moreover, in the final version, the drafters revised 'the State strengthens and improves macro-control of economy' to 'the State sets and implements competition rules suitable for the socialist market-oriented economy, improves macro-control of the economy, and establishes a united, open, competitive, and well-ordered market system' (Article 4). That weakened industrial policy's control of macro-regulation of the economy and paved the way for enforcing the AML in regulated industries in the future.

20 *Ibid.*

21 SAMR, "Shichang Jianguan Zongju Guanyu Shidian Weituo Kaizhan Bufen Jingyingzhe Jizhong Anjian Fanlongduan Shencha De Gonggao" (市场监管总局关于试点委托开展部分经营者集中案件反垄断审查的公告) [Announcement of Trial to Entrust Pilot Agencies to Review Some Merger Cases], *samr.gov.cn*, July 15, 2022, https://www.samr.gov.cn/fldes/sjdt/tpxw/art/2023/art_f239901206cf43c08c649db06578fba4.html

22 Qing Li (李青), *Zhongguo Fanlongduan Shier Nian: Huigu Yu Zhanwang* (中国反垄断十二年：回顾与展望) [*Twelve Years of Anti-Monopoly in China: Review and Prospect*] (CITIC Press Group, 2020), 52–53.

23 *Ibid.*, at 80–81.

Article 7 of the AML (2008),[24] however, buried a seed of conflict and ambiguity when enforcing the AML in regulated industries. The investigation driven by the NDRC on two state-owned telecoms—China Unicom and China Telecom—in the telecom industry was a striking example of that latent conflict.

Before the SAMR was inaugurated in 2018, the authority for AML enforcement was shared by three pre-existing administrative organs: the NDRC and MOFCOM, both ministerial-level departments of the State Council, and the SAIC, a ministerial-level agency under the State Council. Their jurisdiction was roughly divided according to the category of behaviours being investigated, as stated earlier. Normally, they have a similar administrative status to that of industrial regulators in China's government system.

On 9 November 2011, China Central Television (CCTV), China's state television broadcaster, interviewed an official who disclosed that the NDRC was investigating China Unicom and China Telecom.[25] That was the first time the AML had challenged SOEs in the telecom industry. That news report made a big splash in public. Two days later, the *People's Post and Telecommunication*, a newspaper affiliated with the Ministry of Industry and Information Technology (MIIT), the telecom industrial regulator, fought back by publishing an article with the uncommonly aggressive title 'Confusing and Misleading the Public: Refuting CCTV's Report Accusing China Unicom and China Telecom of a Price Monopoly'.[26] That report blamed the CCTV's report for raising monopoly accusations without solid evidence and knowing little about the telecom market. On 14 November, *People's Daily*, the official newspaper of the Central Committee of the Communist Party of China, joined the media fray. The battle centred on three major issues: Did China Unicom and China Telecom really enjoy monopoly power? Was it a violation of professional ethics for the media to disclose the investigation before the NDRC made a decision? And what was the connection to consumer welfare?[27] The anti-monopoly probe became a media extravaganza that grabbed public attention.

24 Article 7 of AML (2008): 'In industries concerning the lifeline of national economy and national security where state-owned economy has a controlling status, or in industries where companies enjoy franchise or monopoly power in accordance with the law, the State shall protect their lawful business operations, regulate and control their behaviors, prices of their commodities and services according to the law, to protect the interests of consumers and promote technological advancement. The undertakings mentioned in the previous paragraph shall operate in accordance with the law, act in good faith, be self-discipline, accept public supervision, and shall not damage consumer welfares by taking advantage of their market power'. This article has been remained in the AML (2022), note 17, Art. 8.

25 Siyu Guo (郭思宇), "Zhongguo Dianxin He Zhongguo Liantong Zao Fanlongduan Diaocha, Biaoshi Quanli Peihe" (中国电信和中国联通遭反垄断调查，表示全力配合) [China Telecom and China Unicom Were Fully Cooperated by the Anti-Monopoly Investigation], *people.com*, November 9, 2011, http://news.cntv.cn/china/20111109/113175.shtml

26 Xiaoli Li (李晓莉), "Wangyou Reyi Dianxin Liantong Longduan An Meiti Chaojia: Daodi She Sahuang?" (网友热议电信联通垄断案媒体吵架：到底谁撒谎？) [Netizens Talk About the Monopoly Case of China Unicom and Media Quarrel], *sohu news*, November 12, 2011, https://news.sohu.com/20111112/n325419467.shtml

27 See Li, note 22, at 54–55.

China Unicom and China Telecom owned 98.8% of market share in the broadband market on the Chinese mainland, a calculation based on turnover.[28] They provided internet access to internet service providers (ISP), which then offered those services to consumers. China Unicom and China Telecom were accused of setting high prices and implementing price discrimination with different ISPs. These two giant SOEs were blamed for the low average rate of broadband internet access in China (which ranked 71st in the world) and the high average cost for accessing the internet (three or four times higher than developed countries).[29]

As one of China's most powerful administrative agencies, the NDRC tried to cement its authority in the anti-monopoly landscape by targeting large SOEs for the first time. The news about the anti-monopoly investigation caused the two companies' share prices to plunge. Under pressure from all sides, on 2 December 2011, less than a month after the NDRC announced the investigation, the two telecom monopolies reached settlements with the NDRC and promised to rectify their behaviours.[30]

Each company released an announcement on its official website admitting that it had abused its dominant market position. However, the strained relations and discontent between the competition authorities and industrial regulators continued to simmer under the apparent cooperation and obedience in the announcement.

Take China Telecom's announcement for example. The announcement initially posted on 2 December 2011 stated that

> China Telecom gives high priority to and actively cooperates with the NDRC's investigation. We have studied *China's Anti-Monopoly Law* and related laws seriously and self-rectified price-related conduct thoroughly…. Regarding the broadband accessing services provided to ISPs, we failed to *properly oversee pricing,* which led to *large price differences*.[31]

However, it seems that China Telecom's managers were not being sincere in their 'confession'. Seven days later, on 9 December, China's Telecom 'sneakily' altered a couple of phrases in the initial announcement to express its disgruntlement: 'We have studied *China's Anti-Monopoly Law* and *China's Telecommunications Regulations* seriously…. Regarding the broadband accessing services provided to ISPs, the *large price differences are due to competition and regulation*'.[32] The changed

28 See Li, note 22, at 421.

29 Hongren Zhou and Yu Xu (周宏仁，徐愈), *Zhongguo Xinxi Hua Xingshi Fenxi Yu Yuce (2011)* (中国信息化形势分析与预测2011) [*Analysis and Forecast of China's Informatization Situation (2011)*] (Social Sciences Academic Press [China], 2011).

30 Xinhua News Agency (新华社), "Dianxin He Liantong Shenqing Zhongzhi Fanlongduan Diaocha" (电信和联通申请中止反垄断调查) [China Telecom and China Unicom Applied for Suspension of the Anti-Monopoly Investigation], *finance.ifeng.com*, December 3, 2011, https://finance.ifeng.com/news/special/fanlongduan/20111203/5190881.shtml

31 Jingjing Zhong and Jin Zhao (钟晶晶，赵谨), "Dianxin Qiaoran Gaidong Longduan Zhenggai Shengming" (电信悄然改动垄断整改声明) [China Telecom Quietly Changed the Monopoly Rectification Statement], *finance.ifeng.com*, December 9, 2011, https://finance.ifeng.com/a/20111209/5239909_0.shtml

32 *Ibid.*

announcement implied that China Telecom's price setting and price discrimination did not violate the law since it complied with industrial regulations.

That discord may root from Article 7 of the AML (2008). Article 7 provides that the State protect monopolistic companies' lawful business operations. Thus, it can be inferred from Article 7 that when companies follow laws and regulations (in most cases, industrial laws and regulations), they can be regarded as engaging in 'lawful business operations', which are beyond the AML's scope, even though laws and regulations are lower in the hierarchy than the AML.

From this perspective, we may understand China Telecom's 'grievance'. China's Telecommunications regulations require broadband owners to charge fees following criteria set by MIIT, the industrial regulator. MIIT adopted a formula[33] for calculating the ceiling price of providing broadband services, which means that companies can set prices freely as long as they are lower than that ceiling price.[34] Thus, if the prices set by China Unicom and China Telecom were lower than the ceiling, it would not be easy to prove the illegality of their behaviour.

The Gordian knot in this story is not whether two giant telecoms indeed abused their dominant market position, but whether the AML should yield when it comes into conflict with industrial regulations. The telecom case was no anomaly. Another high-profile case, nicknamed 'the 3Q War', broke out between two large internet companies who sought to compel consumers to choose either one or the other.[35] When this 'war' broke out, the MIIT had stepped in to urge the two companies to issue customers a 'letter of apology' and restore products' compatibility.[36] It only evolved into an anti-monopoly law issue after the MIIT had already stopped the 'either-or' business squabble.

In these years since the AML's enactment, it became clear in retrospect that industry regulations always cast a shadow on AML enforcement. Some sarcastically described the AML as a 'toothless tiger'. But those circumstances have changed in the last decade. The central government has repeatedly taken steps to strengthen the fundamental status of competition policy. Those changes apparently parallel AML enforcement in the digital market, a topic we will explore in the following section.

33 Measures for the Settlement between the Internet Exchange Center Networks (effective December 1, 2007), Xin Bu Dian [2007] No. 557, CLI.4.100869(EN) (Lawinfochina).

34 Yanbei Meng (孟雁北), *Guanzhi Hangye Fanlongduan Zhifa Wenti Yan Jiu* (管制行业反垄断执法问题研究) [*Research on Anti-Monopoly Law Enforcement in Regulated Industries*] (Law Press (China), 2020), 27.

35 Wenming Zhu and Xinying Dou (祝文明，窦新颖), "Qihu 360 Su Tengxun Gongsi Fanlongduan An Ershen Xuanpan" (奇虎360诉腾讯公司反垄断案二审宣判) [Qihoo 360 v. Tencent Anti-Monopoly Case Second Instance Judgment], *people.com*, October 17, 2014, http://ip.people.com.cn/n/2014/1017/c136655-25855478.html

36 Ministry of Industry and Information Technology of the People's Republic of China, "Guanyu Piping Beijing Qihu Keji Youxian Gongsi He Shenzhen Shi Tengxun Jisuan Ji Xitong Youxian Gongsi De Tongbao" (关于批评北京奇虎科技有限公司和深圳市腾讯计算机系统有限公司的通报) [Notice on Criticizing Beijing Qihoo Technology Co., Ltd. and Shenzhen Tencent Computer System Co., Ltd], (Gong Xin Bu Dian Guan Han [2010] No. 536), *gov.cngov.cn*, November 20, 2010, http://hprc.cssn.cn/gsgl/zyxw/zhongyao_1/201011/t20101122_3999339.html

1.3 The AML enforcement revolution in the digital economy

1.3.1 Dormant period: prior to 2020

Compared to the European Union and the United States, China's competition authorities did not place a watchful eye on the digital market until relatively late. For a long time, it was a mainstream opinion in the Chinese academic community that traditional anti-monopoly theories are not suitable for the digital market.[37] That opinion led the competition authorities to adopt a 'prudent and tolerant' attitude to digital competition. Moreover, the tripartite structure of the competition authorities and the lack of supporting guidelines or regulations for digital issues also contributed to lax anti-monopoly enforcement. During that period, very few notable enforcement actions were launched against digital companies.

The rise of Alibaba's business empire at this phrase can be taken as an example. Alibaba, founded in 1999 by a high-school English teacher, emerged as an e-commerce behemoth in the e-commerce industry in less than 15 years. As one of the top internet enterprises in the Chinese market, Alibaba's market share in the business-to-business (B2B) e-commerce market was 43% in 2016, or 35.5 percentage points higher than the second runner (7.5%), according to a research report issued by a think tank.[38] The report disclosed that as early as 2013, Alibaba started to take the 'either-or' strategy of forcing its business partners to choose between it and its competitors. In 2015, Alibaba signed exclusive agreements with more than 20 well-known brands, such as Timberland and Lafuma, under which they pledged to only operate online shops on Alibaba's platform.[39] In 2017, Alibaba forced business operators to shut down their online shops on competitors' platforms with the threat of reducing advertising resources, downgrading search ranks, blocking search results, and so on, if they refused.[40]

The sharp increase of Alibaba's fees also reflected its increasing market power. From 2003 to 2005, setting up an online shop on Alibaba's e-commerce platform was free of charge. In 2011, however, opening a shop on Alibaba's platform business incurred an annual service fee of RMB 30,00060,000 (about USD 4,200–8,400) and a deposit of RMB 10,000–150,000 (about USD 1,400–21,000), with fees varying with the store's size.[41] However, Alibaba's abusive behaviours did not trigger any official antitrust enforcement actions or penalties until 2021.

Tencent, the other leading tech company, also grasped the opportunity to grow fast in those 'heady' times, when the antitrust sword was growing rusty from disuse.

37 Wang Xiaoye and Gao Yajie, "China's Antimonopoly Law Enforcement in the Digital Economy," *The Antitrust Bulletin* 67 (2022): 562, 562–64.

38 Internet Lab (互联网实验室), "Zhongguo Chaoji Dianshang Pingtai Jingzheng Yu Longduan Yanjiu Baogao" (中国超级电商平台竞争与垄断研究报告) [Research Report on Competition and Monopoly of Super E-commerce Platforms in China], *blogchina.com*, November 24, 2020, https://chinalabs.blogchina.com/696341659.html

39 *Ibid.*

40 *Ibid.*

41 *Ibid.*

In 2013, Tencent was sued by antivirus software developer Qihu 360 for abusing its dominant market position.[42] That landmark case was heard by the Chinese Supreme People's Court (SPC) on 8 October 2014. That was the first time the SPC had considered the abuse of a dominant position in the digital market under the AML.

Although the SPC in this case acknowledged that Tencent held a very high share (almost 90%) of the relevant market (instant messaging), it held that market share was merely a rough indicator of market power, especially in the instant messaging market, where market participants face highly dynamic and intense competition.[43] Therefore, the SPC stated that courts should not rely overmuch on market share to determine market dominance, but should instead focus on the analysis of factors such as the status quo of market competition, the power to control price and products, and the threshold for market entry.[44]

The SPC held that the instant messaging market is a dynamic market with a low threshold to market entry, various competitors, and high pressure on competition. Tencent had to update and innovate its products to survive amid that competition. Moreover, Tencent had no power to control prices or consumers. The free-to-use business model makes consumers very sensitive to any price increases. Furthermore, the 'either-for' dispute between Tencent and Qihu360 only lasted for one day, but the number of active users on MSN, Tencent's major competitor, sharply increased.[45]

Thus, the SPC concluded that Tencent did not hold a dominant market position, even though its market share was exceptionally high. Tencent did not face any antitrust liability in the case either. The SPC adopted a startlingly lenient attitude toward Tencent. But today, just a couple of years later, few people would doubt Tencent's dominant position in China's digital market. It is reasonable to infer that the SPC's decision helped Tencent (perhaps not intentionally) by clearing a stumbling block on the path to its major success today.

The field of merger control is another example where such lax enforcement can be observed. Most digital platforms did not report their mergers and avoided the notification responsibility by claiming their turnover did not reach that threshold. During the 13 years since the enactment of the AML, there have been many mergers between internet-based companies,[46] but few of them have been reported to the competition authorities. As of December 2020, no administrative punishment had

42 Beijing Qihu Ltd. v. Tencent Technology (Shenzhen) Ltd. (北京奇虎科技有限公司诉腾讯科技（深圳）有限公司、深圳市腾讯计算机系统有限公司滥用市场支配地位纠纷案), (2013) Min San Zong Zi Di 4 Hao [(2013) Sup. People's Ct. Final Decision No. 4] (China), Wolters Kluwer.

43 *Ibid.*, at 25–26.

44 *Ibid.*, at 25–27.

45 *Ibid.*, at 27.

46 According to disclosed data, there have been about 542 mergers involving in internet companies from 2010 to 2020. See Jinyu Wang (王进雨), "Hulian Wang Fanlongduan Beihou: Jin Shinian Woguo Hulianwang Qiye Binggou Shijian Da 542 Qi" (互联网反垄断背后：近十年我国互联网企业并购事件达542起) [Behind Anti-Monopoly in the Internet Market: About 542 Mergers So Far], *sina.com.cn*, December 14, 2020, https://finance.sina.com.cn/chanjing/cyxw/2020-12-14/doc-iiznezxs6898584.shtml

been imposed for failure to make pre-merger notification. There has been considerable criticism of these mergers, such as Didi's merger with Uber in 2016,[47] Alibaba's acquisition of Amap (a leading digital map provider on the Chinese mainland) in 2014,[48] and the merger of Meituan (a large platform offering food delivery, restaurant reviews, travel booking, bike-sharing, movie ticketing, and other services) with Dazhong Dianping (China's version of Yelp) in 2015.[49]

1.3.2 New era: active enforcement, shift in central government's policies

1.3.2.1 Turning point: the enforcement campaign in 2021 and a calm after the storm

The year 2021 was a remarkable one in AML history. The sword of Damocles hanging over the heads of China's big tech firms finally dropped.

The first target was big tech's abuse of its dominant market position. On 10 April, Alibaba was slapped with a record fine of RMB 18 billion (USD 2.8 billion) for its 'either-or' abuse of its dominant market position, which was the highest antitrust penalty ever levied against a digital company.[50] Six months later, the sword was wielded against Meituan, the Chinese food delivery giant. A fine of RMB 3.4 billion (USD 534 million) was imposed for its 'either-or' abusive behaviour.[51] Moreover, the regulator ordered Meituan to return deposits amounting to RMB 12.89 billion (USD 2 billion) to its trading partners. The partners had paid these deposits as a guarantee that they would not do business with Meituan's competitors. Thereafter, the baton was passed to the provincial-level competition authority in Shanghai. A fine of RMB 1.2 million (USD 178,500) was given to Sherpa's, a Shanghai-based English-language food delivery app.[52] From my point of view, however, the provincial watchdog's penalty should be reconsidered

47 Yizi Jin (金易子), "Uber Zhongguo Jiangyu Di Di Hebing Hebing Hou Guzhi 350 Yi Meiyuan" (Uber中国将与滴滴合并合并后估值350亿美元) [Uber Merger With Didi, Estimated Value of US$35 Billion], *china.com.cn*, August 1, 2016, http://finance.china.com.cn/stock/xsb/yw/20160801/3838828.shtml

48 Soham Chatterjee, "Alibaba to Buy AutoNavi," *reuters.com*, April 12, 2014, https://www.reuters.com/article/us-autonavi-deals-alibaba-group-idUSBREA3A15620140411

49 Wang Yue, "China's Meituan, Dianping Merge to Create a Mega Online-to-Offline Service Platform," *forbes.com*, October 8, 2015, https://www.forbes.com/sites/ywang/2015/10/08/chinas-meituan-dianping-merges-to-create-a-mega-online-to-offline-service-platform/?sh=7f4a90163e28

50 "Guojia Shichang Jiandu Guanli Zongju Xingzheng Chufa Jueding Shu" (国家市场监督管理总局行政处罚决定书) [SAMR's Administrative Penalty Decision], Guo Shi Jian Chu [2021] No. 28, *samr.gov.cn*, April 10, 2021, https://www.samr.gov.cn/xw/zj/art/2023/art_4966dda92ab34c398615f5878c10c8f1.html

51 "Guojia Shichang Jiandu Guanli Zongju Xingzheng Chufa Jueding Shu" (国家市场监督管理总局行政处罚决定书) [SAMR's Administrative Penalty Decision], Guo Shi Jian Chu Fa [2021] No. 74, *samr.gov.cn*, October 8, 2021, https://www.samr.gov.cn/xw/zj/art/2023/art_31910760066b4f69aa119a20dee250ad.html

52 "Shanghai Shi Shichang Jiandu Guanli Ju Xingzheng Chufa Jueding Shu" (上海市市场监督管理局行政处罚决定书) [Shanghai Municipal Administration for Market Regulation's Administrative Penalty Decision], Hu Shi Jian Fan Long Chu [2020] No. 06201901001, *samr.gov.cn*, December 25, 2020, https://www.samr.gov.cn/xw/df/art/2023/art_fb84525d385a489db74615d1939883d0.html

given doubts about whether this smaller tech firm really enjoyed a dominant market position.

Soon after imposing the penalty on Alibaba, the competition authority summoned 34 major platforms, including Tencent, Alibaba, Baidu, JD.com, and Didi, to a meeting.[53] The regulator ordered these platform companies to review all internal measures within a month, thoroughly rectify any actions violating the AML, and issue a public commitment to operate their business in compliance with the law.[54]

As to the merger control, one reason for the lax enforcement prior to this point was the dilemma arising from the legitimate status of the business category known as variable interest entity (VIE). A VIE is a business structure in which an investor has a controlling interest despite not having a majority of voting rights. The controlling interest is achieved through a series of contractual arrangements. Major Chinese internet companies like Alibaba, Tencent, and Baidu have utilised VIE structures to bypass Chinese regulations and restrictions over overseas financing and foreign investing and get listed on stock exchanges in Hong Kong and the United States.[55] Before 2018, MOFCOM was responsible for reviewing mergers as well as reviewing and approving foreign investment. The validity of VIE has neither been recognised nor denied by China's authorities. In the interest of regulatory flexibility, therefore, MOFCOM was reluctant to clarify the legality of the VIE structure.[56] That placed MOFCOM in the following dilemma: If it reviewed a merger involving a VIE structure, that could be interpretated as signalling official confirmation of VIE's legality. But if MOFCOM turned a blind eye to those mergers, it would be slack in enforcing the AML since the companies in question had failed to report those mergers despite reaching the threshold for pre-merger notification. As a result of that quandary, MOFCOM refrained from making any decisions about merger reviews involving VIE structures after the enactment of AML.

Since 2021, China has moved away from its previous ambiguity and tightened tech companies' overseas listings. China's State Council issued the *Antimonopoly Guidelines on the Platform Economic Sector* ('Platform Guidelines'), the first time the regulator specified that mergers involving VIEs were subject to the AML's

53 SAMR, "Zhongguo Fanlongduan Zhifa Niandu Baogao (2021)" (中国反垄断执法年度报告[2021]) [Annual Report on China's Antimonopoly Enforcement (2021)], *samr.gov.cn*, June 8, 2022, https://www.samr.gov.cn/xw/zj/art/2023/art_bfac0acc333e4bd0be85adf099272047.html

54 Jianing Wang (王佳宁), "Sanbumen Lianhe Zhaokai Hulianwang Pingtai Qiye Xingzheng Zhidaohui" (三部门联合展开互联网平台企业行政指导会) [Three Departments Jointly Held the Administrative Guidance Meeting of Internet Platform Enterprises], *xinhuanet.com*, April 13, 2021, https://www.xinhuanet.com/politics/2021-04/13/c_1127324900.htm

55 Jiaxing Li, "What Are Vies and Why Are They Important for Chinese Tech Companies?" *kr-asia.com*, December 3, 2021, https://kr-asia.com/what-are-vies-and-why-are-they-important-for-chinese-tech-companies

56 Fa Chen, "China's Recent Regulation of Variable Interest Entity Structures Has Led to a Drop in Chinese Companies' US Listings," *blogs.law.ox.ac.uk*, April 19, 2022, https://blogs.law.ox.ac.uk/business-law-blog/blog/2022/04/chinas-recent-regulation-variable-interest-entity-structures-has-led

merger control.[57] As of the end of 2022, 125 non-notification mergers in the digital market have been punished by the newly erected competition authority, the SAMR.

Among the penalties issued for these 125 non-notification mergers, the penalty on Tencent's acquisition of China Music Corporation (Tencent/CMC) is quite striking.[58] In 2016, Tencent gained sole control of CMC by acquiring a 61.64% stake in the company. Besides imposing a penalty of RMB 50,000 for the failure to provide notification, the SAMR also found this merger had the effect of restricting and limiting competition, and it required Tencent to terminate exclusive copyright licensing to restore competition in the relevant market.[59] That was the first time the SAMR imposed behavioural remedies following a failure to file pre-merger notification.

Moreover, in 2021, the SAMR blocked the Huya/DouYu merger launched by Tencent involving video game livestreaming. That was China's third decision to block a merger since the enactment of the AML in 2008.[60] The first merger blocked by China's competition authorities was Coca-Cola's attempted acquisition of Chinese Huiyuan Juice Group Limited, a famous Chinese juice manufacturer.[61] The second such decision was the rejection of a proposed P3 Network, a container shipping alliance between MSC, Maersk, and CMA CGM.[62] The Huya/DouYu merger decision was the first time China's competition authority prohibited a merger between two domestic companies in the digital sector.

The storm of anti-monopoly enforcement grew less furious in 2022 and calmed down in 2023. In the public enforcement area, there were three high-profile cases in the internet field in 2021, but only one penalty for abusing dominant market

57 Guidelines of the Anti-monopoly Commission of the State Council for Anti-monopoly in the Field of Platform Economy (issued by the Antimonopoly Commission of the State Council on February 7, 2021, effective February 7, 2021), Guo Fan Long Fa (2021) No. 1, CLI.4.352590(EN) (Lawinfochina), Art. 11 [Hereinafter Platform Guidelines].

58 "Guojia Shichang Jiandu Guanli Zongju Xingzheng Chufa Jueding Shu" (国家市场监督管理总局行政处罚决定书) [SAMR's Administrative Penalty Decision], Guo Shi Jian Chu [2021] No. 67, *samr.gov.cn*, July 24, 2021, https://www.samr.gov.cn/jzxts/tzgg/xzcf/art/2021/art_58f3ac8703ba450cb11085e16a57beba.html

59 *Ibid.*, at 7.

60 SAMR, "Shichang Jianguan Zongju Guanyu Jinzhi Huya Yu Douyu Guoji Konggu Youxian Gongsi Hebingan Fanlongduan Shencha Jueding De Gonggao" (市场监管总局关于禁止虎牙公司与斗鱼国际控股有限公司合并案反垄断审查决定的公告) [The Notice of SAMR's Anti-Monopoly Decision on Douyu/Huya Merge], *samr.gov.cn*, July 10, 2021, https://www.samr.gov.cn/fldes/tzgg/ftj/art/2023/art_47b307e668484e83a598add8793dcdca.html

61 MOFCOM, "Shangwubu Guanyu Jinzhi Kekou Kele Gongsi Shougou Zhongguo Huiyuan Gongsi Shencha Jueding De Gonggao" (商务部关于禁止可口可乐公司收购中国汇源公司审查决定的公告) [The MOFCOM's Announcement of Blocking the Coca-Cola's Acquisition to Chinese Huiyuan Company], *mofcom.gov.cn*, March 18, 2009, https://www.mofcom.gov.cn/zcfb/zhzc/art/2009/art_be88661e25c147a1bb91776135537d56.html

62 MOFCOM, "Shangwubu Guanyu Jinzhi Mashiji, Dizhonghai Hangyun, Dafei Sheili Wangluo Zhongxin Jingyingzhe Jizhong Fanlongduan Shencha Jueding De Gonggao" (商务部关于禁止马士基、地中海航运、达飞设立网络中心经营者集中反垄断审查决定的公告) [The MOFCOM's Announcement of Blocking the Network Centre Set by MSC, Maersk and CMA CGM], *mofcom.gov.cn*, June 17, 2014, http://www.mofcom.gov.cn/article/b/c/201406/20140600628730.shtml

position in 2022.[63] There were 28 merger review cases related to platforms and 98 penalties for failure to report in 2021, but just 24 and 27, respectively, in 2022. Penalties issued by the competition authorities had a total value of RMB 21.74 billion in 2021, but that value decreased dramatically to RMB 104 million in 2022.[64]

1.3.2.2 State-led regulation model: the central government policies steering anti-monopoly enforcement

It may be possible to infer some of the reasons behind the enforcement campaign and the subsequent calm. Jack Ma, the founder and controlling shareholder of Alibaba, criticised Chinese financial regulation during a speech at a Shanghai summit on 24 October 2020. Ma impassionedly criticised China's traditional financial regulation for being modelled after a pawnshop, stifling innovation and being risk-averse.[65] However, Chinese Vice President Wang Qishan stressed financial security and regulation in a speech at the same summit.[66] Ma's speech touched a nerve in Beijing and set off a series of investigations and anti-monopoly enforcement actions against platforms.

On 2 November, less than 10 days after the speech, Jack Ma and two senior managers of Ant Group, the fintech sector of Alibaba's empire, were summoned before China's regulators.[67] Ant Group was accused of using the technology company as a front for engaging in financial business that bypassed traditional financial regulations. Ant Group's major business was making online loans at the small and micro scale. Qifan Huang, the former mayor of Chongqing City, once said that Ant's original capital of RMB 3 billion had been leveraged about 100 times.[68] Such an extreme amount of leverage poses a serious risk to the security of China's financial market. On 4 November, Ant Group's IPOs on Shanghai's STAR market

63 SAMR, "Zhongguo Fanlongduan Zhifa Niandu Baogao (2022)" (中国反垄断执法年度报告[2022]) [Annual Report on China's Antimonopoly Enforcement (2022)], *samr.gov.cn*, June 9, 2023, https://www.samr.gov.cn/xw/zj/art/2023/art_38056964cf5449daa346237200e24da0.html, at 33.

64 *Ibid.*, at 33.

65 Ziyi Tang, "What You Need to Know About Ant Group's Suspended IPO and the Future of Chinese Fintech," *caixinglobal.com*, January 15, 2021, https://www.caixinglobal.com/2021-01-15/what-you-need-to-know-about-ant-groups-suspended-ipo-and-the-future-of-chinese-fintech-101651386.html

66 Xinhua News Agency (新华社), "Yaojianshou Dixian Yeyao Linghuo Yingdui Fengxian Tiaozhan" (要坚守底线也要灵活应对风险挑战) [Need Stick to the Bottom of Line, Also Need Deal With Risk Flexibly], *xinmin.cn*, October 25, 2020, https://paper.xinmin.cn/html/xmwb/2020-10-25/2/84294.html

67 Global Times, "Jack Ma and Ant Group Management Summoned by Top Chinese Financial Regulatory Authorities," *globaltimes.cn*, November 3, 2020, https://www.globaltimes.cn/content/1205487.shtml

68 Qifan Huang (黄奇帆), "Huangqi fan: Mayi Jinfu 100 Yi Lirun, 45 Yi Lirun Laizi Chongqing Liangge Xiaodai Gongsi" (黄奇帆：蚂蚁金服100亿利45亿利润来自重庆两个小贷公司) [Qifan Huang: Ant Financial Has A Profit of 10 Billion Yuan, and a Profit of 4.5 Billion Yuan Comes From Two Small Loan Companies in Chongqing], *finance.sina.com.cn*, June 16, 2020, https://finance.sina.com.cn/money/bank/2020-11-03/doc-iirczymk7303056.shtml

and the Hong Kong stock market were suspended.[69] Ant Group was required to overhaul its financial business according to the suddenly stricter regulatory requirements.

Didi Chuxing, China's largest online ride-hailing provider, was listed on the New York Stock Exchange (NYSE) without obtaining approval from China's regulator. That ended up being one of several straws that broke the camel's back in terms of regulating platforms. The founder of Didi, Chen Wei, quit his job at Alibaba and set up Didi with RMB 800,000 in start-up capital in 2012. It only took Didi four years to triumph over the online ride-hailing market in China. After an intense investor-subsidised price war, Didi merged Kuaidi and Uber's China division in 2015 and 2016, respectively, which made Didi the largest online ride-hailing service provider in the Chinese market with a market share of about 90%.[70]

After such rapid growth, Didi made its debut on the NYSE on 30 June 2021 at USD 14 a share, valuing the company at USD 68 billion. That was the biggest IPO of a Chinese company on an American stock exchange since Alibaba's IPO in 2014.[71] Didi chose the very low-key listing date of 30 June, just two days before the 100th anniversary of the founding of the Communist Party of China (CPC), with no press briefing or bell-ringing ceremony. Didi's rushed listing was due to concern about stricter regulations on Chinese companies' overseas listing taking effect after July 1. That sleight of hand, however, did not work. Just two days later, the Cyberspace Administration of China (CAC) ordered the removal of Didi's app from domestic app stores and stopped new user registration with the statement that 'Didi has seriously violated laws and regulations in its collection and use of personal information'.[72] Thereafter, the CAC, together with six other top ministries and departments, ordered Didi to undergo a cybersecurity review.[73]

The Ant Group and Didi incidents touched upon two sensitive areas for the Chinese government: financial security and data security, which have a major impact on national security. The State cannot, in any case, tolerate private monopolies' efforts or ambitions to dominate those fields.

Thus, China regulators thought it was time to end the long period of lax regulation over platforms. As an expert with the Antimonopoly Commission of the State Council said in an interview, the giant platforms had already grown from 'toddlers'

69 Tang, note 65.

70 Jingmeng Cai, "The Sharing Economy and China's Antimonopoly Law: From the Didi Case to Regulatory Challenges," *Asia Pacific Law Review* 28 (2020): 159, 164–66.

71 Kara Greenberg, "Didi Global (Didi) IPO: What You Need to Know," *investopedia.com*, July 2, 2021, https://www.investopedia.com/didi-global-didi-ipo-what-you-need-to-know-5191083

72 Wei Han, "China's Cybersecurity Regulator Orders Didi Removed From App Stores," *caixinglobal.com*, July 4, 2021, https://www.caixinglobal.com/2021-07-04/chinas-cybersecurity-regulator-orders-didi-removed-from-app-stores-101735800.html

73 CAC, "Guojia Hulianwang Bangongshi Deng Qibumen Jingzhu Didi Chuxing Keji Youxian Gongsi Kaizhan Wangluo Anquan Shencha" (国家互联网信息办公室等七部门进驻滴滴出行科技有限公司开展网络安全审查) [CAC and Other Six Top Ministries and Departments Stationed at Didi Technology Co. to Carry Out a Cybersecurity Review], *cac.gov.cn*, July 16, 2021, https://www.cac.gov.cn/2021-07/16/c_1628023601191804.htm

to 'youths', and it was time to update the regulatory approach.[74] Therefore, the anti-monopoly law was taken as a powerful club to wield against tech companies.

At the end of 2020, China's annual Central Economic Work Conference—the most important Party-led annual economic meeting that sets the economic policy agenda for the next year—used uncommonly harsh language to require strict regulation of platforms. Officials said that to

> strengthen the anti-monopoly enforcement and prevent disorderly expansion of capital . . . it is necessary to cement regulation and improve regulatory capabilities. Any monopolistic or unfair competition behaviours shall be firmly opposed. Financial innovation must be carried out under prudent regulation.[75]

That augured the storm of anti-monopoly enforcement actions against platforms that struck in 2021. Tightened scrutiny of tech giants rang out like a warning bell, reminding digital tech firms that the digital market is not beyond China's regulatory jurisdiction.

Didi was fined RMB 8 billion (USD 1.2 billion) on 22 July 2022 for illegally collecting and analysing passengers' and drivers' personal and facial information in violation of the newly enacted Personal Information Protection Law (2021),[76] Data Security Law (2021),[77] and Cyber Safety Law (2016).[78] Immediately, Didi expressed a high level of obedience and an attitude of sincere contrition. It announced on its official microblog on Weibo, the Chinese equivalent of Twitter, now known as X, that 'we sincerely accept the administrative penalty and will strictly comply with the regulatory requirements, conduct a thorough and deep internal investigation, actively cooperate with government supervision, and complete a major overhaul.[79]

74 Yuanyang Zhu (朱远祥), "Fanlongduan Shisannian·Zhifa | Jianguan Chixu Fali, Jing Liangbaiyi Danan Fakuan Chuangjilu" (反垄断十三年·执法 | 监管持续发力，近两百亿单案罚款创纪录) [Thirteen Years of Anti-Monopoly Law Enforcement: Regulation Continues, Nearly $20 Billion Single-Case Fines Set Records], *thepaper.cn*, November 3, 2021, https://www.thepaper.cn/newsDetail_forward_15188946

75 Xinhua News Agency (新华社), "Zhongyang JingJi Gongzuo Huiyi Zai Beijing Juxing, Xijingping Likeqiang Zuo Zhongyao Jianghua" (中央经济工作会议在北京举行习近平李克强作重要讲话) [The Central Economic Work Conference Was Held, Jinping Xi and Keqiang Li Delivered Important Speeches], *gov.cn*, December 18, 2020, https://m.mofcom.gov.cn/article/i/jyjl/l/202012/20201203024652.shtml

76 Personal Information Protection Law of the People's Republic of China (promulgated by the Standing Committee of the National People's Congress, issued August 20, 2021, effective November 1, 2021), CLI.1.5055321(EN) (Lawinfochina).

77 Data Security Law of the People's Republic of China (promulgated by the Standing Committee of the National People's Congress, issued June 10, 2021, effective September 1, 2021), CLI.1.5015167(EN) (Lawinfochina).

78 Cybersecurity Law of the People's Republic of China (promulgated by the Standing Committee of the National People's Congress, issued November 7, 2016, effective June 1, 2017), CLI.1.283838(EN) (Lawinfochina).

79 Zhichao Wu (伍智超), "Didi Huiying Beifa 80.26 Yi: Jianjue Fucong Quanmian Zicha Renzhen Zhenggai" (滴滴回应被罚80.26亿：坚决服从、全面自查、认真整改) [Didi Responded to

In January 2023, the CAC permitted Didi to resume new user registration after an 18-month ban.[80]

Then on 7 July 2023, the other shoe finally dropped on Alibaba after a two-year wait. A fine of RMB 7.1 billion (USD 984 million) was imposed on Ant Group after government-led overhaul and restructuring that lasted nearly a year.[81] Jack Ma gave up control of Ant Group, allowing his voting share to decrease from 53.46% to 6.2%.[82] Alibaba has also gone to great lengths to cut ties with Ant Group, removing all Ant Group's executives from its list of owners and terminating a 50-year data-sharing agreement with Ant.[83] There is no actual controller of Ant Group after the restructuring.

Moreover, Alibaba initially announced in March 2023 that it would split into six units—cloud intelligence, online sales, local services (online map and food delivery), international digital commerce, logistics, and digital media and entertainment. While Alibaba retains total control over the Taobao and Tmall e-commerce platforms (its original business areas), the other five units are now free to raise capital and pursue their own sale of public shares.[84]

The storm of platform regulation eventually blew over. The enforcement campaign had been a heavy blow to the digital industry. Along with massive layoffs at major tech firms and falling stock prices at Chinese tech companies listed in the United States, winter seemed to be coming for the internet industry.[85]

Considering the digital sector's massive share of China's GDP and its crucial role in shaping future global competition, appropriate incentives are needed to harness the sector's development. Therefore, after a series of robust anti-monopoly enforcement actions and hefty punishments, a milder tone was adopted in the

Being Fined 8.026 Billion: Resolute Obedience, Comprehensive Self-Examination, and Serious Rectification], *thepaper.cn*, July 21, 2022, https://www.thepaper.cn/newsDetail_forward_19112206

80 Zhiyu Jiang (蒋芷毓), "Huifu Xinyonghu Zhuce, Didi De Zhenggai Jieshu Lema?" (恢复新用户注册，滴滴的整改结束了吗？) [Resumption of New User Registration, Is the Rectification of Didi Over?], *baijiahao.baidu.com*, January 17, 2023, https://baijiahao.baidu.com/s?id=1755250112648910139&wfr=spider&for=pc

81 "Tech Insider: Ant Group Fined," *caixinglobal.com*, July 11, 2023, https://www.caixinglobal.com/2023-07-11/tech-insider-ant-group-fined-zeekr-evs-heading-to-israel-102074518.html

82 Fenghuang WEEKLY (凤凰WEEKLY), "71 Yi Fadan Luodi, Yun Ma He Mayi Dou Anxin Le, Zhuanjia: Pingtai Zhengzhi Jieshu" (71亿罚单落地，马云和蚂蚁都安心了，专家：平台整治结束) [The 7.1 Billion Fine Landed, Ma Yun and Ant Were Relieved, Expert: The Platform Rectification is Over], *new.qq.com*, July 10, 2023, https://new.qq.com/rain/a/20230710A07TQE00

83 Kelsey Cheng, "Ant Group Hit With $984 Million Fine as Years-Long Overhaul Wraps Up," *caixinglobal.com*, July 7, 2023, https://www.caixinglobal.com/2023-07-07/ant-group-hit-with-984-million-fine-as-years-long-overhaul-wraps-up-102073424.html

84 Yunhong Bao, Erchi Zhang, Yunxu Qu, and Kelsey Cheng, "In Depth: Alibaba Has Hurdles to Overcome Before Its Drastic Restructuring Pays Off," *caixinglobal.com*, June 21, 2023, https://www.caixinglobal.com/2023-06-21/in-depth-alibaba-has-hurdles-to-overcome-before-its-drastic-restructuring-pays-off-102068224.html

85 Nancai Compliance Technology Research Institute (南财合规科技研究院), "Hulianwang Fanlongduan Yu Touzi Yingxiang Baogao (2022)" (互联网反垄断与投资影响报告[2022]) [Report of Anti-Monopoly in Internet Field and Investment Impacts (2022)], *m.21jingji.com*, February 28, 2023, https://m.21jingji.com/mall/173.html, at 13.

Central Economic Work Conference in 2021. President Xi Jinping presented a speech about China's attitude toward capital in the conference:

> We must correctly recognise the idiosyncrasies and the operating laws of capital. The socialist market economy is a great creation. Inevitably, there are various forms of capital in the socialist market economy. Capital shall play a positive role as a productive factor, and its negative role shall be controlled. We shall set 'traffic lights' for capital, strengthen effective regulation, and prevent capital from growing wildly. We shall support and guide capital's normative and healthy development and stick to and improve the socialist economy as the fundamental economic system. We will work unswervingly to both consolidate and develop the public sector and encourage, support, and guide the development of the non-public sector.[86]

Toward the end of 2022, the central government made a U-turn on digital platforms. In the Central Economic Work Conference in 2022, government officials made the following statement:

> We shall strive to develop the digital economy and set up regular oversight. Platform enterprises should be supported to fully display their advantages in leading industrial development, creating employment, and competing internationally. Platform enterprises should seize new opportunities that have emerged from changes to the global industrial structure and layout. They should be brave to explore new battlefields and win new games.[87]

Anti-monopoly enforcement has never been a purely legal issue; inevitably, it echoes political impacts, bureaucratic missions, and national macroeconomic targets. Although the AML system may be criticised as being heavily politicised, one advantage is that China, despite being like an ocean liner, can still be steered as nimbly as a yacht to achieve a particular national target. As Huyue Zhang states, 'Beijing's recent efforts to strengthen antitrust regulation in the tech sector could facilitate a larger goal of the Chinese government: to become a technology superpower and achieve self-sufficiency, ending reliance on the West'.[88] This level of government leverage on the digital market might be envied by counterparts in the

86 Xinhua News Agency (新华社), "Zhongyang JingJi Gongzuo Huiyi Zai Beijing Juxing, Xijingping Likeqiang Zuo Zhongyao Jianghua" (中央经济工作会议在北京举行习近平李克强作重要讲话) [The Central Economic Work Conference Was Held, Jinping Xi and Keqiang Li Delivered Important Speeches], *gov.cn*, December 10, 2021, https://www.gov.cn/xinwen/2021-12/10/content_5659796.htm

87 "2022 Zhongyang Jingji Gongzuo Huiyi Gongbao Quanwen" (2022中央经济工作会议公报全文) [Full Text of The Central Economic Work Conference (2022)], *china-cer.com.cn*, December 16, 2022, http://www.china-cer.com.cn/guwen/2022121622596.html

88 Angela Huyue Zhang, "What Does Beijing Achieve From Regulating Its Big Tech?" *usali.org*, April 20, 2021, https://usali.org/usali-perspectives-blog/what-does-beijing-achieve-from-regulating-its-big-tech

United States, where efforts to rein in digital giants are usually uphill battles and where it takes long years to overturn court precedents and amend legislative texts.

1.3.3 The newly amended AML and supporting regulations

If we admit that the impact of non-legal factors on antitrust enforcement is unavoidable, the crucial role of the law is to guarantee those factors' impacts within a manageable range, normalise the authority to enforce the law, and hold authorities within the legal framework. Thus, the newly amended AML, which took effect in 2022, reflects China's determination to constrain enforcement power within the legal framework and limit the influence of non-legal factors. Major Chinese scholars and legislators have also advocated for making AML enforcement more legalised and professional.

The AML was amended for the first time in 2022, with regulation of the digital sector receiving some major updates. Several highlights are discussed next.

1.3.3.1 Substantial revisions in Chapter 1 of AML: general provisions

First, 'encouraging innovation' was added as one of the legislative purposes of the AML. While this revision echoes anti-monopoly enforcement in the digital sector, it has generated considerable controversy. Professor Xiaoye Wang argues that encouraging innovation should not be equal to the purpose of protecting competition.[89] Conduct that has promoted innovation may still injure competition. There is a risk that high-tech companies, especially those with a dominant market position, will lean on the promotion of innovation as an excuse for their abusive behaviours.

Second, the CPC's leadership of anti-monopoly enforcement has been explicitly added to the law with Article 4 of the AML (2022). Meanwhile, Article 4 stresses the market-oriented principle: The rule of law shall be maintained, and the status of competition policy shall be reinforced. This Article sets the primary theme for the AML and underlines the priority of competition policy, which could be effective for resolving conflicts between competition policy and industrial policy in the future.

Third, the amendment incorporates the Fair Competition Review System (FCRS) into the AML for the first time. As early as 2013, China's leader spoke of the need to tame regional protectionism and restrict administrative power to revitalise a uniform national market in China in a significant conference: the Third Plenary Session of the 18th Central Committee of the CPC.[90]

89 Xiaoye Wang (王晓晔), "Fanlongduan Fa (Xiuzheng Caoan) De Pingxi" (《反垄断法（修正草案）》的评析) [Commentary on the Antimonopoly Law (Draft Amendment)], *Contemporary Law Review* 36 (2022): 36, 43–44.

90 Xinhua News Agency (新华社), "Zhonggong Zhongyang Guanyu Quanmian Shenhua Gaige Ruogan Zhongda Wenti De Jueding" (中共中央关于全面深化改革若干重大问题的决定) [Decisions on Major Issues Concerning Comprehensively Intensifying Reform], *gov.cn*, November 15, 2013, https://www.gov.cn/zhengce/202203/content_3635143.htm, Title 3 Art. 9.

The purpose behind the FCRS is to block undue and improper interference in the market and competition by administrative authorities. Three years later, on June 1, 2016, FCRS was officially established in China.[91] It requires all administrative organs, from local governments to the State Council itself, to make sure that all proposed rules and policies would not eliminate or restrict competition before their submission or enactment. Before the AML's 2022 amendment took effect, fair competition review was just an administrative responsibility for governmental organs, and failure to perform that review was only punished on an internal level.

But since the FCRS was written into the AML (2022), it has become a legal obligation for administrative organs to review rules and policies they have drafted and issued. Failure to do so is a violation of the law and not just an internal infraction within the administrative system. That reflects lawmakers' efforts to restrain discretionary power and prevent administrative bodies from unduly interfering in the market and subjugating companies to achieve bureaucratic missions. The AML was once mocked as a toothless tiger against administrative monopolies. The birth of FCRS is expected to equip that tiger with a set of sharp teeth.

Fourth, Article 9 of AML (2022) is a new provision specially designed to regulate the digital sector. It provides that undertakings may not utilise algorithms, technology, capital advantages, or platform rules to engage in any monopolistic behaviours prohibited by the AML.

1.3.3.2 Highlighted modifications in the AML (2022)

The amended AML (2022) addresses vertical agreements—one of the most controversial areas in China's AML enforcement—by setting clearer criteria for distinguishing them from horizontal agreements. The 'safe harbour' mechanism, borrowed from EU competition law, has been imported into China's antitrust regime. But that mechanism can only be applied to vertical agreements, rather than all eligible agreements (including horizontal agreements) as under EU law.

Article 19 is a brand-new provision instituted to punish anybody who organises a monopolistic agreement or makes a substantial contribution to such an agreement. The Article is likely to be applied to rein in digital platforms, which often serve as a hub for conspiracies among companies.

The chapter of AML on merger review has undergone major modifications as well. First, the amended law states that even if a merger does not reach the threshold of pre-merger notification, the competition authorities can still require companies to provide notification if there is evidence of possible anti-competitive effects. This new provision is designed to plug a loophole exploited by many platforms to circumvent the previous merger review system. The Didi/Uber merger in 2016 can be regarded as a 'triumphant trophy' for corporate lawyers in mockery of regulators' weakness.

91 Opinions of the State Council on Establishing a Fair Competition Examination Regime in the Building of the Market System (promulgated by St. Council, June 1, 2016, effective June 1, 2016), Guo Fa (2016) No. 34, CLI.2.272306(EN) (Lawinfochina).

Second, the 'stop-the-clock' mechanism from EU law has been introduced to allow the competition authorities to suspend a merger review under certain conditions. This has, at least to some extent, alleviated the pressure on regulators to complete a merger review within the time limits set by the law. Considering the heavy caseload and staff shortage, this new mechanism can improve the quality of reviews, but it also raises concerns about the risk of officials abusing their discretionary power and unduly extending the review period, creating uncertainty and obstacles for transactions.

Third, the AML (2022) sets up a classified and graded review system in order to strengthen scrutiny in certain areas—finance, media, science, and technology—areas closely tied to people's livelihood, mergers involving start-ups, and labour-intensive industries.[92] Thus, mergers in the digital market will be a key area for China's regulators to review.

Another highlight of the amended law is that it adopts more severe penalties. For example, the monetary penalty on companies reaching monopolistic agreements is calculated based on their sales volume in the last year, varying from 1% to 10% of the sales volume. The 2008 version of the AML provided that if a monopoly agreement has not been carried out the competition authorities can give a maximum penalty of RMB 500 thousand. The 2022 version of the AML, however, raises that threshold to RMB 3 million. In addition, a maximum penalty of RMB 5 million can even be imposed on companies that did not have any sales in the last year. Moreover, the new amendment adds a monetary penalty for individuals, and the threshold of penalties on industrial association has been raised from RMB 500,000 to RMB 3 million. As for failure to make a pre-merger notification, mergers with anti-competitive effects are to be halted, the pre-merger situation restored, and a maximum penalty of 10% of the last year's sales volume imposed, compared to the paltry RMB 500,000 penalty in the AML (2008). Even if the merger in question does not have any anti-competitive effects, a maximum penalty of RMB 5 million can still be imposed.

Notably, Article 67 of the AML (2022) incorporates criminal liability into the AML. This Article states that 'Where a violation of this law constitutes a crime, the offender shall be criminally liable'. Although the criminal liability for violating the AML will need to be finalised in a future revision of the criminal code, adding criminal liability to the AML to cement its deterrent force is itself a milestone. Also, the AML (2022) authorises prosecutors to bring civil public interest lawsuits against companies that engage in monopolistic conduct. That may help accelerate the sluggish development of private enforcement and alleviate the heavy burden of proof for private plaintiffs attempting to demonstrate monopolistic behaviour.

92 Opinions of the CPC Central Committee and the State Council on Accelerating the Construction of a Unified National Market (issued March 25, 2022, effective March 25, 2022), CLI.16.5115681(EN) (Lawinfochina).

1.4 Conclusion

If we admit that anti-monopoly enforcement has never been a purely legal issue, but has inevitably reflected political impacts, bureaucratic missions, and national macroeconomic targets, we can understand the crucial role that the AML has played in normalising enforcement power and binding competition authorities to the legal framework. The amended AML reflects these efforts to make anti-monopoly enforcement more legalised and professional. The AML's enforcement in the digital age reflects the challenges as well as the opportunities brought by technological advances. China's anti-monopoly law has the potential to become a quiet but vital force to shake up the seemingly unbreakable global antitrust order that has formed over the past century in advanced antitrust regimes.

2 Abuse of dominant market position in the digital market

2.1 Early years of AML enforcement: prudent and tolerant regulatory policy for the digital market

The year 2018 was when the three former antitrust authorities were consolidated into a single new agency—the State Administration for Market Regulation—during a massive reorganisation of the Chinese administrative structure. That can be roughly regarded as the watershed year for the discussion of AML enforcement in the digital sector. Prior to 2018, regulators had restrained themselves from interfering with the digital market. Xiaolu Liu, a professor of Renmin University, states that in most cases digital platforms during that period had not been charged with any social responsibilities.[1] Thus, competition in the digital market was very dynamic, and most of today's well-known tech companies sprang up and flourished during that period.

2.1.1 Private enforcement: plaintiffs' ponderous burden of proof

From 2008 to 2017, courts nationwide accepted 700 lawsuits and closed 630 cases involving anti-monopoly issues, more than 90% of which were related to abuse of dominant market position.[2]

As early as 2009, just one year after the AML took effect, China's courts heard a case against Baidu, the largest internet search engine provider in Chinese mainland, for abusing its dominance by lowering the plaintiff's rank in its search results.[3] This

1 Xiaolu Liu (刘小鲁), "Shuzi Jingji Xia De Pingtai Zhili" (数字经济下的平台治理) [Platform Governance in the Digital Economy], *sohu.com*, June 19, 2024, https://www.sohu.com/a/786999065_345245

2 Li Zhu (朱理), "Fanlongduan Minshi Susong Shinian: Huigu Yu Zhanwang" (反垄断民事诉讼十年：回顾与展望) [Ten Years of Antitrust Civil Litigation: A Review and Outlook], "Zhongguo Zhishi Chanquan Bao" (中国知识产权报) [China's Intellectual Property Newspaper], August 24, 2018, A08.

3 Tangshan Renren Information Service Co. Ltd. v. Beijing Baidu Netcom Science & Technology Co. Ltd. (唐山市人人信息服务有限公司诉北京百度网讯科技有限公司垄断纠纷案), (2009) Yi Zhong Min Chu Zi Di 845 Hao and (2010) Gao Min Zhong Zi Di 489 Hao [(2009) Beijing Municipal First Intermediate People's Court Civil First Instance Judgment No. 845 and (2010) Beijing Municipal Higher People's Court Final Civil Judgment No. 489] (China), Wolters Kluwer. [Hereinafter '*Renren v. Baidu*'].

DOI: 10.4324/ 9781003654452-2

case entailed similar legal issues, to some extent, with the *Google Shopping* case heard by the EU General Court about 10 years later, in 2021.[4]

Although Google had not yet pulled out of the Chinese mainland in 2009, Baidu was already the most competitive search engine provider. Baidu's search engine, accessible at www.baidu.com, obtains and displays search results on internet users' screen. Those results are either selected by the search engine according to general criteria or neutral algorithms, without payments from the websites to Baidu ('natural search results') or selected according to a specialised ranking algorithm based on the different amount of fees paid to Baidu ('bidding ranking'). The bidding ranking results appear alongside the natural search results, generally on the right side of the web page under the label of 'ads'.

Tangshan Renren Information Services Co Ltd. ('Renren'), the plaintiff, was a medical consulting service provider. Since March 2008, Renren had paid Baidu for its bidding ranking service. But when Renren reduced its payment that May, it saw the number of its website views dramatically decrease.[5] Thus, Renren sued Baidu for abusing market dominance according to the newly enacted AML.

The case was heard by Beijing First Intermediate Court (the trial court) and Beijing Higher Court (the appellate court). The appellate court by and large supported the trial court's judgement, ruling in favour of Baidu. In short, both courts followed the three steps in abuse of dominance cases: (1) defining the relevant market, (2) determining whether the defendant has market dominance, and (3) determining whether the defendant has abused its dominance. For the convenience of this discussion, the 'Court' refers to the appellate court in the following section.

As to defining the relevant market, the Court rebutted Baidu's argument that the search engine service could not be regarded as the relevant market since it was free. The Court said,

> Users of the search engine service include not only general users who refer to search results without paying, but also commercial websites who intend to pay for Baidu's services.... Moreover, the natural search results and bidding ranking results appear on the same page.... It is untenable for Baidu to rely on the natural search results to claim that its search engine service cannot be defined as a relevant market because it is a free service.[6]

Whether Baidu held a dominant market position was the major battlefield for the litigants. According to the AML and China's civil procedure law, the plaintiff bears the burden of proof for their claims. Therefore, Renren had to first prove that Baidu had the dominant market position before arguing it abused the dominance. Article 19 of the AML (Article 24 of AML [2022]) provides that a dominant market position can be presumed if the defendant controls at least half market share

4 *Google and Alphabet v. Commission* (*Google Shopping*), Case T-612/17, November 10, 2021.
5 See *Renren v. Baidu*, note 3.
6 *Ibid.*

of the relevant market. Renren provided a website article to prove Baidu's market share, but the Court denied the evidentiary capability of that article due to the lack of corroborative evidence.[7] Another piece of evidence presented by Renren was a research report issued by the China Internet Network Information Centre (CNNIC), a research institution under the Ministry of Industry and Information Technology. The report stated that 76.9% of Chinese users had named Baidu as their first choice of search engine. However, the Court determined that without other corroborative evidence, it could not decide that the target market in the research report was the same as the relevant market in this case.[8] The third piece of evidence submitted by Renren was a newspaper article and a consulting agency's article to prove Baidu's market share. Although the Court recognised that the target market in these articles was identical with the relevant market in this case, these articles' conclusion about Baidu's dominance was not persuasive to the Court because they lacked appropriate economic analysis.[9] The last piece of evidence was an article published on Baidu's official website claiming that the company was 'the largest Chinese search engine in the world'. However, the Court held that such a 'self-admission' did not happen during litigation and could not be regarded as Baidu's admission of its own dominance. Thus, the Court concluded that Renren had not proven Baidu's dominance. So the plaintiff's claim that Baidu held dominance in the relevant market could not be upheld.

Even though 15 years have passed since that lawsuit, when I read the judgement, the plaintiff's desperation seems still palpable today. All the evidence presented by the plaintiff to prove Baidu's dominant market position was rejected by the Court without persuasive grounds. Private plaintiffs' burden of proof in abuse of dominance case seems to have become an insurmountable obstacle in AML private enforcement.

As for the third step in such cases (that is, determining whether the defendant has abused its market dominance), Renren had failed to prove Baidu's market dominance in the first place, so it was impossible to establish Baidu's abusive behaviours. Nevertheless, the Court analysed the question of abuse to finalise its analysis. Basing on the evidence presented by Baidu, the Court accepted Baidu's argument that there were 'junk links' to Renren's website, so lowering Renren's ranking in the search results was a punitive measure, rather than retaliation for Renren's payment decrease.[10] Thus, Baidu's behaviour could be justified.

The first antitrust case against a digital giant in the history of China's anti-monopoly regulation ended with Baidu's triumph. Unfortunately, the exceptionally high threshold for the plaintiff proving the defendant's market dominance as well as the plaintiff's 'tainted behaviour' itself (using junk links) kept Chinese judges from continuing with an in-depth analysis of whether the search engine provider abused its dominance by interfering with or manipulating search results.

7 *Ibid.*
8 *Ibid.*
9 *Ibid.*
10 *Ibid.*

That issue would be faced by the EU competition enforcers several years later in the *Google Shopping* case.

In *Renren v. Baidu*, we can detect the judicial decision makers' prudent and tolerant attitude toward digital companies at that stage. They were reluctant to jump to the conclusion that a newly emerging business model violated the law. The case of *Qihu 360 v. Tencent*, already explored in Chapter 1, also mirrored such attitudes. Just as in the case of *Renren v. Baidu*, the courts were reluctant to admit these well-known digital companies' dominant position in the market despite their high market shares.

On the positive side, compared to the decision in *Renren v. Baidu*, China's SPC in *Qihu 360 v. Tencent* spent over 74,000 Chinese characters, including over 30,000 Chinese characters on its reasoning, to explain the internet market's peculiarity and question the effectiveness of traditional antitrust analytical approaches.[11] Despite controversies, the SPC bravely addressed the issues with the relevant market definition, as well as how business models and market dynamics affect the determination of market dominance in the internet and high-tech field, which was a cutting-edge topic even in advanced antitrust jurisdictions. The negative side, however, is that the lawsuit's outcomes significantly impeded the development of private enforcement. The heavy burden of proof noticeably frustrated plaintiffs' motivation to bring antitrust lawsuits in courts, especially against large digital companies. Very few plaintiffs could win cases. A judge in Jiangsu Province stated that, from 2011 to 2019, just 17 civil lawsuits involving anti-monopoly issues were heard by courts in Jiangsu Province, and only in one case was the defendant held as violating the AML.[12] Li Zhu, the SPC's Justice, also acknowledged that 'under the present civil procedure law rules, a high rate of plaintiffs losing cases is almost inevitable'.[13]

Since most potential private plaintiffs got cold feet before the gates of the court due to the difficulty of proving defendants' dominance, readers may be curious about whether public enforcers were in a similar position. The next section will discuss the AML's public enforcement before 2018.

2.1.2 Public enforcement: agencies' bureaucratic missions and styles

Before the SAMR was set up, the authority for investigating abusive dominance was shared by the State Administration for Industry and Commerce (SAIC) and the National Development and Reform Commission (NDRC). (While the Ministry of Commerce (MofCom) was responsible for reviewing mergers, I will set it aside in this chapter.) From 2008 to 2015, the abuse of dominance was not a major task

11 *Beijing Qihu Ltd. v. Tencent Technology (Shenzhen) Ltd.* (北京奇虎科技有限公司诉腾讯科技（深圳）有限公司、深圳市腾讯计算机系统有限公司滥用市场支配地位纠纷案), (2013) Min San Zong Zi Di 4 Hao [(2013) Sup. People's Ct. Final Decision No. 4] (China), Wolters Kluwer.

12 Qing Li, eds., (李青主编), *Zhongguo Fanlongduan Shier Nian: Huigu Yu Zhanwang* (中国反垄断十二年：回顾与展望) [*Twelve Years of Antitrust in China: Review and Prospect*] (CITIC Press Group, 2020), 142.

13 Zhu, note 2.

for both agencies. No company had been investigated or fined by the agency for abusing dominance before 2013, and only 13 cases had involved that issue by the end of 2015.[14] The situation was similar at the NDRC. Among 190 anti-monopoly investigations launched by the NDRC, only 7 cases had concerned the abuse of dominance as of 2015.[15] After 2016, the two agencies turned their attention to the abuse of dominance, though still on a limited scale. From 2016 to 2017, a total of 315 anti-monopoly cases were dealt with by the SAIC and the NDRC along with their local agencies, among which 47 cases involved the abuse of dominance, accounting for 15% of the total.[16]

Based on the disclosed data, the digital market was not the focus of the SAIC and the NDRC during that time. Rather, public utility companies in such areas as water, gas, electricity, and public transportation were their major targets. Thus, proving the market dominance of these companies was not a major obstacle for public enforcers because most of them were natural monopolies, unlike the situation encountered by private plaintiffs.

However, two well-known cases deserve to be discussed here, even though they are not directly related to the digital field. These decisions reflect the NDRC's and the SAIC's analytical approaches and mindsets when dealing with cases related to the abuse of market dominance, which will also be reflected in their future decisions involving the digital field. One is the NDRC's investigation and penalty decision on Qualcomm in 2015,[17] and the other is the SAIC's decision in the *Tetra Pak* case in 2016.[18]

On 2 March 2015, the NDRC published its decision after a 15-month investigation into Qualcomm, the largest smartphone chipmaker in the world. The NDRC awarded damages of RMB 6.088 billion (about USD 975 million), the highest penalty imposed under the AML until that time.[19]

14 The data include cases investigated by the SAIC, the NDRC and their local agencies. Wen Lin (林文), *Zhongguo Fanlongduan Xingzheng Zhifa Baogao (2008~2015)* (中国反垄断行政执法报告2008–2015) [*Report on China's Anti-Monopoly Administrative Law Enforcement (2008~2015)*] (Intellectual Property Publishing House, 2016), 76–79.

15 *Ibid.*, at 143–44.

16 The number is summarized from *Report on China's Anti-Monopoly Administrative Law Enforcement (2008~2015)*. See Lin, note 14.

17 "Guojia Fazhan He Gaige Weiyuan Hui Dui Gaotong De Xingzheng Chufa Jueding Shu [2015]1 Hao Xingzheng Zhifa" (国家发展和改革委员会对高通公司的行政处罚决定书[2015]1号行政执法) [The NDRC's Administrative Penalties Decision on Qualcomm, [2015] No.1], Fa Gai Ban Jia Jian Chu Fa [2015] No. 1, *chinaiprlaw.cn*, December 31, 2015, https://www.chinaiprlaw.cn/index.php?id=935 [[Hereinafter 'NDRC's Administrative Penalties Decision on Qualcomm'].

18 "Guojia Gongshang Xingzheng Guanli Zongju Xingzheng Chufa Jueding Shu" (国家工商行政管理总局行政处罚决定书) [The SAIC's Administrative Penalty Decision], Gong Shang Jing Zheng An Zi [2016] No. 1, November 9, 2016, https://www.samr.gov.cn/zt/qhfldzf/art/2016/art_8ca2ed4b38d842d7b4c363eaac06c103.html [Hereinafter '*Tetra* Case Decision'].

19 Xinhua News Agency (新华社), "Shi Shenme Rang Gaotong 'Renfa' 60 Yiyuan: Jiemi Zhongguo Shishang Zuida Jine Fanlongduan Fadan" (是什么让高通认罚" 60亿元：揭秘中国史上最大金额反垄断罚单) [What Make Qualcomm Accept the Penalty of RMB 6 Billion: Uncover the Secret of the Largest Penalty in China's History], *gov.cn*, February 10, 2015, https://www.gov.cn/xinwen/2015-02/10/content_2817573.htm

With little difficulty, the NDRC proved Qualcomm's dominance in the relevant market. The NDRC concluded that CDMA baseband chips, WCDMA baseband chips, and LTE baseband chips were standard essential patents ('SEPs') that constituted three separate and independent relevant markets.[20] Qualcomm licensed these SEPs collectively, so its behaviour impacted several relevant markets. In each relevant market, Qualcomm enjoyed a 100% market share, amounting to Qualcomm's market dominance under Article 19 of the AML (2008). No evidence had been provided by Qualcomm to rebut the dominance claim. The NDRC's approach to defining relevant market was basically same as that in US and EU competition law.[21]

The NDRC concluded that Qualcomm had abused its dominance in three respects:[22] First, it charged excessive royalties. By refusing to provide patent lists and signing long-term or indefinite licensing agreements with fixed royalty rates, Qualcomm incorporated expired wireless SEPs into its licensing package. In addition, Qualcomm required certain Chinese licensees to counter-license their non-wireless SEPs to Qualcomm without compensation. Second, Qualcomm tied non-SEPs with SEPs without justification. Third, Qualcomm imposed unreasonable sales terms on the baseband chips it supplied. Namely, licensees had to promise not to challenge its licensing agreement as a precondition for purchasing its baseband chips.

The NDRC is not the first antitrust watchdog worldwide to take action against Qualcomm. The European Union, Japan, and Korea had already launched their own antitrust investigations over the previous 10 years.[23] None of them had challenged Qualcomm's basic formula of calculating royalties. The NDRC, however, articulated that 'calculating wireless SEP royalties based on the wholesale price of the entire device' was wrong since that would cause unreasonably high royalties.[24] Professor Xiaoye Wang, an expert who reviewed the NDRC's decision, stated that the NDRC's draft decision proposed making Qualcomm calculate royalties based on the price of the chip, the smallest saleable component, rather than the wholesale price of the entire device.[25] However, that proposal would significantly destroyed Qualcomm's

20 The NDRC's Administrative Penalties Decision on Qualcomm, note 17, at 2.

21 Cleary Gottlieb Steen and Hamilton LLP, "Chinas NDRC Concludes Qualcomm Investigation, Imposes Changes in Licensing Practices," *clearygottlieb.com*, March 16, 2015, https://www.clearygottlieb.com/-/media/organize-archive/cgsh/files/publication-pdfs/chinas-ndrc-concludes-qualcomm-investigation-imposes-changes-in-licensing-practices.pdf

22 The NDRC's Administrative Penalties Decision on Qualcomm, note 17.

23 See European Commission, "Antitrust: Commission Fines Qualcomm €997 Million for Abuse of Dominant Market Position," *ec.europa.eu*, https://ec.europa.eu/commission/presscorner/detail/en/IP_18_421; see also Japan Fair Trade Commission, "Cease and Desist Order Against QUALCOMM Incorporated," *Jftc.go.jp*, September 30, 2009, https://www.jftc.go.jp/en/pressreleases/yearly-2009/sep/individual-000038.html; see also Korea Fair Trade Commission, "Strict Sanctions on Qualcomm's Abuse of Cellular SEPs," *qualcomm.com*, December 28, 2016, https://www.qualcomm.com/content/dam/qcomm-martech/dm-assets/documents/kftc_issued_press_release_dated_december_28-2016-unofficial_english_translation.pdf

24 The NDRC's Administrative Penalties Decision on Qualcomm, note 17.

25 Li, eds., note 12, at 430.

basic global business model and core interests. Thus, the NDRC and Qualcomm negotiated and compromised with each other in the end. The NDRC allowed Qualcomm to continue calculating royalties based on the wholesale price of the entire device, and Qualcomm committed to charging 65% of the current royalties.

The NDRC's investigation of Qualcomm attracted the most attention from the international antitrust community. While the SAIC had been a market regulator even before the AML's enactment, the NDRC stood out among the three antitrust agencies as a macroeconomic planner.[26] The NDRC was criticised for its widely used pre-emptive administrative interventions, which were seen as abusing administrative power and violating due process.[27] In a Reuters report, Kunlin Xu, director general of the NDRC's antitrust bureau at that time, was dubbed 'Mr. Confession'.[28] The report states that 'lawyers and executives describe meetings with the NDRC as "interrogations", where raised voices, flaring tempers and verbal reprimands are commonplace.... A picture emerges of a culture of intimidation under the leadership of Director General Xu Kunlin'.[29] The Reuters report, however, was exaggerated and emotionalised to a large extent and did not draw the whole picture of story.

Frankly speaking, in the *Qualcomm* case, the NDRC went to great efforts to rebut accusations about lacking due process and transparency, especially from the United States. At the beginning of its investigation against Qualcomm, the NDRC held a press conference to disclose that the investigation was launched due to industrial associations and companies (some of them are American companies) tipping the NDRC off about Qualcomm's abuse of dominance, rather than the NDRC selectively enforcing the law against foreign companies.[30] During the investigation, the NDRC invited competition lawyers and experts to attend meetings with Qualcomm and issued timely (and unprecedented) press releases after many meetings with Qualcomm's senior executives.[31] Kunlin Xu stated in public that the NDRC gave Qualcomm sufficient time and opportunities to prepare for its defence. The NDRC met 28 times with Qualcomm, most in the presence of Qualcomm's lawyers.[32]

Therefore, I cannot agree with the eye-catching descriptions in the Reuters report about the NDRC's meetings with companies being mere 'interrogations' and

26 Angela Huyue Zhang, *Chinese Antitrust Exceptionalism: How the Rise of China Challenges Global Regulation* (Oxford University Press, 2021), 44.

27 *Ibid*, at 47–49.

28 Reuters, " 'Mr. Confession' and His Boss Drive China's Antitrust Crusade," *cnbc.com*, September 15, 2014, https://www.cnbc.com/2014/09/15/mr-confession-and-his-boss-drive-chinas-antitrust-crusade.html

29 *Ibid.*

30 "Guojia Fazhan Gaige Wei Jiage Jianguan Yu Fanlongduan Gongzuo Xinwen Fabu Hui Shilu" (国家发展改革委价格监管与反垄断工作新闻发布会实录) [Transcript of the NDRC's Price Regulation and Anti-Monopoly Work Press Conference], *Price Supervision and Anti-Monopoly in China* 3 (2014): 4, 4–8.

31 Cleary Gottlieb Steen and Hamilton LLP, note 21, at 11.

32 "Jiemi Fanlongduan Zuida Fadan: Gaotong Fagai Wei Goutong 28 Ci Xiangjie 60 Yi Fakuan Laili" (揭秘反垄断最大罚单：高通发改委沟通28次详解60亿罚款来历) [Uncover the Largest Antitrust Fines: Qualcomm and the NDRC Communicated for 28 Times, Explore the Origin of the Fine of RMB 6 Billion], *sohu.com*, February 11, 2015, https://www.sohu.com/a/2143612_108342

'reminiscent of Red Guard tactics'. Qualcomm and other investigated companies were given opportunities to argue in those meetings, and their defence indeed influenced the final decision. In the *Qualcomm* case, the NDRC yielded on its original proposal that the royalty be based on the smallest saleable component, as some experts and industrial regulators (e.g., MIIT) had advocated. That was definitely the result of Qualcomm's unstinting appeals during those meetings. The NDRC's investigation of IDC, a US tech company, is another example. Several meetings were also held between the NDRC and IDC in the investigation of IDC's abuse of dominance. Given IDC's active cooperation and responses, the NDRC suspended its investigation.[33] I would like to use the *Qualcomm* and *IDC* cases to argue that meetings with the NDRC were not necessarily about forcing companies to yield to the NDRC's unchallengeable power. Shrewd lawyers and sensible executives should have known how to utilise those meetings, and the opportunities for communication they provided, to avoid the worst penalties and strive for their companies' best interests.

Of course, the NDRC's enforcement was not perfect. The NDRC's bureaucratic culture and the remnants of regulation under a planned economy may cast a shadow on its enforcement. As a macroeconomic planner and price controller, the NDRC may be the most powerful administrative agency in China. That inevitably contributed to a paternalistic and hard-hitting approach to its enforcement of the AML. The fact that an antitrust advisor was dismissed by the State Council's Anti-Monopoly Consultant Committee for providing consulting services to Qualcomm may have further reinforced the NDRC's reputation.[34] Moreover, the decision in the *Qualcomm* case was still unpolished, lacking sufficient economic analysis about the competitive effects of the behaviour. Furthermore, the boundary it drew between defining the relevant market and determining market dominance was blurry.

Compared to the NDRC, the SAIC was the market regulator even before the AML was enacted. The SAIC's predecessor—the Central Administration for Industry and Commerce—was set up as early as 1954. In 1978, the first year of China's reform and opening up, the SAIC was formally established. In 1993, China enacted the AUCL, which was primarily enforced by the SAIC. That law prohibits various anti-competitive behaviours that disturbing or damaging the competition, such as counterfeiting, commercial bribery, false advertising, infringing commercial secrets, unfair prize selling, damaging good will, and some behaviours now regulated by the AML (like tying and administrative monopoly). In 2001, as China was preparing to join the WTO, the SAIC was upgraded to a ministry-level department directly under the State Council and authorised to investigate counterfeiting,

33 The NDRC, "Guojia Fazhan Gaige Wei Dui Meiguo IDC Gongsi Shexian Jiage Longduan An Zhongzhi Diaocha" (国家发展改革委对美国IDC公司涉嫌价格垄断案中止调查) [The NDRC Suspends Investigation of U.S. IDC Corporation for Alleged Price Monopolization], *ndrc.gov.cn*, May 22, 2014, https://www.ndrc.gov.cn/xwdt/xwfb/201405/t20140522_956346.html

34 Lan Lan, "Antitrust Adviser Booted off State Committee for Violations," *chinadaily.com.cn*, August 14, 2014, https://www.chinadaily.com.cn/business/2014-08/14/content_18307258.htm

protect consumer welfare, investigate commercial fraud, break up local protectionism, enforce the AUCL, among other market regulations.

Compared to the NDRC, the SAIC kept a low profile, with less eye-catching enforcement and insignificant fines and remedies, except for its investigations of Tetra Pak and Microsoft.[35] To some extent, that was due to the SAIC's rich experience with market regulation and its bureaucratic culture of being a microeconomic regulator. In other words, it adopted less of a paternalistic style in its enforcement, leaving more space for market mechanisms.

The SAIC's investigation of Microsoft was a case of 'great cry and little wool'. Since no formal decision was ever disclosed, we cannot discern the SAIC's enforcement tendencies or patterns from that case. Therefore, I would like to take a close look at the *Tetra Pak* case here. The decision on *Tetra Pak* is relatively self-contained and detailed, allowing us to discern tendencies and peculiarities in the SAIC's enforcement.

After five years investigating Tetra Pak International SA and five of its Chinese subsidiaries (here collectively called 'Tetra Pak'), the SAIC concluded that Tetra Pak had abused its dominance and issued a fine of RMB 667.7 million (approximately USD 90.7 million), the largest fine imposed by the SAIC as of the end of 2016.[36] The SAIC had conducted a field investigation, surveyed the market, held interviews, and collected a trove of documents and digital data while dealing with this case.[37] Moreover, both the SAIC and Tetra Pak employed external economists to provide expert opinions regarding the definition of relevant market and the evaluation of competitive effects.

Despite being a fledging antitrust enforcer then, the SAIC issued a 47-page, well-organised and well-reasoned decision that exceeded most expectations. The decision, with its clear and logical structure, included a three-part analysis.

Specifically speaking, in the first part, the SAIC identified three separate relevant markets: the supply of aseptic packaging equipment ('equipment market'), the supply of technical services for aseptic packaging equipment ('service market'), and the supply of aseptic packing materials ('materials market').[38] Moreover, the SAIC used economic methods—namely, the rules of demand-side/supply-side substitutability—to determine the relevant markets. For example, the SAIC stated that there was strong demand to deliver milk throughout China (especially southern China) because major milk suppliers were in the north. Given China's vast territory and the insufficiency of cold-chain transportation across the country, aseptic packaging can meet the needs of affordable long-distance liquid milk delivery.[39] No materials were similar enough in function to substitute for aseptic packaging, so

35 See Zhang, note 26, at 44; see also Xiaoting Guo (郭晓婷), "Gongshang Zongju Zhuanan Zu Dui Weiruan Gongsi Jinxing Fanlongduan Diaocha Xunwen" (工商总局专案组对微软公司进行反垄断调查询问) [The SAIC Working Panel Investigates Microsoft Corporation], *gov.cn*, September 1, 2014, https://www.gov.cn/xinwen/2014-09/01/content_2743252.htm

36 *Tetra* Case Decision, note 18, at 47.

37 *Ibid.*, at 2.

38 *Ibid.*, at 3–10.

39 *Ibid.*, at 5.

the supply of aseptic packing materials should be identified as a separate relevant market. The equipment market and the service market were analysed and identified through the same approach.

The second part was to determine Tetra Pak's dominant market position. The SAIC followed the assessment indicators provided by Article 18 of the AML (2008) to conclude that Tetra Pak held dominance in each of the three relevant markets. These indicators included market share, the status quo of competition, the company's ability to control the market, others' level of reliance on the company, and the threshold of market entry. These analyses were not superficial or mere formalities but demonstrated the SAIC's relatively mature administrative enforcement. For example, as to the issue of dominance in the equipment market, Tetra Pak argued that there were a dozen competitors who also manufactured the aseptic packaging equipment, so Tetra Pak did not have the dominance. The SAIC countered that the number of aseptic packaging machines was not enough to demonstrate market share, but that the machines' filling capacity should be taken into consideration. When one machine can fill 6,000 packs per hour and another can fill 24,000 packs per hour, the latter machine's filling capacity is four times that of the former one. Although Tetra Pak had several competitors in the equipment market, a calculation of the number and filling capacity of machines showed that Tetra Pak's market share was over 50%.[40]

In the third part of its analysis, the SAIC addressed whether Tetra Pak had abused its dominance. Three major behaviours were under the SAIC's scrutiny: (1) whether there was illegal tying when Tetra Pak tied equipment and services with packing materials; (2) whether there was a restriction of trade when Tetra Pak required upstream producers of brown paper to deal exclusively with it, and (3) whether loyalty discounts violated the AML.

The SAIC's decision in *Tetra Pak* case used mainstream economic approaches in the antitrust field and reflected the impact of EU and US competition law on China's enforcers.

As to the tying issue, the SAIC noticed the 'leverage' effects of tying. Namely, by requiring its equipment and services customers to use its packing materials as well, Tetra Pak could leverage its market power in the equipment market and services market to the materials market so as to sustain its dominance in the materials market despite increasingly intense competition there. The SAIC seemed to use an approach like the 'rule of reason' to evaluate the anti-competitive and pro-competitive effects of tying. Unfortunately, the SAIC did not go further to explain how tying would substantially injure the market, considering that Tetra Pak only required equipment buyers or renters to use the tied packing materials during the equipment performance trial period and quality warranty period (a maximum 21 months in total). Since the investigation against Tetra Pak had lasted for five years, the conclusion that Tetra Pak had engaged in illegal tying would have been more persuasive if the SAIC had found empirical evidence showing that tying for no more than 21 months had substantially injured or distorted competition.

40 *Ibid.*, at 12.

Regarding the issue of restricting trade, Tetra Pak was accused of restricting raw material producers from trading with others. There were only two producers (one being the other's subsidiary) of brown paper in Chinese mainland. Tetra Pak was their only trading partner, while other packing material producers in Chinese mainland used white paper, rather than brown paper. Tetra Pak and the two brown paper producers signed a cooperation agreement of exclusively producing packing boxes according to parameters and requirements given by Tetra Pak. The SAIC concluded that Tetra Pak's behaviour had restricted and injured competition in the materials market.[41] The SAIC noted that the patent for brown paper was owned by the two material suppliers, rather than Tetra Pak, which was not justified in restricting the suppliers' freedom to supply brown paper to others.

Some, however, argue that the SAIC's conclusion about Tetra Pak's illegal restriction on trade should have been based on more cautious analysis. These critics note that whether restricting trade harms competition is a contentious question in the field of economics and that the supplier's motivation behind accepting the restrictions is the key factor in applying the 'raw material blockade' theory.[42] To some extent, I agree with that opinion that the materials market could not have actually been blocked due to Tetra Pak's restricting behaviours because the white paper supplied by various other producers could fully substitute for brown paper. Moreover, if the two brown paper producers were willing to accept such restrictions, that may have been a rational business strategy for them, considering the large volume and steady orders from Tetra Pak. From this point of view, the SAIC may have unduly interfered in their normal business activities.

The loyalty discounts issue was the SAIC's bold attempt to use the catch-all clause of Article 17 of the AML (2008) to create a new type of abusive behaviour since the AML does not list loyalty discounts as a typical abusive behaviour. The SAIC found that Tetra Pak offered its customers three types of discounts: retroactive rebates, personalised sales target discounts, and special discounts or exceptional discounts.[43] The SAIC adopted an approach akin to the 'rule of reason'. It admitted that giving discounts was a common commercial activity with apparently pro-competitive effects, but under certain circumstances, a company with market dominance could apply discounts to generate clearly anti-competitive effects. In this case, the SAIC found that customers' demand could be divided into a 'non-contestable portion', which could only be provided by Tetra Pak, and a 'contestable portion', which could be provided by both Tetra Pak and its competitors. However, by using the loyalty discounts, 'the dominant company could utilise the "non-contestable portion" of demand to restrict the "contestable portion" of demand'.[44] Thus, the SAIC concluded that, the key to determining the loyalty discounts' anti-competitive effects was whether it has prevented competitors

41 *Ibid.*, at 22.
42 *See* Li eds., note 12, at 460–61.
43 *Tetra* Case Decision, note 18, at 37.
44 *Ibid.*, at 40.

from vying with Tetra Pak at the same or similar costs.[45] That analytical approach reflected the cutting-edge theory of 'raising competitors' costs' that was also adopted by advanced antitrust jurisdictions.[46]

2.1.3 Conclusion

After the AML's enactment, many were delighted to learn about a new means of venting their rage against large enterprises for years of high prices and poor services. Thus, an increasing number of private lawsuits were brought in the courts, 90% of which were about abuse of market dominance in various aspects of people's lives, such as transportation, insurance, medical care, food, household appliances, electricity, and digital activities.[47] The lawsuits against digital and tech giants like Baidu, Tencent, and IDC attracted the most public attention. China's courts, however, were cautious to hold a digital company as being in violation of the AML. That may be because the judicial branch prefers to be discreet about interfering in market mechanisms, especially in newly emerged business areas such as the internet. Therefore, private plaintiffs' winning rate was extremely low in the early years of AML enforcement, and almost all plaintiffs' losses were due to insufficient evidence. That created a significant disincentive for bringing antitrust lawsuits, a negative effect that continues to this day.

Compared to private enforcement, public enforcement did little to target digital companies in this period. Although the burden of proof was not a substantial obstacle for public enforcers, antitrust enforcement in the digital field and cases of abuse of dominant market position were not their main concerns because of the national plan for economic development during that time. Therefore, very few well-known digital companies were investigated. Since few administrative decisions in the digital field has been disclosed, I chose two high-profile cases (*Qualcomm* and *Tetra Pak*), which were respectively decided by the NDRC and the SAIC, to observe the characteristics of the two agencies' enforcement.

As a macroeconomic planner and powerful price controller, the NDRC's enforcement seemed tougher and more unkindly, which received more criticism from overseas observers. Nevertheless, the NDRC's efforts to improve transparency and due process should not be ignored. Compared to the NDRC, the SAIC had a long history of market regulation. On the one hand, the SAIC seldom investigated 'famous' companies to avoid making a big splash. Rather, it authorised its local branches to conduct most investigations. On the other hand, the SAIC was in tune with enforcement trends in advanced antitrust jurisdictions. It proactively adopted economic approaches to analyse the competitive effects of a specific behaviour, and some analysis even reflected up-to-date economic theories. With the *Tetra Pak* decision, the SAIC showed it was able to conduct a relatively

45 *Ibid.*, at 46.
46 See Li eds., note 12, at 461.
47 Zhu, note 2.

complicated analysis about a behaviour's competitive effects, although some conclusions still needed more solid and in-depth reasoning. Observing the SAIC's enforcement patterns is crucial for our following discussion because the antitrust agency that would be established later, the SAMR, largely took up the mantle of the SAIC.

2.2 After 2018: storm and reform of AML enforcement

2.2.1 Changes in legal framework and regulatory regime

In 2018, 10 years after the enactment of the AML, the chariot of China's antitrust enforcement suddenly moved into the fast track. The end of 2020 was when the Central Economic Work Conference first stated, 'To strengthen antitrust efforts and prevent the disorderly expansion of capital, the country will improve laws and regulations regarding the identification of monopolistic practices from Internet platform companies'.[48] Therefore, the abuse of dominance in the digital market came into the spotlight for not only the government but also the whole society. That led to significant reforms and changes in law-making and enforcement.

2.2.1.1 Revisions of laws and regulations

A series of laws and regulations have been drafted and enacted to bridle the digital leviathans. The newly amended AML (2022) inserted a new provision: 'An undertaking with a dominant market position shall not abuse its dominance by utilizing data and algorithms, technology, or platform rules, etc.'.[49] The supporting regulation, *Provisions on Prohibiting Abuse of Dominant Market Positions* ('Provisions on Abuse of Dominance 2023'), was issued by the SAMR in 2023 to clarify the definition of the relevant market and specify elements when defining a market. *Provisions on Prohibiting Abuse of Intellectual Property Rights to Exclude or Restrict Competition* ('Provisions on Abuse of IP Rights 2023') reiterates the fundamental rule that merely having IP rights does not imply the rights holder's dominant market position and further specifies factors for determining an IP rights holder's dominance.

Furthermore, the State Council's Anti-Monopoly Committee issued the *Anti-Monopoly Guidelines for the Platform Economic Field* ('Platform Guidelines') in 2021. Although the Platform Guidelines are not binding, they do point to the direction of China's anti-monopoly enforcement in the future. The chief advisor of the Anti-Monopoly Committee of the State Council, Qiong Zhang, stated that the core purpose of the Platform Guidelines was to encourage platforms to develop

48 Wei Xu, "Nation Sets Its 2021 Goals for Economy," *chinadaily.com.cn*, December 19, 2020, https://www.chinadaily.com.cn/a/202012/19/WS5fdd346ca31024ad0ba9cc00.html

49 Anti-monopoly Law of the People's Republic of China (promulgated by Standing Comm. Nat' l People's Cong., August 30, 2007, effective August 1, 2008, amended August 1, 2022), CLI.1.5128034(EN) (Lawinfochina), Art.18, para. 2. [Hereinafter 'the AML (2022)'].

larger and stronger, and the Guidelines could improve the consistency and transparency of anti-monopoly enforcement in the platform economy.[50]

In Section 2.2.2, several high-profile cases will be discussed. From these cases, we can tell how these newly enacted rules and regulations have affected decision makers' analysis and conclusion, compared to the early years of AML enforcement.

Besides the laws and regulations in the field of anti-monopoly previously mentioned, some newly enacted laws in other fields during that period also address digital platforms' activities. The Personal Information Protection Law, enacted in 2021, imposes extra liabilities on platforms (especially large platforms), to protect personal information.[51] The E-commerce Law,[52] which took effect in 2019, also regulates platforms' abuse of dominance.

These laws have the same legal status as the AML, but some of their provisions are inconsistent (or even contradictory) with it. In the short term, conflicts inevitably arise when applying different laws that aggravate unpredictability and inconsistency when platform companies do business and develop strategies. In the long run, that could even undermine the AML regulatory regime. These conflicts and connections between the AML and other laws leave space for further study and clarification. This topic will be discussed in Chapter 5.

2.2.1.2 Evolving characteristics and development of public and private enforcement

Unlike the United States, China's anti-monopoly regime is centred on administrative agencies, rather than the judicial system. Administrative agencies have been carrying the banner in AML enforcement against digital companies that have abused their dominance. The year 2021 was a banner year in the AML's history. A storm of AML enforcement swept major platforms (such as Alibaba and Meituan) in Chinese mainland. Their 'either-or' behaviour of abusing dominance (namely, the dominant platform forces its trading companies or consumers to choose from it and its competitors) was the major target set by the SAMR. After the record-breaking penalty of RMB 18 billion (USD 2.8 billion) on Alibaba, the SAMR summoned representatives from 34 major platform enterprises and ordered them to scrutinise themselves for irregularities.[53] That instantaneously sent jitters

50 Can Jin (金灿), "Zhuanjia Jiedu Pingtai Jingji Lingyu Fanlongduan 'Zhinan'" (专家解读平台经济领域反垄断《指南》) [Expert Interpretation of the Anti-Monopoly Guidelines for the Platform Economic Field], *jjckb.cn*, March 2, 2021, http://www.jjckb.cn/2021-03/02/c_139776988.htm

51 Personal Information Protection Law of the People's Republic of China (promulgated by the Standing Committee of the National People's Congress, August 20, 2021, effective November 1, 2021), CLI.1.5055321(EN) (Lawinfochina).

52 E-Commerce Law of the People's Republic of China (promulgated by the Standing Committee of the National People's Congress, August 31, 2018, effective January 1, 2019), CLI.1.321035(EN) (Lawinfochina).

53 Global Times, "Chinese Regulators Summon 34 Platforms to Meeting, Ordering Them to Self-Scrutinize Irregularities," *globaltimes.cn*, April 14, 2021, https://www.globaltimes.cn/page/202104/1220928.shtml

throughout the digital market. I once invited a senior manager from Tencent to join my researching project. When he heard the project involved antitrust issues, he politely but promptly turned me down.

That enforcement storm suddenly calmed down toward the end of 2022, due to the pivot in the central government's policy toward the platform economy that was discussed in Chapter 1. Only one platform operator was investigated and fined by the SAMR in 2022, and no company in the digital market was fined in 2023.[54]

Although the judicial system (that is, private enforcement) has played a second fiddle in China's anti-monopoly enforcement system, the role of courts has been continuously stressed in recent years. Indeed, the relationship and connection between private enforcement and public enforcement received considerable attention from the designers of China's anti-monopoly regime.

The SPC issued the new *Judicial Interpretation on Several Issues Concerning the Application of Law in Anti-Monopoly Civil Lawsuits* on 24 June 2024 ('Judicial Interpretation [2024]'). The new judicial interpretation was based on a previous interpretation from 2012, keeping 9 articles unchanged, revising 5, and adding 37 new articles.

Judicial Interpretation (2024) had two main purposes: first, smoothing the connection between judicial decision-making and administrative enforcement from procedural mechanisms to substantial provisions; and second, lightening plaintiffs' burden of proof.[55]

As to the connection between private and public enforcement, Article 2 of Judicial Interpretation (2024) provides that except for merger review decisions, private plaintiffs can bring lawsuits either directly before the courts or after administrative agencies have reached an effective decision. Courts, however, may not hear lawsuits that merely argue a defendant's behaviour is monopolistic without demanding any compensation. The purpose of that provision is to prevent a flood of lawsuits that could squander judicial resources.

Article 10 of Judicial Interpretation (2024) addresses the evidentiary capability of administrative decisions in follow-on private lawsuits. An earlier draft of Judicial Interpretation (Article 11) provided that when anti-monopoly agencies have determined a behaviour to be monopolistic, the plaintiff can assert it is monopolistic without providing any other evidence, unless there is sufficient counterevidence to rebut that conclusion. However, that provision was revised in the final version of the interpretation, which narrows the evidentiary scope of administrative decisions. Article 10 states that if an administrative decision in force has established a monopolistic behaviour, the plaintiff of a following lawsuit need not prove the basic facts ascertained by that decision. For example, in a private litigation

54 The China National Knowledge Infrastructure (CNKI), the country's largest online academic database and library, was the only case of abuse decided by the anti-monopoly agency in 2022.

55 "Zuigao Fa Fabu Xinde Fanlongduan Minshi Susong Sifa Jieshi" (最高法发布新的反垄断民事诉讼司法解释) [The Supreme People's Court Issues New Judicial Interpretations on Anti-Monopoly Civil Litigation], *ipc.court.gov.cn*, June 24, 2024, https://www.court.gov.cn/zixun/xiangqing/435731.html

regarding abuse of dominance, the plaintiff does not need to prove the exact percentage of market share if that percentage, as a factual issue, has been held by a previous administrative decision. But the plaintiff still needs to prove the legal issue, namely that with that percentage of market share, the defendant enjoys a dominant market position. Presumably, the reason for such a change is that the drafters of Judicial Interpretation (2024) were cautious about giving administrative decisions such strongly determinative and probative capability, given some innate defects of public enforcement. Nevertheless, it seems that the new judicial interpretation does indeed alleviate, but not thoroughly solve, the chronic problem of plaintiffs' difficulty in meeting the burden of proof.

Moreover, Article 13 of Judicial Interpretation (2024) provides that when an anti-monopoly authority has begun investigating an alleged monopolistic behaviour, courts may suspend lawsuits about the behaviour in question. Clearly, courts' right to suspend litigation can save judicial resources and alleviate plaintiffs' burden of proof, as well as avoid inconsistency in the results of public and private enforcement. However, considering that information about launching anti-monopoly investigations is generally not disclosed to the public, it is not certain whether such a provision will improve the transparency of public enforcement in the future or just become a formality.

Concerning the abuse of dominance in the digital market, several new provisions of Judicial Interpretations (2024) deserved to be discussed here.

First, Article 14 provides that plaintiffs may no longer assume the burden of proof of defining the relevant market if the defendant has a dominant market position or the behaviour with effects of restricting and eliminating competition. That opinion has already been reflected in the SPC's previous decisions. In the *Qihu 360 v. Tencent* case, the SPC stated that the relevant market definition was only a tool, but not the purpose, for assessing a business's market power and evaluating a behaviour's effect on competition. Even without defining the relevant market, therefore, a court can still evaluate dominance and competition effects so long as there is direct evidence to prove an alleged behaviour is restricting or eliminating competition.[56]

However, in my opinion, that position may contain a logical paradox. Without defining the relevant market, how could the court determine a defendant's dominance, when market power is to a large extent determined by the scope of the market? In the *Qihu 360 v. Tencent* case, the SPC concluded that the relevant market definition was not a necessary step, but it still defined the relevant market as the instant messaging market in Chinese mainland. I worry that this new provision may give courts too much discretion, making anti-monopoly lawsuits more uncertain and less predictable.

Second, Paragraph 2 of Article 16 specifies the approaches for defining the relevant market involving digital platforms. It provides that the relevant market may

56 *Beijing Qihu Ltd. v. Tencent Technology (Shenzhen) Ltd.* (北京奇虎科技有限公司诉腾讯科技（深圳）有限公司、深圳市腾讯计算机系统有限公司滥用市场支配地位纠纷案), (2013) Min San Zong Zi Di 4 Hao [(2013) Sup. People's Ct. Final Decision No. 4] (China), Wolters Kluwer. [Hereinafter '*Qihu 360 v. Tencent*'].

generally be defined according to a platform's alleged monopolistic behaviour. Namely, if there are multiple markets, the relevant market is the one closely related to the alleged monopolistic behaviour. Also, when the alleged monopolistic behaviour is involved in multiple markets, the court can define several relevant markets separately or, if necessary, define all markets involved as a single one. From my point of view, this provision has valuable foresight. Given digital platforms' networking and multi-homing characteristics, it provides a flexible framework for courts to explore approaches for evaluating platforms' competition and business. Since it is a cutting-edge issue, China's experience and attempts may provide possible solutions to global antitrust community in future.

Third, Article 29 of Judicial Interpretation (2024) further specifies plaintiffs' burden of proof for defendants' dominance. With the purpose of lightening plaintiffs' burden of proof, it provides that courts may determine defendants' dominance, if plaintiffs can prove (1) that the undertaking maintains a price significantly higher than what is competitive for a long period, or the quality of its commodities significantly decreases for a long period without substantial loss of users, and the relevant market lacks competition, innovation and new players; (2) that the undertaking has maintained a significantly high market share over a long period, and the relevant market lacks competition, innovation, and new players.[57] Moreover, the last paragraph of Article 29 states, 'Information released to the public by the defendant may be taken as *prima facie* evidence to prove the defendant's dominance, unless there is other contrary evidence to rebut it'. That provision appears to be a lesson learned from the *Renren v. Baidu* case to correct the Court's conclusion that Baidu did not have dominance even though its own official website claimed it was 'the largest Chinese search engine in the world'.

Furthermore, Article 32 lists factors that courts may take into special consideration when determining a platform's dominance, which include (1) the platform's business model and the actual competitive pressure it suffers; (2) the platform's market share and the duration it has held such a share; (3) whether the platform generates significant network effects, scale effects, and scope effects, among others; (4) data, algorithms, and technologies, among other advantages held by the platform; (5) its impact on adjacent markets; (6) users' reliance on the platform, lock-in effects, usage habits, multiple platform usage, and the cost of switching to other platforms; (7) new entrants' willingness and ability to compete with incumbents and entry barriers due to scale and technical reasons as well as policy and legal restrictions; and (8) innovative and technological developments in the relevant market. Therefore, in private lawsuits related to platforms, courts must determine the defendant's dominant market position from various aspects, which not

57 It deserves to note that the Judicial Interpretation (2024) firstly includes the 'time factor' into consideration when the court determines the market dominance. Considering the dynamic of the digital market, the time factor is crucial to determine a market dominance. As an expert stated in an OECD report that 'as an unscientific rule-of-thumb, one could consider a market-leading firm to be dominant for competition law purposes if it remains unchallenged for five years, or if it very easily defeats any challenges that do arise'. See OECD, The Digital Economy, DAF/COMP (2012)22, at 146.

only gives courts more discretion but also leaves more room for litigants to debate that determination.

The following sections, which cover public and private enforcement, respectively, will discuss several high-profile cases that reflect how these changes in the legal framework and regulatory regime have impacted decision makers' analyses and judgements.

2.2.2 After 2018: public enforcement and high-profile cases

2.2.2.1 The opening of the enforcement storm: the Alibaba case

The penalty of RMB 18.228 billion against Alibaba Group Holding Limited ('Alibaba') on 10 April 2021 kicked off a storm of public enforcement. Since the background of this case has already been addressed in Chapter 1, I will not go further here but only focus on the administrative decision itself and the administrative instruction issued by the SAMR.

By using the demand and supply substitution test, the SAMR defined the relevant market as the online retail platform services market in Chinese mainland. First, the SAMR distinguished online retail platform services from brick-and-mortar retail services based on the different demands of three groups: namely, platform operators, consumers, and retailers. Second, given various aspects—like trading customs, service language, payment settlement, after-sale services, and the government approval required to operate value-added internet-based telecommunication services in the Chinese mainland—the SAMR decided the relevant geographic market was the Chinese mainland market.[58]

As to the issue of dominant market position, the SAMR encountered challenges from the new forms of competition. Alibaba argued that there were various indicators to define the market share of online retail platform services; online platform services were highly reliant on technological development, third-party payment methods, and logistics, which significantly lowered the threshold of market entry and encouraged new entrants. Alibaba also said that thanks to the development of platforms, there were now more diverse channels for distribution, which decreased business operators' reliance on any one platform, and that migration costs were not high.[59] The SAMR, however, turned down Alibaba's arguments without a detailed explanation, merely noting that the company had held a high market share for a long time with a high market reputation and strong consumer stickiness, which actually creates a high cost for migrating to other platforms.[60]

The SAMR chose to analyse Alibaba's dominance normatively under Articles 18 and 19 of the AML (2008), while addressing the peculiarities of the platform

58 "Guojia Shichang Jiandu Guanli Zongju Xingzheng Chufa Jueding Shu" (国家市场监督管理总局行政处罚决定书) [SAMR's Administrative Penalty Decision], Guo Shi Jian Chu [2021] No. 28, *samr.gov.cn*, April 10, 2021, at 3–8, https://www.samr.gov.cn/zt/qhfldzf/art/2021/art_74b2593fd32a432baf3dcbd163935167.html [Hereinafter referred to 'SAMR Penalty Decision on Alibaba'].

59 *Ibid*., at 8.

60 *Ibid*., at 8.

economy. First, after calculating the service revenue and commodity transaction volume on the platform, the SAMR concluded that Alibaba's share of the relevant market was over 50%.[61] Second, the SAMR used the Herfindahl-Hirschman (HHI) and CR4 indexes to conclude that over the past five years, the relevant market had been highly concentrated with very few competitors.[62] Third, the SAMR deemed Alibaba with strong control power over the market, from setting prices and controlling data traffic to making platform rules and algorithms and owning major distribution channels for business operators.[63] Fourth, Alibaba had deep financial pockets with which to expand its business and advanced technology to collect big data on trading, logistics, and payments. Moreover, Alibaba was the largest public cloud service provider in China, which gave its business operators a suite of services for cloud computing and big data analysis to boost their business. In addition, Alibaba had established a reliable security system powered by advanced AI technology. Fifth, Alibaba's platform had strong network and lock-in effects, a very strong reputation recognised by consumers, and a high cost of migrating to other platforms, which altogether proved business operators' high reliance on Alibaba.[64] Sixth, considering the network effects and two-sided nature of the platform, it was becoming increasingly difficult for potential entrants to reach a critical mass. Also, operating a platform requires a massive investment as well as a combination of logistics, payments, and data systems and substantial inputs for advertising and marketing, making market entry of online retail platforms very difficult.[65] Last, the SAMR noted that Alibaba had endeavoured to build its own ecosystem, including not only online retail services but also logistics, payments, and data processing, which in turn cemented its dominance.[66]

The main portion of the penalty decision centred on this last question—whether Alibaba had abused its dominant market position. The agency carried out a two-step analysis of Alibaba's behaviours: first, examining whether it was abusive; second, assessing its competitive effect.

As to the first step, the SAMR concluded that Alibaba had engaged in three types of behaviours to abuse its dominance without justifiable excuses, violating Article 17.1(4) of the AML. It described those three types of behaviours as follows:[67] (1) Alibaba ranked business operators on its platforms into seven levels and prohibited business operators at the top three levels (core operators) from operating stores on any other competitive platforms. (2) Alibaba prohibited business operators (especially core operators) from joining sales or advertising activities held by rivals' platforms. As everyone in China knows very well, each year's e-commerce promotions like 'Double 11' and '618' (comparable to Black Friday in the United States and Boxing Day in Britain), are national carnivals of consumerism. Thus, such an

61 *Ibid.*, at 9.
62 *Ibid.*, at 9.
63 *Ibid.*, at 10.
64 *Ibid.*, at 11.
65 *Ibid.*, at 12.
66 *Ibid.*, at 12.
67 *Ibid.*, at 13–18.

'either-or' rule could be significantly detrimental to retailers' profits. (3) Alibaba used various carrot-and-stick measures to implement its either-or strategy with the help of platform rules, algorithms, and data-processing technology. For example, if an operator violated Alibaba's either-or rules, Alibaba would degrade the operator's commodities in search results and disqualify it from promotion activities. Since online retail is a competition for grabbing consumers' attention, those punishments were very intimidating for business operators on Alibaba's platform. When retailers complied with the either-or rules, Alibaba would increase the traffic of their online stores as rewards.

In the last part of the penalty decision, the SAMR analysed the either-or behaviours' effect on restricting or eliminating competition from four perspectives.

First, the SAMR concluded that Alibaba's either-or behaviours damaged competition among providers of online retail platform services. Due to the network and lock-in effects, that behaviour not only resulted in losses for business operators but also damaged consumer welfare, becoming a feedback loop that further weakened rival platforms' ability to compete. Evidence showed that when implementing the either-or strategy, Alibaba deliberately targeted certain commodities and brands to successfully make rival platforms less competitive. Also, the either-or strategy deterred many potential players from entering the relevant market.[68]

Second, the SAMR said business operators on the platform were victims as well. Alibaba's behaviours impaired operators' freedom to run their business on the one hand, and the punishments Alibaba administered for violations of its either-or rules injured operators' legitimate profits on the other hand.[69]

Third, the SAMR stated that Alibaba's behaviours hindered resource optimisation and hampered innovation.[70] It is interesting to note that innovation in SAMR's decision was taken as an independent factor in evaluating the behaviour's competitive effects, which mirrored lawmakers' major concern about the impact of monopolistic behaviour on innovation. That may also explain why innovation was added to Article 1 as one of the achieving purposes of the AML when it was amended in 2022, even though some scholars have expressed opposition or doubts about that revision.[71]

68 *Ibid.*, at 18–20.

69 *Ibid.*, at 20–21.

70 *Ibid.*, at 21–22.

71 For example, Professor Xiaoye Wang opposes to include 'encouraging innovation' as one of the AML's major purposes. She states it is wrongful to set 'innovation encouragement' as the AML's legislative purpose since it may conflict with the AML's fundamental purpose—competition protection—and it may cause confusion with the goal of Intellectual Property Law. See Xiaoye Wang (王晓晔), " 'Fanlongduan Fa (Xiuzheng Caoan)' De Pingxi" (《反垄断法（修正草案）》的评析) [A Commentary on the Anti-Monopoly Law (Draft Amendment)], *Contemporary Law Review* 36 (2022): 36, 43–44; also see, Lei Wang argues that encouraging innovation can be covered by the purpose of improving efficiency, so it should not be set as an independent purpose in Article 1 of the AML. See Lei Wang (王磊), "Chuangxin Mubiao Zai 'Fanlongduan Fa' Shang De Dingwei Yu Shixian–Jianping 'Fanlongduan Fa (Xiuzheng Caoan) 'Di 1 Tiao' (创新目标在《反垄断法》上的定位与实现—兼评《反垄断法（修正草案）》第1条) [Orientation and Realization of Innovation Goal in Anti-Monopoly Law: Comment on Article 1 of the Anti-Monopoly Law (Draft Amendment], *Journal of China University of Political Science and Law* 87 (2022): 173, 176.

Fourth, injury to consumer welfare was the last point that the SAMR addressed. It is reasonable for a modern anti-monopoly law to consider harm to consumer welfare. The definition of consumer, however, is always contentious.[72] In the digital market, consumer welfare is much harder to define since every individual has various expectations and varying degrees of tolerance about technology, privacy, and value of personal data, among other matters. The terms used to define consumer welfare—such as 'wealth', 'satisfaction', and 'consumer choice'—are full of subjectivity and uncertainty, especially in the digital era, so it is difficult for anti-monopoly enforcers to evaluate harm to consumer welfare. Therefore, in my opinion, the SAMR addressing consumer welfare here was more intended to position it as a modern competition agency than to substantively or thoroughly discuss the actual issue here.

Thus concludes the reasoning part of the SAMR's decision. Compared to the decision in the *Qualcomm* case, the reasoning of the decision on *Alibaba* is evidently more mature and sophisticated, with clear logic and careful organisation. The analytical and economic approaches adopted by the SAMR were largely consistent with international practices. Moreover, the SAMR reiterated that all facts and findings were supported by solid evidence, such as the company's financial reports, working summaries, agreements signed with business operators, data issued by national statistical departments and third parties, interviews and inquiries with business operators on the platform, and data from competing platforms' operations, among others.[73]

The *Alibaba* decision has been widely praised by domestic experts as well as overseas observers. Professor Jianzhong Shi, a leading antitrust expert in China as well as the advisor of the State Council's Anti-Monopoly Consultant Committee, spoke highly of it:

> The *Alibaba* case demonstrated that anti-monopoly enforcement in the platform economy had entered a new stage, sending a clear signal that the State had enhanced its regulation over platforms. Thus, the investigation and decision in this case played a significant exemplary role.[74]

The *Alibaba* decision has also been affirmed by legal experts at international law firms, who comment that '[The] decision on Alibaba is thoughtful and impressive, in particular considering that it took the authority only three months to close the investigation'.[75] Professor Sandra Marco Colino opined that as a young antitrust

72 'The term consumer welfare is the most abused term in modern antitrust analysis. Sometimes consumer welfare is used as a synonym for economic efficiency, in which case it becomes an unnecessary and confusing redundancy'. Joseph F. Brodley, "The Economic Goals of Antitrust: Efficiency, Consumer Welfare, and Technological Progress," *New York University Law Review* 62 (1987): 1020, 1032.

73 See SAMR Penalty Decision on Alibaba, note 58, at 1.

74 Jianzhong Shi (时建中), "Ali Beifa 182.28 Yiyuan, Shifang Shenme Xinhao?" (阿里被罚182.28亿元，释放什么信号？) [Alibaba Was Fined RMB 18.228 Billion, What Signal Did It Send?], *thepaper.cn*, April 10, 2021, https://www.thepaper.cn/newsDetail_forward_12141281

75 Yong Bai, Dave Poddar, Masafumi Shikakura, and Helen Wang, "Antitrust in China and Across the Region (Quarterly Update, January–March 2021)," *cliffordchance.com*, October 10, 2024, https://www.cliffordchance.com/content/dam/cliffordchance/briefings/2021/04/asia-pacific-quarterly-antitrust-briefing---q1-2021.pdf

jurisdiction, it was impressive for China to 'take swift, effective steps to tame its big tech giants', but in the European Union, 'resolving an instance of abuse of dominance in just a few months is nothing short of a pipe dream'.[76]

From my point of view, besides the aforementioned reasons, another reason the penalty decision on *Alibaba* is regarded as a landmark case is because it demonstrated an official modus operandi for helping companies predict how administrative agencies would analyse their behaviours when determining whether it constitutes abusive dominance. That can contribute to the transparency and predictability of the AML's public enforcement.

As for the penalty, besides ordering Alibaba to terminate illegal activities and imposing a fine of RMB 18.228 billion (4% of Alibaba's annual sales in Chinese mainland in 2019), the SAMR issued an administrative instruction requiring Alibaba to rectify all the shortcomings addressed and report its efforts to the SAMR by 31 December on a yearly basis for the next three consecutive years.

The administrative instruction may sound strange to Western ears. Here I would like to further discuss its impact on the future of China's public enforcement, as well as related concerns.

The administrative instruction was issued by the SAMR along with the penalty decision. It includes 16 specific requirements in five major areas: First, Alibaba is to comprehensively rectify its competitive behaviours. That includes not only rectifying any behaviour utilising technology, platform rules, or algorithms to abuse its dominant position, but also rectifying other monopolistic behaviours, including monopolistic agreements and illegal mergers.[77] Clearly, the requirements raised in the administrative instruction go beyond the abuse of dominance that was the subject of this case.

Second, Alibaba is required to strictly assume its responsibilities as a platform, which include improving its management rules, setting neutral rules for search and rank algorithms, using data fairly and impartially, improving the transparency of platform operations, and protecting consumer information and privacy. Besides that, Alibaba should cooperate with business operators on its platform in a manner that is fair, reasonable, and non-discriminatory, without abusing its dominance. Moreover, it shall build up an external supervisory mechanism to improve the platform's internal governance.[78]

For the third and fourth obligations, the SAMR requires Alibaba to improve its internal compliance system and protect the legal interests of business operators on the platform and consumer welfare.[79]

For its last obligation, Alibaba is to take on the burden of improving fair competition and promoting innovation. Those tasks entail increasing the openness of data,

76 Sandra Marco Colino, "The Case Against Alibaba in China and Its Wider Policy Repercussions," *Journal of Antitrust Enforcement* 10 (2022): 217, 228.

77 "Guojia Shichang Jiandu Guanli Zongju Xingzheng Zhidao Shu" (国家市场监督管理总局行政指导书) [SAMR's Administrative Instruction], Guo Shi Jian Xing Zhi Fan Long [2021] No. 1, *samr.gov.cn*, April 6, 2021, at 1, https://www.samr.gov.cn/zt/qhfldzf/art/2021/art_74b2593fd32a432baf3dcbd163935167.html [Hereinafter referred to 'SAMR Administrative Instruction to Alibaba'].

78 *Ibid.*, at 1–2.

79 *Ibid.*, at 2–3.

payment channels, intra-platform applications, and other application programming interface on the platform; respecting users' choices; not refusing to deal with other market participants unless with justifications; and improving cross-platform interconnection and interoperability.[80] Furthermore, Alibaba is required to take the lead in enhancing self-discipline and innovation in the industry and to adhere to the principles of inclusiveness and sharing by providing business operators on the platform (especially small- and medium-sized ones) with high-quality services.

Thereafter, the term 'administrative instruction' has been frequently mentioned in China's anti-monopoly community. Six months later, the SAMR issued a similar administrative instruction to Meituan (a very popular platform offering food delivery, restaurant reviews, travel booking, bike-sharing, movie ticketing, and other services) after an investigation and decision to impose a penalty for its either-or abusive behaviours.[81] The SAMR, together with the Central Network Information Office and the State Administration of Taxation, held a meeting on administrative instructions and emphasised the rectifying requirements for platforms.[82] In response to the central agency's actions, some provincial-level agencies held meetings regarding administrative instructions for platforms in their regions as well.[83]

Mainstream academics have given high marks to the role played by these administrative instructions. Shiying Xu, a professor at East China University of Political Science and Law, opined that issuing an administrative instruction was an effective way to save cost on AML enforcement.[84] Guohai Li, a professor at Central South University, claimed that using this 'soft enforcement' of administrative instructions together with normative AML enforcement could better achieve the AML's fundamental purpose. He even predicted that administrative instructions would be used much more frequently in practice and become a regular form of law enforcement.[85]

However, I am concerned that the frequent use of administrative instructions may reinforce the stereotype of the administrative agency's paternalism and the absence of judicial review in public enforcement. Administrative instructions cannot be deemed an equivalent to the 'commitment' mechanism provided in Article 53 of the AML. Under that mechanism, the company under investigation offers to make a commitment in exchange for the agency suspending its investigation. That sets up a bargaining process between companies and the agency, providing an opportunity for them to defend their interests.

80 *Ibid.*, at 3.

81 "Guojia Shichang Jiandu Guanli Zongju Xingzheng Zhidao Shu" (国家市场监督管理总局行政指导书) [SAMR's Administrative Instruction], Guo Shi Jian Xing Zhi Fan Long [2021] No. 2, *samr.gov.cn*, October 8, 2021, https://www.samr.gov.cn/xw/zj/art/2023/art_31910760066b4f69aa119a20dee250ad.html

82 Detong Zhuang (庄德通), "Fanlongduan 'Xingzheng Zhidao' Huocheng Chanagtai Hua Zhifa Moshi" (反垄断" 行政指导" 或成常态化执法模式) [Antitrust 'Administrative Instruction' May Become a Normalized Law Enforcement Model], *mzyfz.com*, May 13, 2021, http://www.mzyfz.com/index.php/cms/item-view-id-1482154

83 *Ibid.*

84 *Ibid.*

85 *Ibid.*

On the contrary, an administrative instruction is unilaterally given by the anti-monopoly agency, akin to an administrative order. Since an administrative instruction is not legally binding, it is not within the scope of judicial review. However, considering the vast authority wielded by administrative agencies in China's antitrust regime, every company operating in China keenly knows the enormous risk of ignoring or defying those instructions. Thus, administrative instructions may play the role of 'regulation by shaming', as Professor Huyue Zhang pointed out in her book.[86] Orders given in administrative instructions vividly reflect the paternalistic and domineering image of regulators. For fear of shares plummeting and market reputation deteriorating, most investigated companies, such as Alibaba and Meituan, would wisely choose to abide by these instructions and waive their rights of defence.

Therefore, I do not support the wide and regular use of administrative instructions, which lack a review mechanism and afford administrative agencies enormous discretion. If administrative instructions must be used on a regular basis, I suggest two ways to maximise their merits and rein in the risks. First, the AML incorporated the issuance of administrative instructions into the law, which makes them an administrative action under judicial review. Second, as we can learn from EU competition law, a mechanism akin to the gatekeeper should be set up, along with explicit stipulation of the criteria for designating gatekeepers, their obligations, the review of their status, and so on. Administrative instructions should strictly follow the regulations for gatekeepers, which can only be issued within a prescribed legal framework.

2.2.2.2 The epilogue of the enforcement storm: the CNKI *case*

As stated in Chapter 1, an enforcement campaign in the digital field was launched in 2021 and soon subsided in early 2023. Nevertheless, such a sudden shift in enforcement was easily understandable. 'The developments also fit within a wider antitrust invigoration strategy pursued by the Chinese government, as well as a traditional modus operandi whereby and observation phase during which companies are allowed to thrive is followed by intervention',[87] as Sandra Marco Colino observes. After the heavy punches thrown at giant platforms, it was necessary to let the digital industry return to a normal operating environment under normalised regulation, rather than leaving companies in a panic about dawn raids and the next record penalty. Therefore, it was clarified during the Central Economic Work Conference 2022, in December 2022, that '[the government] shall strive to develop the digital economy and set up normalized oversight'.[88] That signalled the end of the enforcement campaign in the digital field.

86 Zhang, note 26, at 89–105.
87 Colino, see note 76, at 226.
88 "2022 Zhongyang Jingji Gongzuo Huiyi Gongbao Quanwen" (2022中央经济工作会议公报全文) [Full Text of The Central Economic Work Conference (2022)], *china-cer.com*, December 16, 2022, http://www.china-cer.com.cn/guwen/2022121622596.html

The penalty of RMB 87.6 million (about USD 12.6 million) imposed on China National Knowledge Infrastructure (CNKI), the country's largest online academic database and library, for abusing its market dominance was the only case of abuse in the digital sector decided by the anti-monopoly agency in 2022.[89] The agency's annual report states that the investigation against CNKI was due to public concern.[90] That means that CNKI's choice as a target of investigation was neither random nor of the SAMR's own doing, but a response to public demand.

Even before the case, it was commonly said in Chinese society that 'people have been suffering from CNKI for such a long time!'[91] The Chinese Academy of Sciences, the top public academic institute in China, announced it had to unsubscribe from CNKI's databases since it could not afford the exorbitant subscription fee in April 2022.[92] The Chinese Academy of Sciences was not the first to complain about CNKI. In the 2010s, several universities complained about the high price of CNKI's products and terminated their subscriptions for a while.[93] However, they finally had to yield to CNKI, which provides the largest and most complete set of academic databases, including master's and doctoral dissertations. In December 2021, a lawsuit that an 89-year-old retired professor successfully filed against CNKI for a copyright infringement[94] finally brought the public's outrage to a boil.

Against that backdrop, the SAMR launched its antitrust probe on 13 May 2022 and decided to penalise the company only seven months later, on 26 December 2022.[95] Undoubtedly, the speediness of the *CNKI* case was significant given the chronic problem of lengthy antitrust proceedings, especially when timeliness is crucial in the rapidly growing and changing digital market. Meanwhile, concerns about how to guarantee fair, transparent, and fully reviewed administrative proceedings became salient, especially from overseas observers.[96]

89 SAMR, "Zhongguo Fanlongduan Zhifa Niandu Baogao (2022)" (中国反垄断执法年度报告[2022]) [Annual Report on China's Antimonopoly Enforcement (2022)], *samr.gov.cn*, September 20, 2023, https://www.samr.gov.cn/xw/zj/art/2023/art_38056964cf5449daa346237200e24da0.html

90 *Ibid.*, at 12.

91 Xuan Jia (佳璇), "Tianxia Ku Zhiwang Jiuyi" (天下苦知网久矣) [The World Has Endured China's National Knowledge Infrastructure for a Long Time], *thepaper.cn*, April 23, 2022, https://www.thepaper.cn/newsDetail_forward_17763685

92 Xinghang Ge, Hongyao Wu, and Xintong Wang, "China's Top Science Academy Scraps Subscription to Biggest Research Database Over High Prices," *caixinglobal.com*, April 19, 2022, https://www.caixinglobal.com/2022-04-19/chinas-top-science-academy-scraps-subscription-to-biggest-research-database-over-high-prices-101872889.html

93 Jia, note 91.

94 Yuyao Lin and Yan Liao (林珏瑶，廖艳), "Zhiwang Yin Qinquan Zao Jiaoshou Qisu Hou Xiajia Qi Wenzhang, Shifou Hefa Heli" (知网因侵权遭教授起诉后下架其文章，是否合法合理) [Is It Legal and Justify for CNKI to Remove a Professor's Articles After Be Sued for Copyright Infringement], *thepaper.cn*, December 11, 2021, https://www.thepaper.cn/newsDetail_forward_15790420

95 "Guojia Shichang Jiandu Guanli Zongju Xingzheng Chufa Jueding Shu" (国家市场监督管理总局行政处罚决定书) [SAMR's Administrative Penalty Decision], Guo Shi Jian Chu Fa [2022] No. 87, *samr.gov.cn*, December 26, 2022, https://www.samr.gov.cn/fldes/tzgg/xzcf/art/2023/art_27cab7312a424e0ea46c6fa9e5044371.html [Hereinafter 'SAMR's Administrative Decision on CNKI'].

96 Colino, see note 76, at 228–29.

Just as with its decision in the *Alibaba* case, the SAMR once again followed four steps—defining the relevant market, determining market dominance, deciding whether behaviour was abusive or not, and reviewing the competitive effects of the alleged behaviour—in its analysis.

First, the SAMR defined the relevant market as online academic Chinese literature database services. In this market, database providers—through selection, collection, and arrangement—digitise and update Chinese academic journals, dissertations, conference papers, and other academic literature. These products and services include online publishing, works dissemination, data integration, document classification and navigation, literature research, statistical analysis, paper ranking, online reading, and document downloads, among others.[97]

The SAMR realised that the market concerned is a typical multilateral market that connects publishers, universities, academic institutes, and public libraries. They are academic resource providers but also users. It has prominent characteristics of network effects, so the SAMR followed the rule of demand-side/supply-side substitutability to consider each side's demand and supply in defining the relevant market.[98] It differentiated the market concerned in this case from the e-book database service, the academic literature online search service, and the online academic foreign language literature database service.

From the demand side, the SAMR first explained that an online academic literature database tends to be timely, cutting-edge, and dynamic, in contrast to online book databases, which tend to be more stable, less frequently updated, and less responsive to change. Thus, users generally take the two databases as supplements, rather than substitutes.[99] Second, an online academic literature database can provide users with in-depth search results including citations, keywords, author or institution's names, themes, and so forth that cannot be provided by an e-book database or an academic literature online search service. Moreover, some search results required by universities and academic institutions—like quotation rates and impact factors—can only be provided by an online academic Chinese literature database. Third, the charge for accessing an online academic Chinese literature database is obviously different from other databases.[100]

From the supply side, the SAMR's major reasons are as follows. First, operating an online academic literature database requires obtaining copyright authorisation from academic journal publishers, universities, and authors, setting up a high threshold for market entry.[101] Second, the provider of an online academic literature database needs to establish infrastructure and marketing channels to attract enough users if it is to reach the critical mass point and exert the network effects it needs to be profitable.[102] Such factors make it hard for new entrants to vie with incumbents.

97 SAMR's Administrative Decision on CNKI, see note 95, at 3.
98 *Ibid.*, at 4.
99 *Ibid.*, at 4.
100 *Ibid.*, at 7.
101 *Ibid.*, at 5.
102 *Ibid.*, at 5.

Third, anyone who wants to operate an online academic Chinese literature database must obtain an online publishing license as well as relevant administrative approval. Thus, in practice, no provider of academic literature online search services or online academic foreign language literature database services had ever changed its business to online academic Chinese literature database service.[103] That demonstrated the high barriers to market entry.

As to the second issue, the SAMR addressed market dominance. After the relevant market was defined, it was not difficult to establish CNKI's dominance since hardly anybody could name a rival that could threaten CNKI. Based on CNKI's annual revenue, the volume of downloaded literature, the quantity and quality of literature in its database, and the HHI index of the relevant market, the SAMR concluded that CNKI enjoyed a very high market share.[104] Furthermore, the SAMR stated, evidence demonstrated that CNKI was highly capable of setting prices and imposing conditions on users' subscription agreements.[105] Due to the network effects of the database and the current academic evaluation system adopted by most Chinese academic institutes (which will be discussed later), the SAMR found that users were highly reliant on CNKI and that the market entry barrier was very high.[106]

Regarding the third issue, on the question of abusive behaviour, CNKI was accused of signing exclusive agreements with academic journals, publishers, and universities to corner academic papers and doctoral and master's dissertations and used multiple rewards and penalties to ensure the implementation of these exclusive partnerships. Besides, CNKI was alleged to sell access to its databases at unfairly high prices through continuous steep price increases, as well as through indirect hikes from splitting databases.[107]

Finally, the SAMR analysed the competitive effects of CNKI's behaviours. Those behaviours not only restricted or eliminated competition in the relevant market but also injured the legitimate interests of academic journal presses, universities, and authors.[108] Further, CNKI's behaviours ruined the academic ecosystem and hampered the industry's innovation and development.[109] The SAMR's analysis of the competitive effects reflected the AML's plural values, as articulated in Article 1.

There was little room for creativity in the *CNKI* case since the SAMR followed the established analytical pattern and theories of harm to tackle CNKI's abusive behaviours. However, after reading its seemingly unquestionable reasoning, I find myself suspecting that the current evaluation system used in China's academic community, rather than the database's network effects, largely contributed to CNKI's monopoly power and the success of its abusive behaviour. In other words, the fact that the majority of Chinese academic institutions regarding CNKI's search

103 *Ibid.*, at 7–8.
104 *Ibid.*, at 11–12.
105 *Ibid.*, at 12–13.
106 *Ibid.*, at 13–14.
107 *Ibid.*, at 20.
108 *Ibid.*, at 24–26.
109 *Ibid.*, at 26–27.

results as the most accepted (if not the only accepted) credible sources is the main factor enabling CNKI to retain its dominant position in the market. That also helps explain why leading academic institutes, such as Peking University and the Chinese Academy of Sciences, have to use CNKI's database despite the high price and unfriendly subscription terms.

Therefore, I suggest that the agency should not limit itself to an economic and antitrust theoretical framework when analysing the network effects of a relevant market in this case, but allow non-legal or non-economic factors to affect its conclusion. The agency put much effort into discerning the characteristics of the online database market and analysing its scale effect and network externality. The online academic database, however, is not identical to other two-sided (or multisided) platforms, such as online hailing services or online retailing services. CNKI's products and services cannot be purely regarded as commodities; they involve public interests like education and academic research. Thus, I doubt that orthodox antitrust theories about platforms and relevant market can be bookishly applied to this case. Given the non-rivalry and multi-homing of the data, there could be many substitutes in theory—platforms like ResearchGate, Citationsy, SSRN, or Chinese equivalents—but only if China's academic community adopts more diverse evaluation criteria. Ironically, the current academic evaluation system is not set by CNKI, but by the academic institutes, the victims in this case.

2.2.2.3 The first public enforcement against 'data monopoly': the real-time bond trading data monopoly case

On 6 September 2024, SAMR's local agency in Shanghai City (the 'Shanghai AMR') disclosed a punishment involving data monopoly, which was the first time for China's anti-monopoly regulator dealing with such issue.[110]

The penalised party, a financial information technology company, is engaged in business related to real-time trading data. These data are collected when currency brokerage companies conduct voice brokage of bond trading. The voice brokage of bond trading refers to brokerage activities that facilitate bond transaction through telephone or other electronic technology. Companies engaging in such business shall apply for approval from the state, so there are only six currency brokerage companies in Chinese mainland that are permitted to engage in the voice brokage of bond trading business.[111] The penalised company has signed exclusive agreements with the six currency brokerage companies to obtain data about these companies' voice brokage of real-time bond trading. Thus, Shanghai AMR concludes that the penalised company enjoys 100% market share of the relevant market.[112]

110 "Shanghai Shi Shichang Jiandu Guanli Ju Xingzheng Chufa Jueding Shu" (上海市市场监督管理局行政处罚决定书) [Shanghai Municipal Administration for Market Regulation's Administrative Penalty Decision], Hu Shi Jian Fan Long Chu [2024] No. 202302, *samr.gov.cn*, August 13, 2024, https://www.samr.gov.cn/fldes/tzgg/xzcf/art/2024/art_a98612333b5f48ca98e3ce1c5710dde4.html

111 *Ibid.*, at 3.

112 The relevant market is defined by the agency as the voice brokage of real-time bond trading data services in Chinese mainland.

After the penalised company has obtained these data, it processes and integrates the data to produce a comprehensive data product ('voice bond data product'), which is sold to bond agencies and investors. Therefore, the penalised company monopolises the voice bond data product, and it refuses to trade the data product with certain companies or imposes unreasonable conditions. Shanghai AMR concluded that the penalised company's behaviours constitute the abuse of dominant market position according to the AML and imposed RMB 4.53 million, 2% of the company's sale volume of the previous year.[113]

There are two highlights of Shanghai AMR decision deserved to be addressed here. First, when determining the relevant market, the Shanghai AMR relies on the analytical approach for standard essential patents (SEP) to treat the alleged product as an independent relevant market to stress the data product's uniqueness and non-substitutability.[114] Second, the administrative decision does not bother to discern the data product's ownership, but focuses on the data's usership, which echoes the essence of *Opinions of the CPC Central Committee and State Council on Setting up a Fundamental System for Data to Better Explore The Data's Role* (known as 'the 20 Articles for Data').[115] In the 20 Articles for Data, the central government raises a proposal to design a new data framework, which weakens the importance of data's ownership, emphasises data's usership, and pays attention to the circulation of data.[116] It unprecedently raises a 'three-rights' of regulation system over data, which includes data's possessing right, processing right, and data product's operating right.[117]

In sum, regulators in various jurisdictions keep a more watchful eye on the data monopoly issue, especially in recent years. The US Securities and Exchange Commission, for example, investigated the fees that exchanges charged market participants for market data.[118] Also, the EU Commission investigated Thomson Reuters for imposing restrictions on its business partners from using Reuters Instrument Codes.[119] China, despite starting a bit late, has also joined the antitrust activities against big data giants.

113 *Ibid*., at 17.

114 Xuanfeng Ning, eds. (宁宣凤等), "Woguo Shuju Fanlongduan Diyi An De Qishi" (我国数据反垄断第一案的启示) [The Enlightenment of China's First Data Anti-Monopoly Case], *kwm.com*, September 7, 2024, https://www.kwm.com/cn/zh/insights/latest-thinking/china-s-first-antitrust-case-concerning-data-application.html

115 Opinions of the CPC Central Committee and the State Council on Establishing a Data Base System to Maximize a Better Role of Data Elements (issued December 2, 2022, effective December 2, 2022), CLI.16.5146045(EN) (Lawinfochina) [Hereinafter 'The 20 Articles for Data'].

116 Jia Tang (唐佳), "Hua Zhongdian! 'Shuju Ershi Tiao' You Naxie Liangdian Zhide Zhuyi?" (划重点！“数据二十条”有哪些亮点值得注意？) [Key Points! What Are the Highlights Worth Noting in the 'Twenty Data Articles'?], *people.com*, December 20, 2022, http://www.people.com.cn/n1/2022/1220/c32306-32590557.html

117 The 20 Articles for Data, note 115, Art. II, section 3.

118 Chairman Jay Clayton, "Statement on Market Data Fees and Market Structure," *sec.gov*, October 16, 2018, https://www.sec.gov/newsroom/speeches-statements/statement-chairman-clayton-2018-10-16

119 European Commission, CASE AT, *39654-Reuters Instrument Codes*, December 20, 2012, https://ec.europa.eu/competition/antitrust/cases/dec_docs/39654/39654_2861_16.pdf

2.2.3 After 2018: private enforcement and high-profile cases

Private enforcement plays a different role in the anti-monopoly regime from public enforcement. In contrast to private antitrust enforcement in the United States, the major principle followed by China's private enforcement is 'compensating' injured parties, rather than 'punishing' the monopolists, which is the job of public enforcement. That principle is also reflected in the newly issued judicial interpretation for 2024. Judicial Interpretation (2024) amends Judicial Interpretation (2012) in two respects: lightening plaintiffs' burden of proof and clarifying civil responsibilities.[120] Two high-profile cases will be discussed in this section, which mirror the characteristics of AML private enforcement at the present stage. Then, we will discuss trends in private enforcement moving forward and examine existing problems.

2.2.3.1 A follow-on lawsuit to the Alibaba *case:* JD.com v. Alibaba[121]

JD.com, China's second-largest e-commerce player, initially sued Alibaba for abusing its market dominance via its either-or strategy in 2017. That litigation was dragged into a lengthy quagmire due to thorny questions about jurisdiction. More than two years passed before the lawsuit finally began in December 2020. Three years later, on 29 December 2023, the Beijing High People's Court ('Beijing High Court') held in favour of JD.com, ordering Alibaba to pay compensation of RMB 1 billion (about USD 141 million).[122]

This was a typical follow-on lawsuit to an administrative decision. After the SAMR's decision to penalise Alibaba for its abusive behaviour (hereinafter referred to as 'Decision No. 28'), JD.com immediately submitted Decision No. 28 as supplementary evidence.

The Court affirmed the conclusion about the definition of relevant market, Alibaba's market dominance, and the determination of abusive behaviours in Decision No. 28. That significantly lightened the plaintiff's burden of proof. Otherwise, the Beijing High Court focused on two other issues: (1) whether there was a causation

120 Chenying Zhang (张晨颖), "Fanlongduan Minshi Susong De Dingwei Jiqi Shijian Luoji: 2024 Nian Sifa Jieshi Yaoyi Shiping" (反垄断民事诉讼的定位及其实践逻辑—2024年司法解释要义释评) [Positioning and Practical Logic of the New Interpretation: Comments on the Interpretation of the Application of Law in the Trial of Civil Dispute Cases Arising From Monopolistic Conduct of 2024], *Journal of Law Application* 8 (2024): 84, 89.

121 *JD.com v. Zhejiang Tmall Network Co., Ltd., Zhejiang Tmall Technology Co., Ltd.* (京东诉浙江天猫网络有限公司、浙江天猫技术限公司滥用市场支配地位纠纷案), (2017) Jing Min Chu Di 152 Hao [(2017) Beijing High People's Ct. Civil Ruling Paper No.152] (China). The full judgement has not disclosed to the public yet. I happened to have had a chance to read the judgement. Thus, all information about the judgement is from my notes, so I could not identify specific pages when I cited some information from the judgement in this section.

122 CPI, "JD.com Wins Antitrust Case, Beijing Court Orders $141M Damages Against Alibaba," *pymnts.com*, January1, 2024, https://www.pymnts.com/cpi-posts/jd-com-wins-antitrust-case-beijing-court-orders-141m-damages-against-alibaba/

between the defendants' abusive behaviours and the plaintiff's damages; and (2) how the damages should be calculated.

In regard to the question of causality, the Court emphasised that the abusive behaviour indeed had anti-competitive effects on the market, but it could not necessarily infer that the behaviour had caused damages to the plaintiff in the relevant market. When the plaintiff claimed damages, therefore, it had to prove the causation between the alleged damages and the abusive behaviours. Moreover, the Court stated that the plaintiff's claimed damages could include not only direct damages (the actual loss of profits) but also indirect damages. This latter category included the foreseeable benefits (including market share, commissions, more business operators on the platform, advertising revenue, and greater number of consumers) that would have accrued had the defendant not engaged in the abusive behaviours. Moreover, the Court recognised that the loss in foreseeable benefits would be affected by various factors, such as time and market changes, so the calculation should not be rigid.

Also, the Court considered whether the abusive behaviour could generate foreclosure effects for the plaintiff. If the plaintiff's turnover dropped significantly and there was no other factor contributing to that drop during the period the defendants were engaging in those abusive behaviours, that could be *prima facie* evidence of the plaintiff's damages according to the rule of preponderance of evidence under the civil procedure law. Notably, the Court pointed out that various factors should be taken into consideration to determine plaintiff's losses—such as the competition structure, both parties' business patterns, and methods of attracting consumers and consuming habits, among others. The Beijing High Court stressed that determining plaintiff's damages should accommodate the rules of the market economy without deviating from people's common sense and logic by improperly expanding or narrowing the scope of damages.

Regarding the second issue (the calculation of damages), the Court reiterated the fundamental principle of granting 'compensation' in antitrust civil litigation. Due to the impact of various non-repeatable factors, such as timing, market structure, means of competition, business strategies, and macroeconomic environment, it is often difficult to accurately calculate damages in anti-monopoly lawsuits. However, the fundamental principle of 'filling the gap' (the compensatory rule) in civil procedural law should still be adhered to. To ensure that the amount of compensation is consistent with the plaintiff's actual losses, an economic approach is typically used when estimating damages to avoid arbitrary calculations. The plaintiff should bear the burden of proof in calculating damages. In this case, both parties hired economic experts from academic institutes and industrial experts to support their arguments for calculating damages.

After receiving the judgement, JD.com made a joyful statement on social media praising it as not only being 'a fair verdict, but also a momentous landmark of maintaining fair competition order and a significant brushstroke in the developing history of China's antimonopoly law'.[123] Meanwhile, Alibaba stated that it 'respects the court's decision'.

Some legal experts favourably predicted that *JD.com v. Alibaba* 'would play a crucial guiding role in future anti-monopoly civil litigation and would contribute to the determination of damages in similar cases'.[124] Although it is a remarkable case, it actually represents a clash of the titans. Honestly, the outcome of this case cannot cheer one's heart greatly, presuming that one wants the AML to rein in digital behemoths and protect small- and medium-sized competitors.

Indeed, we should not conclude from *JD.com v. Alibaba* alone that AML private enforcement has reached a new stage that will boost private lawsuits by substantially lightening plaintiffs' burden of proof or predict that private enforcement will flourish very soon. Even though conclusions and findings from administrative decisions have now been directly affirmed as evidence by the Court, the JD.com legal team acknowledged that 'the case encountered difficulties in obtaining evidence and calculating losses'.[125] Even for this follow-on lawsuit, JD.com employed a huge and impressive legal team including leading lawyers, economics professors, and industrial experts, something that small- and medium-sized companies in the digital field cannot afford.

Therefore, though I undoubtedly agree with the significance of the case, I would not say the judgement in *JD.com v. Alibaba* is a typical or model one. I hope more lawsuits will be filed with the courts in the future to provide more empirical data for studying AML private enforcement and foreseeing its developing trends.

2.2.3.2 First private lawsuit about 'data monopoly': Eefung v. Weimeng

Unlike the battle between the two digital giants in *JD.com v. Alibaba*, this case is a story about 'an ant shaking a tree', to borrow a Chinese proverb. Eefung Software, a small software company, sued Weimeng, the owner of the biggest microblogging platform Weibo (China's equivalent of X, formerly called Twitter) for abusing its market power by restricting access to data in a way that 'directly destroyed' Eefung's business model.[126] The lawsuit was heard by Changsha Intermediate Court in Hunan Province at the end of 2022, but the judgement has not been issued yet. Interestingly, the name Eefung in Chinese means 'ants' workshop'. I look forward to the final judgement to see whether the ant has indeed shaken the tree.

123 JD.com (京东集团), "Jingdong: Su Ali Baba 'Er Xuanyi' An Yishen Shengsu, Huopei 10 Yiyuan" (京东：诉阿里巴巴"二选一"案一审胜诉，获赔10亿元) [JD.com: Successfully Won the First Instance Lawsuit Against Alibaba, Receiving a Compensation of 1 Billion Yuan], *thepaper.cn*, December 29, 2023, https://www.thepaper.cn/newsDetail_forward_25836561

124 "JD.com Wins RMB1bn in Anti-Monopoly Lawsuit Against Alibaba," *law.asia*, January 23, 2024, https://law.asia/jd-wins-1bn-antimonopoly-alibaba/

125 *Ibid.*

126 Jessica Seah, "Weibo Faces 'Anticompetitive' Lawsuit as China Cracks Down on BigTech," *Law.com*, November 12, 2021, https://www.law.com/international-edition/2021/11/12/weibo-faces-anticompetitive-lawsuit-as-china-cracks-down-on-bigtech/?slreturn=20241114-15144

There has been a long grudge between the two companies. Eefung was sued for illegally accessing and collecting Weibo's data in 2021. The Beijing IP Court held in favour of Weibo and ruled that Eefung had engaged in unfair competition behaviour.[127] Since the lawsuit was brought under the AUCL, the Court need not to define the relevant market or determine Weimeng's market dominance, but only to decide whether the behaviour was unfair to competition and violated widely accepted business ethics. In that case, the Court held that Eefung had scooped up data (some open to the public and some not) on the Weibo platform by destroying or circumventing Weibo's technical barriers and protection measures, which constituted unfair competition behaviour.[128]

Under the AUCL, Eefung's behaviour may be condemnable, given the assumption that both litigants are undertakings with equal status. From the perspective of the AML, however, Eefung's behaviour may be acceptable because the law imposes extra responsibilities on the market-dominant company. In other words, if Weibo did not have market power, it could justifiably refuse to let Eefung scrape data from its platform at its own discretion. But when Weibo enjoys market dominance, its refusal to make a deal and its foreclosure of access to data may injure competition, squeeze out competitors, and cement its dominance.

Therefore, in this antitrust lawsuit, defining the relevant market and proving Weibo's market dominance are crucial for Eefung. Only if Eefung can prove that Weibo has abused its dominance in the relevant market is it likely to win the case. The facts of the case share some similarities with *HiQ v. LinkedIn*.[129] However, Eefung scraped some non-public and backstage data from Weibo, whereas the data that HiQ scraped from LinkedIn was set as 'open to the public' by users. It is presumably a challenge for Eefung in its lawsuit to justify scraping that non-public data.

Although the case is still pending, I think the judgement may generate more far-reaching influence on AML private enforcement than that *JD.com v. Alibaba*. On the one hand, it will demonstrate whether, and in what ways, the plaintiff's burden of proof has been lightened. On the other hand, the court must answer some more complicated questions: Who owns the data? Can the data be owned, controlled, collected, shared, or substituted by various entities? Is the defendant's market power due to (or mainly resulting from) its ownership of the data? Under certain conditions, should a dominant platform be forced to let competitors access its data? What are these 'certain conditions'? What scope of data should platforms be forced to give access? None of these questions will be easy to answer.

127 Hunan Ant Fang Software Ltd. v. Beijing Weimeng Chuangke Network Technology Ltd. (湖南蚁坊软件股份有限公司与北京微梦创科网络技术有限公司不正当竞争纠纷), (2019) Jing Qi Shi San Min Di 3789 Hao [(2019) Beijing Intellectual Property Ct. Final Decision No.3789] (China), PKILAW CLI.C.311990203.

128 *Ibid.*

129 *HiQ Labs, Inc. v. LinkedIn Corp*, 273 F.Supp.3d 1099 (N. D. Cal. 2017).

2.2.3.3 *A private lawsuit's influence:* Xin Jin v. Apple

Apple has been facing antitrust probes in various jurisdictions over the past three years. The US Justice Department sued Apple for monopolisation of smartphone markets in 2024;[130] the EU antitrust watchdog also fined Apple over €1.8 billion for abusing dominant position for the distribution of music streaming apps to iPhone and iPad users.[131] Similar probes have happened in Korea and Japan as well.[132] Those investigations have forced Apple to reduce the commission fee (known as 'Apple taxes') in varying degrees in those markets.[133]

Surprisingly, Apple has not been investigated by China's competitive authorities. As of 2023, the Chinese market contributed more than RMB 3.76 trillion to App Store's turnover with Apple charging the highest commission fee, compared to other countries' markets.[134] Therefore, many criticisms attribute Apple's huge monopoly profits to Chinese competitive authorities' silence.[135]

Although the government keep dormant to Apple, consumers 'wage the war' against Apple. Xin Jin, a user of iPhone, sued Apple for abusing its dominant market position by charging over high prices for iOS apps and preventing cross-platform third-party digital wallets. The case was heard by Shanghai IP Court for the first trial and issued the judgement on 29 May 2024.[136] Although the court held Apple

130 "Justice Department Sues Apple for Monopolizing Smartphone Markets," *justice.gov*, March 21, 2024, https://www.justice.gov/opa/pr/justice-department-sues-apple-monopolizing-smartphone-markets

131 European Commission, "Commission Fines Apple Over €1.8 Billion Over Abusive App Store Rules for Music Streaming Providers," *europa.eu*, March 4, 2024, https://ec.europa.eu/commission/presscorner/api/files/document/print/en/ip_24_1161/IP_24_1161_EN.pdf

132 See Ben Lovejoy, "Korean Antitrust Regulators Find Apple and Google Guilty of Anti-Competitive Behavior," *9to5mac.com*, October 6, 2023, https://9to5mac.com/2023/10/06/korean-antitrust-regulators-aapl-goog/; see also Japan Fair Trade Commission, "Closing the Investigation on the Suspected Violation of the Antimonopoly Act by Apple Inc.," *jftc.go.jp*, September 2, 2021, https://www.jftc.go.jp/en/pressreleases/yearly-2021/September/210902.html

133 For example, iOS apps in the European Union can pay a commission of 17% to Apple, plus 3% if apps are using Apple's In-App Purchase system. It is a significant cut from the old 30% rate. Small business program developers will pay commission of 10%, plus 3%, down from 15%. See, Benjamin Mayo, "Apple Announces Reduced Commission Structure for Apps in Europe," *9to5mac.com*, January 25, 2024, https://9to5mac.com/2024/01/25/apple-announces-reduced-commission-structure-for-apps-europe/

134 Yangyu Wu and Shuqi Wen (伍洋宇，文姝琪), "Zhongguo App Store Qunian Chuangshou 3.8 Wanyi, Xuyao Jiao 'Pingguo Shui' De Zhiyou 5%" (中国App Store去年创收3.8万亿，需要交"苹果税"的只有5%) [The Chinese App Store Generated 3.8 Trillion Yuan in Revenue Last Year, But Only 5% of it Needs to Pay the "Apple Tax"], *news.qq.com*, November 19, 2024, https://news.qq.com/rain/a/20241119A04JWY00

135 See Efe Udin, "Is the 30% 'Apple Tax' High? Experts Say It Constitutes a De Facto Monopoly," *gizchina.com*, June 25, 2022, https://www.gizchina.com/2022/06/25/is-the-30-apple-tax-high-experts-say-it-constitutes-a-de-facto-monopoly/; see also Hairu Zhang, Yongjian Li, and Yan Jiang (张海汝，李勇&坚蒋艳), "'Pingguo Shui' Fan Jingzheng Xing Yanjiu: Genyuan, Biaoxian Ji Zhili Jinlu" ('苹果税'反竞争性研究：根源、表现及治理进路) [Study on Anti-Competition of 'Apple Tax': Origins, Manifestations, and Governance Strategies], *Enterprise Economy* 44 (2025): 59, 60.

136 *Xin Jin v. Apple Computer Trading (Shanghai) Co., Ltd., Apple Inc* (金鑫与被告苹果电脑贸易（上海）有限公司、被告苹果公司 (Apple Inc) 垄断纠纷案), (2021) Hu 73 Zhi Min Chu 220 Hao [(2021) Shanghai IP Court First Instance Decision No. 220] (China).

enjoying a dominant position in the relevant market, it did not uphold the plaintiff's assertion for Apple abusing the dominant position.

The court still follow the traditional analytical steps for abusing dominance case: (1) defining the relevant market; (2) determining whether Apple has a dominant position; (3) analysing whether Apple's alleged behaviours constitute abusive behaviours and violate the AML.

As to the first issue, the court defines the relevant market as the application programme trading platform with iOS system in the Chinese mainland market.[137] For the second issue, the court holds that Apple is the major operator of iOS system, which is a closed system and cannot be substituted easily by Android system, so Apple has the dominant position in the relevant market.[138]

The third issue is the focus addressed in the court's reasoning. As to the first claim, the plaintiff argued that Apple charged a high commission fee (30%) on iOS apps' providers and the fee was then transferred to consumers, which let consumers pay a higher price for the same apps in the App Store than those on other platforms. The court, however, stated that due to the huge scale of Apple's operating system, the cost for running Apple's system is hardly to be calculated, so the court could not decide whether the commission was overly high by evaluating the gap between the cost and charged commission.[139]

Furthermore, in order to determine whether Apple's commission fee was an unfair price, the court compared Apple's commission with other the application programme trading platforms (such as Xiaomi and Huawei) for same or similar apps.[140] The court found that the lowest commission fee charged by Apple was 15%, but that charged by most Android system's apps stores was over 15%; the highest commission fee charged by some Android system's apps stores can reach 50% (some app stores would also deducted trading fee before distributing profits to app providers), but the highest fee charged by Apple was 30% without deducting any trading fee.[141] Thus, the court concluded that no evidence proves that Apple charged an unfairly high price compared to the same or substitute apps' sales on the platforms of Apple's competitors. Moreover, the court stated that no evidence proved that the higher price paid by the plaintiff for an app on Apple platform than the app on other Android system platforms was due to the commission fee charged by Apple.[142] The price of a certain app was set by the app's developer/provider and changed from time to time, which may be affected by various factors, such as operating cost, market situation, users, types of services, etc.[143] Thus, the plaintiff's allegation that the higher purchasing price paid for iOS app was due to the 'Apple taxes' did not upheld by the court.

137 *Ibid.*, at 51.
138 *Ibid.*, at 46–51.
139 *Ibid.*, at 52.
140 *Ibid.*, at 53.
141 *Ibid.*, at 54.
142 *Ibid.*, at 54.
143 *Ibid.*, at 54.

Table 2.1 Apple's policy in different markets[144]

Markets	*Permit External Payment Link*	*Allow Third-Party App Stores on iOS*	*Commission Fee 'Apple Taxes'*	
			Standard Business	*Small Business*
China	No	No	30%	15%
European Union	Yes	Yes	17%	10%
United States	Yes	No	27%	12%
Korea	Yes	No	26%	11%

As to the plaintiff's claim for Apple's illegal behaviours of tying, restricting trade, and refusal of dealing, the court did not hold in favour of plaintiff either. The plaintiff claimed that Apple requires all app developers to imbed the in-App Purchases (IAP) module in the apps, and all payments are firstly transferred to an Apple's affiliated company and then distributed to app developers, rather than directly paying to developers.[145] The Court held that the plaintiff, as a consumer, did not have a standing for such a claim. Even if Apple's behaviour of forcing app developers to use the IAP module constitutes illegal tying and restriction of trade, consumers' benefits have not been injured since they still can connect third-party digital wallets (such as WeChat Pay, Alipay, or debit/visa card) to Apple Pay.[146] Moreover, the court said that IAP module was a part of iOS system, rather than an independent product, so it cannot be regarded a tying. Also, the court stated that requiring app developers to exclusively use the IAP could guarantee the data security and facilitate iOS apps' trading, which did not restrict or eliminate competition.[147]

Compared to other antitrust jurisdictions, China's decision makers seem unexpectedly tolerable toward Apple. Criticisms and doubts against Shanghai IP Court's judgement have arisen.[148]

Although the court states that the prices of iOS apps are not absolutely higher than those at app stores run by Android system, undoubtedly, Apple charges the highest commission fee and has the strictest trading conditions in China. Table 2.1 shows the difference in various markets.

Despite the fact that Apple achieved the victory in the private lawsuit, the resentment and complaints against Apple seem become more serious. In order to avoid

144 The table is cited from a blog article written by Qiongfei Wang, the plaintiff's lawyer in *Xin Jin v. Apple*.

145 *Ibid.*, at 55.

146 *Ibid.*, at 55.

147 *Ibid.*, at 57.

148 Na Li (李娜), "Zhongguo Xiaofei Zhe Su Pingguo Fanlongduan An Yishen Baisu, 'Pingguo Shui' Zhengyi Youcun" (中国消费者诉苹果反垄断案一审败诉，'苹果税'争议犹存) [Chinese Consumers Lost Antitrust Case Against Apple for the First Instance Trial, Controversies About 'Apple tax' Still Exist], *sina.com.cn*, May 30, 2024, https://finance.sina.com.cn/jjxw/2024-05-30/doc-inawzrpm0175791.shtml

any further antitrust probes by public enforcers in future and appease consumers, Apple invited an expert, a professor of economics from Shanghai University of Finance and Economics, to issue a study report to justify the commission and other policies adopted by Apple in the Chinese market.[149] However, the effect of that study report is not as ideal as Apple envisages. Some argue that data provided in that study report is not accurate and is misleading. For example, the study report states that as of 2023 the revenue of App Store is more than RMB 3.76 trillion, but to more than 95% of that revenue, app developers/providers do not need to pay 'Apple taxes'.[150] However, an expert points out that the revenue include offline and online consumption (such as take-away ordering, online shopping, online hailing a ride, advertisements, etc.); for these consumptions, Apple has not and cannot charged commission, which is only charged for in-app purchase.[151] Thus, the study report deliberately exaggerates the portion that has not been charged 'Apple taxes'. Many critics argue that the report does not well explain whether a 30% commission charged for the Chinese market is reasonable: Why does Apple charge different commission rate in China, the United States, and the European Union? Are the different rates in various markets due to different costs or actually because of Apple's fear of the tough antitrust enforcement in certain jurisdictions?[152]

It seems that the sword of Damocles is still hanging over Apple, and it is likely to become the next target for China's competitive authorities, largely because of the complaints from consumers and concerns of academics and practitioners. If there is an investigation over Apple in future, the impetus for the AML enforcement should be from bottom to up, rather than *vice versa*.

2.2.3.4 *Supreme People's Court's final decision on Didi's market dominance:* Li v. Didi Chuxing

When I intended to finalise the manuscript of this book, the SPC's final judgement[153] about a consumer suing Didi Chuxing's abuse of dominant market position

149 Heng Ju (居恒), "Apple Shengtai Xitong Zai Zhongguo Duiyu Yonghu Yu Kaifa Zhe De Jiazhi Yanjiu" (Apple生态系统在中国对于用户与开发者的价值研究) [Research on the Value of Apple Ecosystem for Users and Developers in China], *sccio.cn*, November 28, 2024, http://www.sccio.cn/uploads/20241128/11f43c504c6cff0277262b167bde54eb.pdf

150 *Ibid.*, at 1.

151 Xiao Xiao (肖潇), "Pingguo Huiying Guonei 'Pingguo Shui' Zhengyi: 95% De Kaifa Zhe Shouru Weibei Choucheng?" (苹果回应国内”苹果税”争议：95%的开发者收入未被抽成？) [Apple Responds to Domestic Debates Against 'Apple tax': 95% of Developers Not Be Charged Commissions?], *21jingji.com*, November 20, 2024, https://www.21jingji.com/article/20241120/herald/fe14507ed18a5bb832edfaf8a127a510.html

152 Jing Fu (付静), "Hanjian 'Baogao' Huiying 'Pingguo Shui' Zhiyi! Keyi Huibi Qubie Duidai Zhongguo Shichang? Pingguo: Ying Buhui Gongkai Zhiping" (罕见《报告》回应”苹果税”质疑！刻意回避区别对待中国市场？苹果：应不会公开置评) [Rare Report Responds to Debates Over 'Apple Tax'! Deliberately Avoiding Differential Treatment in the Chinese Market? Apple: Not Giving Comments], *cls.cn*, November 23, 2024, https://www.cls.cn/detail/1867809

153 *Li v. Didi (Beijing) Network Platform Technology Co., Ltd. and Didi Technology Co., Ltd.* (李某某诉滴滴出行（北京）网络平台技术有限公司、滴滴出行科技有限公司), (2024) Zui Gao Fa Zhi Min Zhong 452 Hao [(2024) Sup. People's Ct. Final Decision No. 452] (China).

was disclosed to the public in January 2025, despite the judgement was made on 25 November 2024.

Li, the plaintiff, logged into Didi Chuxing app ('Didi'), the largest transportation network provider in the Chinese market, with different mobile phone numbers to hail online rides within the four-month period from April to August 2021. He found that by using different accounts the riding prices, waiting times, and choices of rides were various. Thus, he sued Didi for engaging in differential treatment based on big data and algorithms, and he claimed Didi had abused its market dominance in violation of the AML.

The trial court ruled in favour of Didi, and the SPC heard the plaintiff's appeal on 27 March 2024. Eight months later, the Court made its final decision. The Court still followed the typical three steps in abuse of dominance cases: What is the relevant market? Does Didi have the market dominance? Had Didi abused its dominance? But there are two highlights of this judgement that deserve to be discussed.

First, the Court held that the online ride hailing service cannot be defined as a separate relevant market; instead, the relevant market in this case should at least encompass the online ride hailing service and cruising cabs that also could be booked online.[154] The geographic market is Beijing city. Considering most of cruising cabs in Beijing can be ordered online, this relevant market definition actually includes all online and offline ride hailing services.

Although there are criticisms about such relevant market definition, I agree with the Court's definition of the relevant market. Truly, the online ride hailing service providers and cruising cab operators are subject to different administrative regulatory requirements and adopt various business models; but based on the rules of demand-side substitutability, the two services can substitute for each other in the majority of cases. Based on my daily experience, when I use Didi to hail a ride, I can choose multiple types: cruising cabs, Didi Express (with a lower fare), Didi Premier (with higher fare but luxury and comfortable vehicles), or car-pooling, etc. In order to hail a ride as soon as possible, people always select multiple types of vehicles on the Didi app. It means that for consumers, cruising cabs and online rides are indeed substitutes for each other. Moreover, based on my personal experience, when I book a ride on the Didi platform, there is a probability of more than 50% that the platform will dispatch a cruising cab to me.

Thus, this case is a typical example to show how the development of technology blurs the boundary of different markets, especially the border of traditional and digital markets, which in turn affects the antitrust enforcement. The SPC's ruling, which does not stick to traditional antitrust theories but is aware of the market changes, should be applauded.

Second, the Court states at the end of the judgement that

> the conclusion is made based on the presented evidences in this case and taking the time point when the alleged monopolistic behaviour occurred as the

154 *Ibid.*, at 14.

> benchmark, so it has limitations and is subject to the constraints of time and location. Thus, the judgement does not have generally applicable effects.[155]

Such a statement is not common in a SPC's judgement. In this case, the Court held Didi neither has a market dominance nor abuses its market power. It can be inferred the reasons for such a statement that the decision makers are fully aware of the dynamics and rapid changes of the digital market, so they prefer a case-by-case analysis and are prudent to grant a precedent binding effect at present, before the SPC develops a consistent and certain approach based on sufficient practical data and trial experience.

2.3 Conclusion

Since China's AML moved into the 'fast lane' after 2018, enforcement about abuse of market dominance has been prominent and productive. Administrative decisions, judicial judgements, and academic discussions centring on this issue have reflected enforcement tendencies and problems that can help us sketch the contour of China's AML during this stage.

Compared to the early years of AML enforcement, enforcement since 2018, both by administrative agencies and through the judicial system, has been unprecedentedly active. The reasons for that are partly due to changes in national policy and partly because the platform market has been growing so fast over the last five years. Cases of companies abusing market dominance are the main targets of AML enforcers since they always attract the most attention from the media and the public.

AML enforcement during this period exhibits at least three tendencies: First, the storm of public enforcement after 2021 sent a signal to the digital market that the lax regulatory time was over and that all business operators in the digital field should be more cautious about their competitive behaviours. Once that purpose had been achieved, the enforcement storm subsided. The decisions reached by public enforcers during this period were more mature and sophisticated, with clear logic and solid organisation. They demonstrated an official modus operandi of administrative enforcement that, to a large extent, can contribute to the transparency and foreseeability of the AML's public enforcement.

Second, creating fresh motivation to bring anti-monopoly lawsuits so that the judicial system can play a crucial role in the anti-monopoly system is a major task for the courts. Compared to bureaucratic authorities, judges, who normally have received a proper legal education, pay more attention to reasoning and to the analysis of a behaviour's competitive effects in their judgements. Since a judgement that is well-organised and soundly reasoned can earn a judge a good reputation,[156]

155 *Ibid.*, at 21.

156 Periodically, the Supreme Court chooses several judgements from all levels of courts as model cases to distribute in the judicial system and disclose to the public. It has largely motived judges to improve judgements they issued with well-organised and soundly reasoned merits.

judges are willing to be influenced by economic theories and analytical approaches adopted by advanced antitrust jurisdictions to show their professionalism. Whereas administrative enforcers value their political performance and are greatly affected by short-term policies, judicial decision makers seem to be more prudent and take into consideration their judgements' long-term impact on society.

Third, from the legislative perspective, more regulations, rules, and guidelines have been successively issued to make the AML's abstract and general provisions more specific and applicable based on previous enforcement and the experience of advanced antitrust jurisdictions (especially the United States and European Union). The legal regime has yet to be perfected, however. The conflicts and connections between the AML and other laws of comparable status remain to be addressed.

3 Merger control in the digital market

3.1 Introduction to merger control in the digital sector

In recent years, there has been a growing number of mergers involving data-intensive companies in the digital market. A series of mergers launched by giant platforms like Google, Amazon, Meta, and Apple (GAMA) in the global market and by Baidu, Alibaba, and Tencent (BAT) (later replaced by Alibaba, Tencent, and Meituan [ATM])[1] in the Chinese market. Leading economists, expert panels, and major competition authorities around the world have expressed grave concerns about mergers in the digital market, discussed the current merger control regime's difficulty in catching them, and explored possible solutions.[2]

In traditional anti-monopoly theory, most mergers raise no competition concerns, and competition authorities normally view vertical mergers and conglomerate

1 The so-called 'BAT' has been increasingly challenged. Since 2012, Baidu lost its first place and has not caught up with the other two giants since then. JD.com and Xiaomi were rising rapidly and ready to replace Baidu to form a new troika. They almost succeed but failed at last. In 2019, Meituan rose quickly and finally suppressed Baidu with the market value three times more than that of Baidu. But Meituan has suffered intensive pressure from Pin Duoduo and TikTok. The ATM is not stable either. See Gu Wen (温故), " 'Dachang Xipai: Cong BAI Dao TTMAP' "(大厂洗牌：从BAT到TTMAP) [Big Platforms Shuffle: From BAT to TTMAP], *thepaper.cn*, 19 October 19, 2023, https://www.thepaper.cn/newsDetail_forward_24964761

2 For example, discussions can be found in reports issued by competition authorities and scholars in major anti-monopoly jurisdictions. See Stigler Center, "Stigler Committee on Digital Platforms–Final Report," chicagobooth.edu, September 16, 2019, https://www.chicagobooth.edu/research/stigler/news-and-media/committee-on-digital-platforms-final-report; see also FTC, "The 'Sharing' Economy: Issues Facing Platforms, Participants and Regulators," *ftc.gov*, November 17, 2016, https://www.ftc.gov/reports/sharing-economy-issues-facing-platforms-participants-regulators-federal-trade-commission-staff; see also OECD Secretariat, "Roundtable on Conglomerate Effects of Mergers—Background Note," DAF/COMP(2020)2, *one.oecd.org*, April 30, 2020, https://one.oecd.org/document/DAF/COMP(2020)2/en/pdf; see also Jacques Crémer, Yves-Alexandre de Montjoye, and Heike Schweitzer, *Competition Policy for the Digital Era: Final Report* (Publications Office of the European Union, 2019); see also Jerrold Nadler and David N. Cicilline, "Investigation of Competition in Digital Markets (U.S. Majority Staff Subcommittee on Antitrust, Commercial and Administrative Law, 2020)," *govinfo.gov*, August 2, 2023, https://www.govinfo.gov/content/pkg/CPRT-117HPRT47832/pdf/CPRT-117HPRT47832.pdf?stream=top

DOI: 10.4324/ 9781003654452-3

mergers as benign. Since the enactment of AML in 2008, China's competition authority has approved more than 5,258 mergers—over 98% of which were cleared unconditionally—while blocking only three.[3]

This generally permissive and tolerant attitude toward mergers, however, has been increasingly called into question in the context of the digital era. One specific concern is how to evaluate a digital merger's effect on competition. Can the traditional approaches and analytical tools of merger control still be effectively applied? The other concern is how to evaluate and control mergers among big platforms and start-ups to avoid 'killer acquisitions'.

Generally speaking, there are two types of mergers attracting most concerns in the digital market. One is data-driven mergers, whose major purpose is to access, collect, or utilise the targeted companies' data to expand business lines and set up an ecosystem; the other is 'nascent mergers', which aim to wipe out potential competitors in their infancy. Thus, in this book, the discussion will be focused on these two types of mergers.

Specifically speaking, the AML regulates three kinds of mergers and acquisitions: (1) mergers among undertakings (in which at least one of the undertakings loses its independent legal status); (2) an undertaking acquiring control over another by purchasing voting shares or assets (normally referred to as 'acquisition', after which each undertaking retains its own legal status); (3) an undertaking gaining control over another or having a decisive impact on it through contracts or other arrangements. In this book, 'mergers' are used in a broad sense that includes the three kinds of concentrations among undertakings.

This chapter will firstly address procedural review issues to sketch a brief picture of the AML's digital merger control framework and show the latest adjustments and improvements. Then the focus will shift to substantive review issues—namely, the difficulty of defining the relevant market and assessing competition damage—to discuss the challenges and dilemmas faced by the competition authority. Based on this analysis of traditional antitrust theories and discussion of high-profile cases with media coverage and social repercussions, I try to offer possible solutions and raise theoretical and practical issues that are worthy of further discussion.

3.2 Procedural review issues: latest changes of the merger control regime

In 2022, the AML was amended for the first time.[4] One of the major adjustments was adding several provisions concerning the digital market to respond to issues and practical disputes.

3 The data is calculated based on all disclosed decisions issued by China's competition authority, and the period of the data statistics is from 1 August 2008 to 20 August 2023.

4 Anti-monopoly Law of the People's Republic of China (promulgated by Standing Comm. Nat'l People's Cong., August 30, 2007, effective August 1, 2008, amended August 1, 2022), CLI.1.5128034(EN) (Lawinfochina). [Hereinafter the AML (2022)].

3.2.1 Pre-merger notification thresholds

3.2.1.1 Problems arising from the turnover-based threshold[5]

The merger control under the AML (2008) was based on the turnover threshold. *Provisions on the Pre-Merger Notification Thresholds for Businesses Undertaking Concentrations (2018)* ('Pre-merger Notification Provisions [2018]')[6] specifies the notification thresholds as follows: When the turnover of all merging parties exceeds 10 billion yuan in the global market or exceeds 2 billion yuan in the Chinese mainland market in the last accounting year, and the turnover in the Chinese mainland market of at least two merging parties exceeds 400 million yuan separately in the last accounting year, the merger shall be notified to China's competition authority before the transaction is carried out.[7]

Most digital platforms, however, did not report their mergers and avoided the notification responsibility by claiming that their turnover did not reach that threshold. During the past 13 years since the enactment of the AML, there have been many mergers between internet-based companies,[8] but few of them have been reported to China's competition authority. As of December 2020, no administrative punishment had been imposed for failure to make a pre-merger notification. These mergers have drawn much criticism, such as Didi's merger with Uber in 2016,[9] Alibaba's acquisition of Amap (a leading digital map provider in Chinese mainland) in 2014,[10] and Meituan's (a large platform offering food delivery, restaurant reviews, travel booking, bike-sharing, movie ticketing, etc.) merger with Dazhong Dianping (Chinese Yelp) in 2015.[11]

This lax enforcement may be due to the dilemma arising from the legitimate status of the business category known as variable interest entity (VIE). A VIE refers to a business structure in which an investor has a controlling interest despite not

5 Discussions of Didi-launching mergers is excerpted from my previous published article, with revisions: Jingmeng Cai, "The Sharing Economy and China's Antimonopoly Law: From the Didi Case to Regulatory Challenges," *Asia Pacific Law Review* 28 (2020): 159.

6 Provisions of the State Council on the Standard for Declaration of Concentration of Business Operators (2018 Revision) (Decree No. 703 of State Council, issued August 3, 2008, effective August 3, 2008, revised September 18, 2018), CLI.2.322430(EN) (Lawinfochina).

7 *Ibid.*, Art. 3.

8 According to disclosed data, there have been about 542 mergers involving internet companies from 2010 to 2020. See Jinyu Wang (王进雨), "Hulianwang Fanlongduan Beihou: Jinshinian Woguo Hulianwang Qiye Binggou Shijian Da 542 Qi" (互联网反垄断背后：近十年我国互联网企业并购事件达542起) [Behind the Antimonopoly Enforcement in the Internet Market: About 542 Mergers So Far], *finance.sina.com.cn*, December 14, 2020, https://finance.sina.com.cn/chanjing/cyxw/2020-12-14/doc-iiznezxs6898584.shtml

9 "Uber Zhongguo Jiangyu Didi Hebing Hebinghou Guzhi 350 Yi Meijin" (Uber中国将与滴滴合并合并后估值350亿美元) [Uber Merger With Didi, Estimated Value of US35 Billion], *finance.china.com.cn*, August 1, 2016, http://finance.china.com.cn/stock/xsb/yw/20160801/3838828.shtml

10 Reuters, "Alibaba to Buy AutoNavi," *reuters.com*, April 11, 2014, https://www.reuters.com/article/us-autonavi-deals-alibaba-group-idUSBREA3A15620140411

11 Yue Wang, "China's Meituan, Dianping Merge to Create a Mega Online-to-Offline Service Platform," *forbes.com*, October 8, 2015, https://www.forbes.com/sites/ywang/2015/10/08/chinas-meituan-dianping-merges-to-create-a-mega-online-to-offline-service-platform/?sh=7f4a90163e28

having a majority of voting rights. The controlling interest is achieved through a series of contractual arrangements. China's major internet giants, like Alibaba, Tencent, and Baidu, have utilised VIE structures to bypass Chinese regulations and restrictions over overseas financing and foreign investing to list in Hong Kong and/or the US stock exchanges markets.[12] Before 2018, the MOFCOM was responsible for merger reviewing. Besides, the MOFCOM was also responsible for reviewing and approving foreign investment. The validity of VIE has neither been recognised nor denied by China's authorities. They were reluctant to clarify the legality of the VIE structure to remain the regulatory flexibility.[13] Thus, the MOFCOM was in a dilemma: If it reviewed a merger involving VIE structure, it may be interpretated as a signal of confirming the VIE's legality by China's authority, so no merger review decision involving VIE structure has been made by MOFCOM.[14]

Since 2021, China has changed its previous ambiguous attitude and tightened the tech companies' overseas listings. China's State Council issued *Antimonopoly Guidelines on the Platform Economic Sector* ('Platform Guidelines'), which was the first time the regulator had articulated mergers involving in VIEs are subject to the AML's merger control.[15] From 2021 to 2022, 125 non-notification mergers in the digital market were punished by the State Administration for Market Regulation (SAMR).[16] The Appendix lists merger control decisions involving China's digital giants since 2021, among which there are punishments on failure of notification before carrying out mergers.

Since the enactment of Platform Guidelines, all mergers in the digital market reaching the notification threshold should be under the AML's scrutiny, making the notification threshold a major issue driving concerns and disputes. Some scholars stand for broadening the pre-merger notification threshold.[17] They suggest referring to the experience of Austria and Germany, which traditionally relied on turnover

12 See Jiaxing Li, "What Are VIEs and Why Are They Important for Chinese Tech Companies?" *kr-asia.com*, December 3, 2021, https://kr-asia.com/what-are-vies-and-why-are-they-important-for-chinese-tech-companies

13 Fa Chen, "China's Recent Regulation of Variable Interest Entity Structures Has Led to a Drop in Chinese Companies' US Listings," *blogs.law.ox.ac.uk*, April 19, 2022, https://blogs.law.ox.ac.uk/business-law-blog/blog/2022/04/chinas-recent-regulation-variable-interest-entity-structures-has-led

14 See Zhisong Deng and Jianmin Dai (邓志松，戴健民), "'Shouli' VIE Jiagou Binggou Jiaoyi Jingying Zhe Jizhong Lian: Bu Yifa Shenbao Falv Fengxian Zhousheng" ("首例" VIE架构并购交易经营者集中立案：不依法申报法律风险骤升) [The First Merger Case Involving in VIE: Illegal Risk Sharply Rising Due to a Failure of Notification], *lvdao.sina.com.cn*, May 22, 2020, https://lvdao.sina.com.cn/news/2020-05-22/doc-iircuyvi4433399.shtml

15 *Guidelines of the Anti-Monopoly Commission of the State Council for Anti-Monopoly in the Field of Platform Economy* (issued by the Anti-monopoly Commission of the State Council on February 7, 2021, effective February 7, 2021), Guo Fan Long Fa (2021) No. 1, CLI.4.352590(EN) (Lawinfochina), Art. 11 [Hereinafter 'Platform Guidelines'].

16 For example, the SAMR imposed penalties on Alibaba, China Reading Limit, Fengchao Network Technology, Didi, and other companies for their failure to report mergers. See Appendix.

17 See Xiaoye Wang (王晓晔), "Woguo 'Fanlongduan Fa' Xiuding De Jidian Sikao" (我国《反垄断法》修订的几点思考) [Some Reflections on Anti-Monopoly Law Amendment in China], *Law Review* 38 (2020): 11, 14–15.

thresholds but have recently widened the notification threshold by introducing a transaction value-based threshold.[18]

Partially as a result of the discussion in the field and academia, the 'transaction amount' threshold was included in Platform Guidelines, which was issued in 2021:

> [T]he turnover of operators includes income obtained from their sale of commodities and provision of services. The calculation of turnover may vary with industry practice, fee collection method, business model, and platform operators' role, among other factors. For platform operators that only provide information matching and collect commissions and other service fees, turnover may be calculated on the basis of the service fees collected by the platform and other platform revenues; for platform operators that directly participate in market competition on one side of the platform or are a leading player in that competition, the transaction amount on the platform may be calculated.[19]

The 'transaction value-based threshold' brings a great many platforms into the notification category. Since most large platforms have engaged in an intensive investor-subsidised price war to squeeze out competitors and obtain more market share, they are likely to sustain losses for a long time. As a result, their turnover is most likely to fall short of the notification threshold and thus escape anti-monopoly scrutiny. However, the 'transaction value-based threshold' bring those mergers under the scope of merger review.

To take the Didi-launching mergers as an example. Didi, an online hailing ride platform, took only four years to triumph over the online ride hailing market in Chinese mainland. The founder of Didi, Chen Wei, quit his job at Alibaba and set up Didi with about USD 120,000 in start-up capital in 2012.[20] In order to beat its first major rival Kuaidi, in which Chen's former employer Alibaba had invested, Didi received financing from Tencent (Alibaba's major rival in China) to engage in an intensive investor-subsidised price war. An investor of Didi stated in an interview that: 'If they [Kuaidi] subsidize RMB 10 for each ride, we will give RMB 11; if they raise the subsidy to RMB 12, we will provide a random subsidy, with a range from RMB 10 to 20, so the rival cannot follow us'.[21] The intense price war was ended by Didi merging Kuaidi in February 2015, and Didi obtained 90% market share of the online ride hailing market at that time.[22]

18 Jacques Crémer, et al., note 2, at 115.

19 Platform Guidelines, note 15, Art. 18.

20 Hao Li (李好), "Didi Ruhe Yong Bashi Wan Chengwei Baiyi Meijin Gongsi" (滴滴如何用八十万成为百亿美金公司？) [How Didi Grew into a Company With Billions Worth Company With RMB 0.8 Million], *tech.163.com*, February 26, 2015, http://tech.163.com/15/0226/18/AJDAUI79000940DU.html

21 "Wanggang: Didi Chuangye Sannian Chengzhangshi" (王刚：滴：创业三年成长史) [Gang Wang: Didi's Three Years' Growing Path], *baixiaosheng.net*, February 25, 2015, http://baixiaosheng.net/5970

22 "Didi De Liangda Zuiqiang Duishou: Yige Beikao Ali Caituan, Yige Nianxiao 150 Wanliang Qiche" (滴滴的两大最强对手：一个背靠阿里财团，一个年销150万辆汽车！) [Didi's Two Powerful

After the merger with Kuaidi, the investor-subsidised price war broke out between Didi and Uber. Uber China's unit announced USD 1billion to put in its Chinese business, while Didi responded with USD 1.5 billion to subsidise rides to buy market share.[23] The escalated price war imposed heavy financial burden on the two companies, and they had constantly to raise new fund to back up 'burning' money. Uber's former CEO, Travis Kalanick, once expressed his dislike of the price war:

> We're profitable in the USA, but we're losing over USD 1 billion a year in China . . . I prefer building rather than fundraising . . . But if I don't participate in the fundraising bonanza, I'll get squeezed out by others buying market share.[24]

In July 2016, Didi and Uber's China unit announced a merger; since then Uber stepped out of the Chinese market.[25]

Neither merger, however, has been reported to the competition authority. Many criticisms against this merger claimed that this merger was completed without going through any anti-monopoly scrutiny.[26] The SAMR has announced that it is investigating the merger of Didi/Uber according to the AML, but the SAMR has not released any decisions yet.[27]

The notification threshold would be the key reason for letting Didi escape from the notifying obligation. If 'turnover' is understood to be the income earned by platforms, both Didi and Uber are likely to claim that their turnover in 2015 (the year before the merger) did not reach the merger control threshold, exempting them from the obligation of notification. During Uber's and Didi's fierce price war

---

Rivals: One Backed Up by Alibaba and the Other With a Sale of 1.5 Million Vehicles a Year!], *sohu.com*, February22, 2019, http://www.sohu.com/a/296463857_100120495

23 Paul Armstrong and Yue Wang, "Didi Chuxing Faces Stiff Competition in Race to Dominate China's Ride-Sharing Market," *forbes.com*, April 11, 2018, https://www.forbes.com/sites/ywang/2018/04/11/didi-chuxing-faces-stiff-competition-in-race-to-dominate-chinas-ride-sharing-market/

24 Adam Jourdan and John Ruwitch, "Uber Losing $1 Billion a Year to Compete in China," *reuters.com*, February 18, 2016, https://www.reuters.com/article/uber-china-idUSKCN0VR1M9

25 Alyssa Abkowitz and Rick Carew, "Uber Sells China Operations to Didi Chuxing," *wsj.com*, August 1, 2016, https://www.wsj.com/articles/china-s-didi-chuxing-to-acquire-rival-uber-s-chinese-operations−1470024403

26 See Yinghua Liu (刘映花), "Shangwubu Erci Huiying Didi Youbu Hebing: Weishixian Shenbao Xuchengdan Falv Zeren" (商务部二次回应滴滴优步合并：未事先申报需承担法律责任) [MOFCOM Reiterated: Unreported Merger Should Be Imposed as Legal Liability], *it.people.com.cn*, August 18, 2016, http://it.people.com.cn/n1/2016/0818/c1009-28645240.html; see also Xu Liu (刘旭), "Didi De Fanlongduan Miti" (滴滴的反垄断谜题) [The Riddle of Didi/Uber Merger], *thepaper.cn*, December 5, 2018, https://www.thepaper.cn/newsDetail_forward_2708193

27 Xinhua News Agency (新华社), "Guojia Shichang Jianguan Zongju: Yiju Fanlongduan Fa Ji Youguan Guiding Dui Didi Shougou Youbu Anjian Jinxing Diaocha" (国家市场监管总局：依据反垄断法及有关规定对滴滴收购优步案件进行调查) [SAMR: Investigating the Didi/Uber Merger Pursuant to the AML], *gov.cn*, November 16, 2018, https://www.gov.cn/xinwen/2018–11/16/content_5341128.htm

before 2016, both companies offered substantial subsidies to private drivers and passengers, so it is indeed plausible that Didi's and Uber's respective revenue in the Chinese market was less than RMB 0.4 billion before the merger. Therefore, broadening the notification threshold to 'transaction value' can capture some transactions without sizeable revenue that nevertheless have an anti-competitive impact.

Furthermore, the newly revised *Provisions of the State Council on the Notification Threshold of Business Concentration* (Provisions on Notification Threshold [2024]) took effect on 22 January 2024. On the one hand, the Provisions on Notification Threshold (2024) largely raise the amount of the turnover threshold with the purpose of exempting small- and medium-size transactions from the pre-merger notification obligation to increase transaction's efficiency, reduce companies' burden, and encourage innovation. On the other hand, it broadens the threshold for large platforms to impose heavier reporting obligations on them.

Two of the revisions in the new provision merits a closer look. First, Article 3 raises the notification threshold from turnover of RMB 10 billion to RMB 12 billion in the last accounting year for all merging parties in the global market and from RMB 2 billion to RMB 4 billion for all merging parties in the Chinese mainland market. The notification threshold for separate turnover in the Chinese mainland market of at least two merging parties is also raised from RMB 400 million to RMB 800 million.

Second, Article 4 is designed with the main purpose of regulating mergers launched by large platforms and 'killer acquisitions'. The version for soliciting public opinion issued in 2022 provides more specific thresholds: If (1) the turnover of one merging party in the Chinese mainland market exceeded RMB 100 billion in the last accounting year; and (2) the market value or the estimated value of the merged company is at least RMB 800 million, and its turnover in the Chinese market accounts for more than one-third of its global turnover, the merge must be notified to the competition authority even if it does not reach the threshold provided in Article 3. The final effective version, however, deletes such provisions but only remains a more general stipulation: 'Although a merger does not reach the threshold provided in Article 3, there are evidence showing that the merger has or may generate effects of eliminating or restricting competition, the competition authority can require undertakings to notify'.

The change in the final version, as observed by practitioners, shows the competition authority's prudent attitude toward the regulation over 'killer acquisitions' to avoid using a 'one-size-fits-all approach' to apply all nascent mergers.[28] Indeed, China's competition authority may need more practical experience to regulate 'killer acquisitions' and determine specific reporting thresholds. Also, the value of Article 4 is not only to grant the competition authority authority to review a merger even though it does not reach the reporting threshold but also leave possibility of importing non-price factors to the merger review mechanism.

28 Li Cai and Zhengyang Cang (蔡丽，苍证阳), "Xin Jingyingzhe Jizhong Shenbao Biaozhun Chutai: Licheng Ji Yaodian Jiedu" (新经营者集中申报标准出台：历程及要点解读) [New Issued Provisions on Notification Threshold: History and Key Points], *dowway.com*, February 6, 2024, https://dowway.com/news/2024-03-11/436.html

3.2.1.2 The potential introduction of non-price factors

Although legislators have taken into account the traits of the digital market to adjust the notification threshold, they have not completely solved all problems arising therein. Both 'turnover' and 'transaction amount' are still based on price parameters, but other nonprice factors also play a significant role in digital mergers, which have not been included in the legal texts.

In the digital field, mergers usually happen between established firms and start-ups. According to the *Provisions on Notification Threshold (2024)*, the notification requirement only applies when at least two merging parties' turnover (or transaction value) reaches 800 million yuan separately. Therefore, these mergers can still escape the scrutiny of China's competition authority if they take place before the start-ups generate enough turnover or have enough transaction value to hit the notification threshold.

Compared to anti-monopoly regulations over other monopoly behaviours (abuse of dominant position and monopoly agreements, for example), merger control is an *ex ante* regulation. Due to the information asymmetry between regulators and business operators, as well as the dynamic nature and complexity of the market, especially the digital market, it is difficult for regulators to foresee or assess a merger's impact on the future market by relying entirely on the turnover or transaction parameters.

There have been proposals to incorporate non-turnover factors in the notification threshold, such as data acquisition, impact on innovation, the possibility of establishing an enclosed business ecosystem, and so on. As we have seen in the mergers of Google/Nest,[29] Google/Dropcam,[30] and Facebook/WhatsApp,[31] what the large platforms really care about is the value of data.

However, some competition authorities, such as the European Commission, worry about that broadening the 'merger control jurisdiction to cover competitively relevant transactions irrespective of turnover raises a set of difficult issues'.[32] Such an approach could cause legal uncertainty while increasing the administrative burden and transaction costs.

In light of these disputes and concerns, Article 26 of the AML (2022) revises the notification threshold as follows:

> Where a business concentration reaches the pre-merger notification thresholds prescribed by the State Council, the undertakings shall report in advance to the anti-monopoly authority under the State Council, and the concentration shall not be implemented if the concentration is not reported.

29 FTC, "Google Inc./Nest Labs, Inc," Transaction Number: 20140457, *ftc.gov*, February 4, 2014, https://www.ftc.gov/legal-library/browse/early-termination-notices/20140457

30 FTC, "Google, Inc./Dropcam, Inc," Transaction Number: 20141171, *ftc.gov*, July 10, 2014, https://www.ftc.gov/legal-library/browse/early-termination-notices/20141171

31 EC, Facebook/WhatsApp (Case Comp/M.7217), Commission Decision (2014) 7239 Final, October 3, 2014.

32 Jacques Crémer, et al., note 2, at 114.

> If a business concentration does not reach the notification threshold prescribed by the State Council, but there is evidence to show that the concentration has or may have the effect of excluding or limiting competition, the antimonopoly authority under the State Council may require the business operators to make a notification.

The second paragraph of Article 26 authorises competition authority to initiatively launch a merger review, even if the merger does not reach the notification threshold. This power could make up for the defects of the turnover-based threshold to bring some data-driven mergers, and especially 'nascent mergers', under the AML's scrutiny. That would also make it possible to introduce some non-price factors for evaluating mergers in the future.

However, the AML (2022) does not specify the criteria or rules that the competition authority must abide by when initiating a review for mergers that do not reach the notification threshold. That leaves room for academic research and practical exploration about how to respond to improving transaction efficiency in the digital market and how to normalise agencies' discretionary power.

3.2.2 'Stop-the-clock' mechanism

The AML (2022) introduces the 'stop-the-clock' mechanism to allow the competition authority to suspend a merger review under certain conditions. That solves, at least to some extent, the issue that has long bothered China's competition authority: when a merger involves in a complicated transaction or complex market condition, the near impossibility of completing a merger review within the time limits set by the law.

The AML gives the competition authority 30 days for a preliminary review. If the competition authority cannot make a decision within that time and needs a further review, it can extend the review for another 90 days. After that period, the competition authority can have another 60 days for a prolonged review, provided that the following conditions are met: (1) the merging parties agree to extend the review period; (2) documents or materials submitted by the merging parties are inaccurate; or (3) substantial changes happened after notification.[33] Thus, according to the law, the longest reviewing period is 180 calendar days in total.

In practice, however, due to the heavier caseload and the complexity of transactions, the competition authority sometimes is not able to complete the review within the time limits. Some merger reviews that could have been completed at the preliminary review stage were delayed to the extended review stage. And in other cases, when the review could not be finished within 180 days as restricted by the law, the merging parties had to withdraw their notification and then resubmit it to earn another 180 days. This is burdensome for both the companies and the competition authority.

33 The AML (2022), note 4, Art. 31.

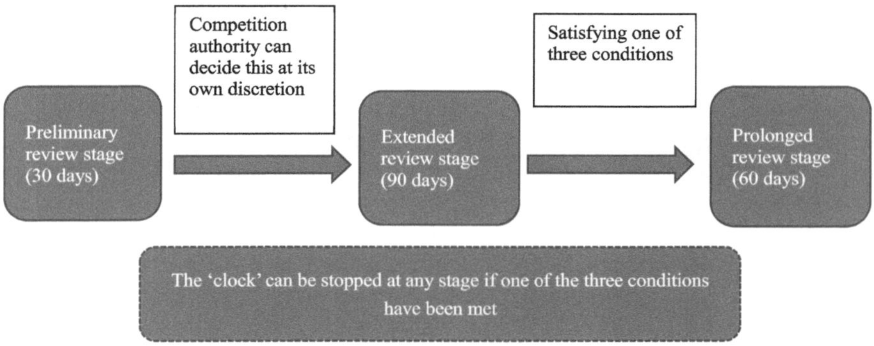

Figure 3.1 Three merger review stages

Table 3.1 Difference between 'stop-the-clock' mechanism and prolonged review stage

Triggered Condition / *Stages*	*'Stop-the-Clock' Mechanism*	*Prolonged Review Stage*
1	Undertakings fail to submit documents and materials as required, making the review impossible.	Documents and materials submitted by undertakings are inaccurate and need to be further verified.
2	New developments or information arise that have a material impact on the merger and must be verified if the competition authority is to proceed with the review.	Relevant circumstances changed significantly following notification about the merger.
3	The competition authority needs to further assess restrictive conditions attached to a merger, and the undertakings request such a suspension.	Undertakings agree to extend the review period.

The stop-the-clock mechanism[34] is designed to address the aforementioned procedural problems. The conditions triggering the stop-the-clock mechanism look similar to the conditions triggering a prolonged review of 60 days, but they are different in essence. Figure 3.1 clarifies the three review stages, and Table 3.1 compares the conditions triggered the prolonged review stage and the stop-the-clock mechanism.

In regard to the submission of defective materials, it would appear that 'stopping the clock' requires a more serious degree of defect than that for pushing the review to the prolonged stage because suspension can happen at any stage of the review and the specific period of suspension has not stipulated by the law yet. To avoid a review suspension, therefore, the merging parties must be more conscientious

34 The AML (2022), note 4, Art. 12.

about submitting the required materials. As to the second condition, the competition authority can only stop the review if new developments or information have arisen that would prevent the review from proceeding. To move into a prolonged review stage, in contrast, the changed circumstances do not have to be as serious as the obstacles preventing the review from proceeding.

For the third condition, under this scenario, it is the merging party that applies for a suspension, rather than the competition authority stopping the review on its own initiative. When the competition authority considers assessing the restrictive conditions that may be imposed, the merger is likely to be the one restricting or limiting the market. The stop-the-clock mechanism gives the merging parties more time to negotiate with the competition authority and persuade them to accept the proposed remedies that the merging parties offered with more elaborate and rigorous competitive analyses and economic arguments. That also gives the competition authority sufficient time to assess the proposed remedies and can keep the competition authority from blocking a merger or imposing harsher restrictive conditions due to a hasty review.

After the stop-the-clock mechanism took effect, the MaxLinear/Silicon Motion merger seems to be a case affected by this mechanism. MaxLinear, an American company designing connectivity and infrastructure solutions for broadband, connectivity, and infrastructure applications, acquired Silicon Motion, a developer of SSD controllers and turn-key solid-state drives, in May 2022; they filed a pre-merger notification to the SAMR on 15 September 2022.[35] According to the disclosed decision, the SAMR decided to suspend the merger review on 6 January 2023, and the review was restarted on 14 July 2023. It seems that the merger review has been suspended for about six months. Unfortunately, the SAMR did not specify which one of the three conditions had triggered the 'stop-the-clock' in this case. In the decision, the SAMR stated that it informed the merging parties that this merger had or might have effects of eliminating or restricting competition and thus conducted several rounds of negotiations with the merging parties about how to reduce anti-competitive effects that the transaction may cause. Thus, it is reasonable to suspect that the stop-the-clock mechanism was triggered in this case due to the third condition, namely, the need of further assessing restrictive conditions attached to the merger. This merger was approved with restrictive conditions on 26 July 2023, but one day later MaxLinear announced the termination of this acquisition.[36] It is reasonable to assume that the SAMR's review decision made beyond the merging parties' expected timeline might be a contributing factor to the termination of acquisition.

35 SAMR, "Shichang Jianguan Zongju Guanyu Fujia Xianzhixing Tiaojian Pizhun Mailing Gongsi Shougou Huirong Keji Gongsi Guquan An Fanlongduan Shencha Jueding De Gonggao" (市场监管总局关于附加限制性条件批准迈凌公司收购慧荣科技公司股权案反垄断审查决定的公告) [Announcement by SAMR on Approving Acquisition of Equity Interests in Silicon Motion Technology Corporation by MaxLinear Inc. With Restrictive Conditions], *samr.gov.cn*, July 26, 2023, https://www.samr.gov.cn/fldes/tzgg/ftj/art/2023/art_a685ac0dd85647b3898dff75f68fa2c4.html

36 "MaxLinear Provides Update on Proposed Acquisition of Silicon Motion," *investors.maxlinear.com*, July 26, 2023, https://investors.maxlinear.com/press-releases/detail/509/maxlinear-provides-update-on-proposed-acquisition-of

Although the newly established stop-the-clock mechanism can make up for some defects of the current review regime, it raises concerns about the risk of officials abusing their discretionary power and greater uncertainty for transactions. My suggestion is to issue more specific supporting guidelines or regulations soon to normalise competition authority's discretionary power and provide companies with more explicit, measurable, and predictable principles and guidance. These provisions, for example, should include a maximum time for 'stop-the-clock' and remedies or punishments for competition authority's abuse of invoking the stop-the-clock mechanism.

3.3 Substantive review issues: puzzles and challenges

In traditional anti-monopoly theory, mergers are classified into three categories: horizontal mergers, vertical mergers, and conglomerate mergers. Horizontal mergers are generally subject to the strictest review since they directly reduce the number of competitors and change the market structure. In contrast, vertical and conglomerate mergers are treated with more tolerance, especially in jurisdictions influenced by Chicago School, which advocates full trust in the market mechanism and minimal government regulation. In the case of conglomerate mergers, competition authorities lack 'an existing guideline (or analytical framework) to assess the merger. It will likely close the investigation (if it even opened one). But that does not mean that these mergers are harmless'.[37]

In the digital sector, a large number of mergers fall into the category of conglomerate mergers: They share data, make it much easier to move beyond the relevant market, create new markets for consumption, and squeeze start-ups, among other effects. There are plenty of examples: Microsoft, a leading developer of personal-computer software and applications, acquired Skype, an instant message software, in 2011.[38] Google spent USD 3.2 billion to buy Nest Labs, a manufacturer of thermostats and carbon monoxide detectors, and USD 555 million to purchase Dropcam, a producer of home monitoring cameras, in 2014.[39] Tele Atlas, a provider of a navigable digital map database, was acquired by TomTom, Europe's largest portable navigation service provider, in 2008.[40] Also, the 2014 merger of Alibaba Group, China's largest online platform, with Amap, a leading digital map provider, can be seen as part of Alibaba's efforts to build its business empire and ecosystem.[41]

37 Maurice E. Stucke and Allen P. Grunes, *Big Data and Competition Policy* (Oxford University Press, 2016), 128.

38 Microsoft/Skype (Case Comp/M.6281) Commission Decision C 7279 [2011], October 7, 2011.

39 See Ankit Ajmera, "Google's Nest to Buy Dropcam for $555 Million: Report," *reuters.com*, June 22, 2014, https://www.reuters.com/article/us-google-nest-dropcam-idINKBN0EW02820140622; see also Nick Statt, "Google's Nest Labs Acquires Dropcam for $555M," *cnet.com*, June 20, 2014, https://www.cnet.com/home/smart-home/googles-nest-labs-acquires-dropcam-for-555m

40 TomTom/Tele Atlas (Case COMP/M.4854), Commission Decision C 1859 [2008], May 14, 2008.

41 Zhe Meng and Lei Bi (孟哲，毕磊), "Ali Wancheng Quanzi Shougou Gaode" (阿里完成全资收购高德) [Alibaba Accomplishes the Acquisition of Amap], *it.people.com.cn*, July 20, 2014, https://it.people.com.cn/n/2014/0720/c1009-25304347.html

These mergers usually span a variety of markets, services, and products; sometimes, they even create a new market. The competition authorities lack economic tools, analytical approaches, technical knowledge, and practical experience that would be needed to *ex ante* assess these mergers' impact on competition. Major jurisdictions' competition authorities have been criticised for underenforcement in the digital market.

In most jurisdictions, the merger review should follow certain fundamental rules. In the United States, a merger must be prohibited where its effect 'may be substantially to lessen competition, or to tend to create a monopoly', according to Section 7 of the Clayton Act. In the European Union, the EC Merger Regulation (139/2004) sets up the rule that a concentration shall 'not significantly impede effective competition in the common market or in a substantial part of it, in particular as a result of the creation or strengthening of a dominant position'. China's AML provides that a merger shall not have the effect of 'restricting or limiting competition'. This section will mainly discuss how these review rules could be applied in the digital market and challenges that China's competition authority may face when enforcing the AML in the digital sector.

3.3.1 Difficulties of defining the relevant market

When reviewing a merger, defining the relevant market is normally the first step. However, it is contentious whether a relevant market should or even can be defined in each merger review case.

In traditional antitrust theory, supply and demand for a product or service are normally used to examine whether there are roughly identical or at least very close substitutes.[42] Since the product or service competes with the substitutes, they can be regarded as being within one relevant market. The rule of relevant market definition is crucial because competition authorities rely on that definition to determine whether a merging party obtains market power or cements that power after the merger. The HHI, which is widely used to determine market competitiveness and the degree of market concentration, also relies on the relevant market definition. Thus, an erroneous market definition may lead to a misguided or wrongful merger review decision.

In her well-known article 'Amazon's Antitrust Paradox', Lina Khan vividly described how Amazon aggressively expanded its business lines through a series of acquisitions and finally established an business empire that crosses multiple markets, from retailing and marketing to delivery and logistics networks, payment services, auctioning, book publishing, television and film producing, fashion design, hardware manufacturing, cloud server space, and computing power.[43] There have been similar developments in China as well. Alibaba and Tencent, the country's two largest e-commerce giants, merged a series of enterprises in different fields

42 Herbert Hovenkamp, "Digital Cluster Markets," *Columbia Business Law Review* 1 (2022): 246, 248.
43 Lina M. Khan, "Amazon's Antitrust Paradox," *Yale Law Journal* 126 (2017): 710, 754.

to expand their business into retailing, logistics services, cloud computing, instant messaging, digital media and entertainment, online finance and payments, and so on. More information of these mergers can be found in the Appendix.

As we can see from the previous examples, it is difficult to arrive at an accurate definition of relevant market in the digital sector, which frustrates China's competition authority and erodes its confidence in enforcing the AML. China's SPC has taken the lead in seeking solutions to this problem. In *Qihu 360 vs. Tencent* in 2013, a landmark decision under the AML, an antivirus software developer called Qihu 360 sued Tencent, a massive instant messaging software platform in China, for abusing its dominant market position.[44]

In this case, the SPC first stated that

> it is not necessary to explicitly define a relevant market in every abusive dominant market position case.... The function of defining the relevant market is to assess the alleged company's market power and evaluate the alleged behaviour's impact on competition, so market definition is not a purpose, but just a tool.[45]

However, the SPC's opinion generated much debate. Some scholars claimed that while it is not always necessary to explicitly define a relevant market, it can still be 'roughly' defined by identifying related factors restricting competition.[46] Others argued that the market definition is a crucial step in determining monopolistic behaviour that cannot be skipped.[47] Scholars in the middle acknowledged that for cases in the digital market involving monopoly agreements or merger review, the AML enforcers may skip defining the relevant market, but market definition is still necessary for cases of abusive behaviour.[48]

Impacted by the SPC's decision and the academic discussion, *Anti-Monopoly Guidelines on the Platform Economic Sector (Draft)*, issued by the SAMR in 2020,

44 *Beijing Qihoo Technology Co. Ltd. v. Tencent Technology (Shenzhen) Co. Ltd. and Shenzheng Tencent Computer System Co. Ltd.* (北京奇虎科技有限公司诉腾讯科技（深圳）有限公司、深圳市腾讯计算机系统有限公司滥用市场支配地位纠纷案), (2013) Min San Zong Zi Di 4 Hao [(2013) Sup. People's Ct. Final Decision No. 4] (China), Wolters Kluwer.

45 *Ibid.*, at 20.

46 Ping Li and Junqi Hao (李平， 郝俊淇), "Hulianwang Hangye Lanyong Shichang Zhipei Diwei Rendingzhong Xiangguan Shichang Jieding Wenti De Yanjiu-Jiyu 'Qihu Su Tengxun Longduanan' Zhongshen Panjue De Sikao" (互联网行业滥用市场支配地位认定中相关市场界定问题研究——基于"奇虎诉腾讯垄断案"终审判决的思考) [Research on the Relevant Market Definition in Abusive Dominant Case in the Internet Market: Thoughts on the Final Judgement of Qihu v. Tencent], *Western Law Review* 4 (2015): 60.

47 See Xiaoye Wang (王晓晔), "Lun Xiangguan Shichang Jieding Zai Lanyong Xingwei Anjian Zhongde Diwei He Zuoyong" (论相关市场界定在滥用行为案件中的地位和作用) [The Functioning and the Roles of the Market Definition in Antitrust Cases Involved Abusive Behaviors], *Modern Law Science* 40 (2018): 57.

48 Maozhong Ding (丁茂中), "Shuzi Jingji Lingyu 'Xiangguan Shichang' Jieding De Shouzheng Yu Biange" (数字经济领域"相关市场"界定的守正与变革) [Preservation and Reform of Definition of 'Relevant Market' in the Field of Digital Economy], *Law Science* 500 (2023): 179, 182–83.

provided that, in specific cases, enforcers may make a decision directly without defining the relevant market as long as certain conditions are satisfied.[49] However, that provision aroused many concerns, like giving the competition authority broad discretionary power to circumvent market definition at will. Due to this controversy, the drafters deleted that provision in the Guideline that was enacted in 2021 and instead stipulated that 'when the AML enforcers investigate cases of monopoly agreements and abusive behaviour or merger review, the relevant market generally needs to be defined'.[50]

3.3.2 Assessment of competition damages

3.3.2.1 Motivations and traditional damage theories

As discussed earlier, one of the most intriguing features in the digital sector is that big tech platforms vigorously pursue a series of conglomerate mergers to expand into business areas that are weakly related (or totally unrelated) to their primary business. In this section, therefore, I focus on digital conglomerate mergers, but some analysis and conclusion can also be applied to horizontal and vertical mergers in the digital sector.

Marc Bourreau and Alexandre de Streel, two European scholars, summarise four theories about the motivations of conglomerate mergers.[51] Then they argue that except for 'agency theory', the other three theories along with two additional new theories effectively explain the rise of conglomerate mergers in the digital sector:

- **Market power theory:** Firms expand into neighbouring markets to increase their market power indirectly and have incentives to create product ecosystems.
- **Resource theory:** Digital players sometimes have an excess of various kinds of important resources, such as conssumer data, logistics services, and cloud computing and storage. The excess capacity in these resources incentivises these firms to expand the business lines.
- **Internal capital markets theory:** Conglomerates have advantages in obtaining funding and redeploying assets. For digital players, the ability to reallocate assets can neatly offset the inherently great risks of new product development.
- **New theories:** The authors raise two theories to explain the rise of digital conglomerates. On the supply side, economies of scope can be a key factor explaining companies' diversification strategies; on the demand side, consumption synergies give firms incentives to expand product lines or create product ecosystems.[52]

49 These conditions include the following: there is sufficient direct evidence; the alleged behavior can only perform with the market dominant position; the behavior lasts for a long time and the damages are apparent; and it lacks conditions or it is difficult to define a relevant market.

50 Platform Guidelines, note 15, Art. 4–(3).

51 Marc Bourreau and Alexandre de Streel, "Digital Conglomerates and EU Competition Policy," *cerre.eu*, March 13, 2019, https://cerre.eu/wp-content/uploads/2020/08/march_2019_digital_conglomerates_and_eu_competition_policy_marc_bourreau_alexandre_de_streel.pdf

52 *Ibid.*, at 6–13.

From Bourreau's and Streel's analysis, we can easily find that conglomerate mergers in the digital market can generate both pro- and anti-competitive effects. Thus, the major issue is whether the competition authorities can still rely on traditional damage theories to assess the effects and make a decision.

According to traditional antitrust theories, the major competition concern for horizontal mergers is that reducing the number of competitors in the relevant market will facilitate the tacit coordination of behaviour. Competition damage is presumed from 'undue concentration in the market for a particular product in a particular geographic area'.[53] Concerns about vertical mergers arise from the reasonable belief that after the merger, the company will have the ability and incentive to exclude competitors or raise their costs.

Merger guidelines in both the European Union and the United States can be generally said to rely upon two merger theories of damage: unilateral effects (foreclosure effects) and coordinated effects. Although EU enforcers and academics are discussing new theories of damage (referred to as 'conglomerate theories'), they still believe that conglomerate theories are rooted in the two traditional merger theories previously mentioned.[54] US antitrust enforcers are not interested in 'inventing' a new damage theory but believe that their 'standard theories of horizontal and vertical harm capture most modern, economically sound theories of what the OECD Secretariat describes as "conglomerate" effects'.[55] China's competition authority has not formed a mature and systemic set of theories for assessing mergers in the digital market yet, but from certain disclosed decisions we can get a glimpse of competition authority's analytical approach and its attitude to digital conglomerate mergers. We will return to these cases later.

Traditionally, competition authorities have generally tolerated conglomerate mergers. The only major concern raised about them in the EU Commission's guidelines is the case of tying and bundling (foreclosure effects).[56] Influenced by the Chicago School, US competition authorities have fewer concerns about conglomerate mergers unless they present the potential of serious vertical or horizontal merger damage. The entrenchment theory of the 1960s and 1970s, embodied in *FTC v. Procter & Gamble Co.*, claims that when a dominant firm acquires a small and non-rival product producer, it may substantially reduce the competitive structure, raise entry barriers, and squeeze smaller firms.[57] This theory, however, has been viewed as obsolete and discarded by US competition authorities.[58] But the rise of New Brandeis movement seems to try to pull the US antitrust chariot back

53 *United States v. Anthem, Inc.*, 855 F.3d 345, 349 (2017).

54 OECD Secretariat, note 2, at 9–10.

55 OECD, "Conglomerate Effects of Mergers—Note by the United States," DAF/COMP/WD(2020)7, *justice.gov*, June 4, 2020, https://www.justice.gov/atr/page/file/1316666/dl?inline, at 2.

56 Bourreau and Streel, note 51, at 13.

57 *FTC v. Procter & Gamble Co*, 386 U.S. 568, 578 (1967).

58 OECD, note 55, at 4–5.

to the theory of structuralism again, and the 2023 *Merger Guidelines of the United States*,[59] to some extent, reflects such efforts.

In the digital sector, conglomerate merger damage can still be implied by unilateral effects and foreclosure effects. However, the effects of digital mergers on competition and efficiency are amplified by digital platforms' network characteristics, two-sided (or multisided) traits, feedback effects, economies of scale, and consumption synergies.

3.3.2.2 Competitive effects and damage assessment

Maurice Stucke and Allen Grunes summarise the network effects into four categories: traditional network effects, scale of data/trial-by-error, scope of data, and spill-over.[60] I will base my discussion of the network effects generated by digital platforms on their classification and focus on enhanced foreclosure resulting from platforms' network effects.

Traditional network effects are generated in a market that is subject to economics of scale. Those effects can be direct, occurring when the value of a product, service, or platform increases with the number of users. They can also be indirect, occurring when there is more than one group of users: As more users from one group join the platform (or use the product or service), the other group receives a greater value.

The WhatsApp/Facebook merger is a typical example of direct network effects. When the European Commission reviewed the merger, it recognised that

> the size of the network of a consumer communications app can have a value for customers in two ways: (i) a larger network implies that it is more likely that existing contacts will already be using a consumer communications app; and (ii) a larger network will afford greater opportunities for contact acquisition and discovery.[61]

Didi, China's largest online ride hailing service provider, survived what was dubbed the 'money-burning war' to acquire Kuaidi and Uber China, explains indirect network effects.[62] Since drivers are inclined to register on the platform with the greatest number of users and *vice versa*, the platform spares no efforts to squeeze out competitors and gain more market share.

However, competition authorities have held that these mergers were unlikely to harm the competition. For example, the European Commission approved the WhatsApp/Facebook and Microsoft/Skype mergers on similar grounds, stating that since users in those markets were multi-homing, the merging parties were unlikely to raise the barrier of market entry after the mergers.[63]

59 U.S. Department of Justice, "Merger Guidelines U.S. Department of Justice and the Federal Trade Commission," *justice.gov*, December 18, 2023, https://www.justice.gov/atr/merger-guidelines
60 Stucke and Grunes, note 37, Chapter 11–13.
61 *Facebook/WhatsApp*, note 31, para 88.
62 See Cai, note 5, at 163–166.
63 *Facebook/WhatsApp*, note 31, at para 105; *Microsoft/Skype*, note 37, at para 92.

Maurice Stucke and Allen Grunes, however, argue that even if users are multi-homing, network effects can still confer platforms' market power.[64] Taking WhatsApp/Facebook merger as an example, WhatsApp's reputation has diminished after the merger,[65] but there has been no apparent migration of users elsewhere. Facebook has less motivation to protect consumers' privacy or improve service quality because it knows the market power endowed by network effects will keep users from leaving its apps.[66]

Scale of data/trial-by-error, scope of data, and spill-over, as discussed by Maurice Stucke and Allen Grunes in their book, are kinds of new network effects that are evident in the digital market. The network effects derive from the scale of data and the merits of algorithm learning-by-doing, which means that the more people providing data (actively or passively), the better the quality and the higher the accuracy of the products or services the platforms can provide and in turn the more users it can attract.[67] Search engines and online navigation maps effectively demonstrate this network effects derived from the scale of data and algorithm's trial-by-error.

Some may argue that the scale of data obviously makes a data-driven merger's pro-competitive effects outweigh its anti-competitive effects because data's non-rivalry, multi-homing, and long-tail effects do not substantially hinder market entry. But the other two effects (scope of data and spill-over) can grant digital platforms the ability to obtain market power and the incentive to abuse such power. The more data a user provides a platform and the more time they invest on the platform, the more information the platform can learn about their preferences and the more accurate profile it can develop for them, besides providing them better-quality goods or services.[68] Once they own these relevant and accurate user profiles, platforms have a strong incentive to monetise the profiles, as well as consumers' attention. Thus, platforms expand their primary business into multiple business lines (spill-over effects).

For example, by collecting data from my shopping at the largest online retailing platform Taobao, owned by Alibaba, in the Chinese market, Alibaba sends me personalised advertisements on its online payment app. The payment information I left (including daily payments such as water and electricity bills) is collected and mined again to offer me customised financial and insurance products. These data are collectively analysed and become the basis for my credit rating. My credit rating then determines the level of discounts and the conditions on instalment payments when I purchase commodities on Taobao. All these products and services I previously mentioned are provided by the Alibaba Group. Considering such a story is very likely to happen in our daily life, I can hardly agree with the European Commission's conclusion that users as well as data are multi-homing.

64 Stucke and Grunes, note 37, at 169.

65 See Lily Hay Newman, "WhatsApp's New Privacy Policy Just Kicked In. Here's What You Need to Know," *wired.com*, May 15, 2021, https://www.wired.com/story/whatsapp-privacy-policy-facebook-data-sharing/

66 Stucke and Grunes, note 37, at 169.

67 *Ibid.*, at 170.

68 *Ibid.*, at 186–89.

This is a chicken-or-egg question. We do not know whether digital products and services necessarily involve various modules and strong economies of scope, enabling platforms to collect a huge amount of consumer data; or whether platforms' ability to obtain massive consumer data inherently gives them the incentives and capacities to create product ecosystems and expand multiple business lines.

There is no need to investigate the original reason, but the potential anti-competitive effects are clear: These network effects can empower large platforms to foreclose competitors (in the relevant market or neighbouring markets), kill innovative new entrants ('killer acquisitions'), and finally build a competitive ecosystem run by one or a couple of super platforms.

In the next section, a couple of cases in Chinese jurisdiction will be addressed. They have testified, to some extent, the theories and conclusions discussed earlier, while they also expose new issues that cannot be explained by existing theories yet.

3.4 High-profile cases

3.4.1 Huya/DouYu

The Huya/DouYu merger in 2021 represented China's third decision to prohibit a merger since the enactment of the AML in 2008.[69] The first blocking decision made by China's competition authority is the acquisition initiated by Coca-Cola to Chinese Huiyuan Juice Group Limited, a famous Chinese juice manufacture.[70] The second blocking decision was denying the approval of the contemplated P3 Network, a container shipping alliance between MSC, Maersk, and CMA CGM.[71] The Huya/DouYu merger decision is the first time China's competition authority prohibited a merger between domestic companies in the digital sector. In its review decision, the SAMR discusses and analyses the 'foreclosure effects' that could be generated by the merger. Although the decision's analysis is not yet mature, it may be a good starting point for the SAMR to form economically sound theories and build up practical experience for the merger control regime in the digital sector in the future.

69 "Shichang Jianguan Zongju Guanyu Jinzhi Huya Gongsi Yu Douyu Guoji Konggu Youxian Gongsi Hebing An Fan Longduan Shencha Jueding De Gonggao" (市场监管总局关于禁止虎牙公司与斗鱼国际控股有限公司合并案反垄断审查决定的公告) [Announcement of the SAMR on the Anti-monopoly Review Decision of Prohibiting the Merger Between HUYA Inc. and DouYu International Holdings Limited], *samr.gov.cn*, July 10, 2021, https://www.samr.gov.cn/fldes/tzgg/ftj/art/2023/art_47b307e668484e83a598add8793dcdca.html [Hereinafter '*Douyu/Huya*'].

70 MOFCOM, "Shangwu Bu Guanyu Jinzhi Kekou Kele Gongsi Shougou Zhongguo Huiyuan Gongsi Shencha Jueding De Gonggao" (商务部关于禁止可口可乐公司收购中国汇源公司审查决定的公告) [Announcement of MOFCOM of Blocking the Coca-Cola's Acquisition to Chinese Huiyuan Company], *mofcom.gov.cn*, March 18, 2009, https://www.mofcom.gov.cn/zcfb/zhzc/art/2009/art_be88661e25c147a1bb91776135537d56.html

71 MOFCOM, "Shangwubu Guanyu Jinzhi Mashiji, Dizhonghai Hangyun, Dafei Sheili Wangluo Zhongxin Jingyingzhe Jizhong Fanlongduan Shencha Jueding De Gonggao" (商务部关于禁止马士基、地中海航运、达飞设立网络中心经营者集中反垄断审查决定的公告) [Announcement of MOFCOM of Blocking the Network Centre Set by MSC, Maersk and CMA CGM], *mofcom.gov.cn*, June 17, 2014, http://www.mofcom.gov.cn/article/b/c/201406/20140600628730.shtml

Huya Inc. (Huya), which is listed on the New York Stock Exchange, is mainly engaged in interactive entertainment video services, like video game livestreaming. Huya is a wholly owned subsidiary of Tencent Holdings Limited (Tencent). DouYu International Holdings Limited (DouYu), listed on the NASDAQ, does business that overlaps with Huya. While superficially a horizonal merger, this is in essence a vertical merger, considering that Tencent operates in the upstream market—online gaming operation services. Also, it can be regarded as a conglomerate merger as well since Tencent has business lines in various markets.

As to the relevant market definition, the SAMR found that Huya and DouYu have horizontal overlaps in the video game livestreaming, entertainment livestreaming, e-commerce livestreaming, and short-form video markets. Then, the SAMR recognised that the video game livestreaming, entertainment livestreaming, e-commerce livestreaming, and short-form video markets are different (whether from the demand side or supply side, which cannot substitute for each other) and thus constitute separate and independent relevant markets.[72]

In this case, therefore, the SAMR defines the relevant market in an ambiguous way. It recognises that there are multiple independent relevant markets involved in this case but does not clarify whether the video game livestreaming market is the market on which it based its review decision or explain the merger's impact on each relevant market either. The SAMR's attitude may reflect some academic opinions that in merger review cases it is not always necessary to provide an accurate market definition.

In its antitrust analysis, the SAMR raises two issues: First, the merger would strengthen Tencent's dominant position in the video game livestreaming market in Chinese mainland and have the effect of eliminating and restricting competition.[73] Second, the merger would enable Tencent to foreclose competitors in both the upstream market (the online gaming operation services) and the downstream market (the video game livestreaming), which is referred to as 'two-way foreclosure'.[74]

In its review decision, the SAMR first concluded that after the merger the entity would have more than 60% market shares in revenue, number of active users, and commentator resources in the video game livestreaming market. In the upstream market, Tencent has already controlled the market share of more than 40%, ranking first in China.[75] Therefore, the SAMR held that Tencent would have enough market power to control both the upstream and downstream markets after the merger and would be able to carry out a two-way vertical foreclosure. Moreover, the upstream market has a high entry barrier and is unlikely to have any new entrants in a short term due to the high capital and time investment, the application of certification for online game operating, and game copyright licenses.[76] Furthermore, publicity from video game livestreaming plays a significant role in promoting online games.

72 *DouYu/Huya*, note 69, at 2–3.
73 *Ibid.*, at 4.
74 *Ibid.*, at 5–6.
75 *Ibid.*, at 5.
76 *Ibid.*, at 5.

Tencent's market power in the downstream market could, in turn, cement or even raise the high market entry barriers of the upstream market.[77]

Second, after the merger, the SAMR held that Tencent has the motivation to carry out the strategy of two-way foreclosure.[78] The SAMR's reasonings are as follows: On the one hand, obtaining game copyright licenses from video game service providers is a prerequisite for engaging in the video game livestreaming business. Thus, Tencent has the incentive and ability to restrict competition in the downstream market by refusing to give game licenses to Huya's competitors. On the other hand, video game livestreaming is an important channel for promoting video games. A mass of promotion would increase payments from players and advertisers, which are a major source of profit for online gaming operation service providers. Tencent thus has a strong motive to utilises its competitive advantages in the downstream market to cement its market power in the upstream market and stifle competition there.

The SAMR's attempts to use the traditional foreclosure effects to assess competition damage in a digital merger should be applauded. In regard to certain key issues, however, its decision lacks solid reasoning, sound economic theory, and in-depth and convincing analysis. For example, it seems that having market power in the upstream market is key to successfully implementing the strategy of 'two-way foreclosure' since video game copyright licenses substantially raise the barrier of market entry for the upstream market and the upstream market power can then be easily leveraged to the downstream market. However, the SAMR does not clearly explain how Tencent is confident that its 'two-way foreclosure' strategy would be successful, considering its market share in the upstream market is only 40%. Actually, Tencent has powerful competitors such as Baidu and Netease in the upstream market. If Tencent restricts downstream market competition, limits the choices of consumers, impairs bargaining ability of video game commentators, or decreases service and product quality, as the SAMR contends, Tencent's competitors in the upstream market would offer more favourable terms to attract consumers and commentators, in turn promoting competition.

Huya/DouYu merger case shares some similarities with Microsoft's acquisition of Activision Blizzard. Microsoft paid USD 69 billion to acquire Activision Blizzard, the maker of Candy Crush and Call of Duty, which would immediately turn Microsoft, the maker of the Xbox gaming system, into one of the world's largest video game companies.[79] The US Federal Trade Commission (FTC) was seeking to block this merger due to the deal's possible anti-competitive effects.

Similar to the vertical relations between DouYu and Tencent, Microsoft, owning Xbox Series S and Series X as two types of high-performance video game

77 *Ibid.*, at 6.

78 *Ibid.*, at 6.

79 Matt O'Brien, "Microsoft Buys Game Maker Activision Blizzard for About $70B," *apnews.com*, January 19, 2022, https://apnews.com/article/microsoft-activision-blizzard-acquisition-call-of-duty-7a9e2bcc8f0b7b9049e4f93fe3e0a4dd

consoles, is actually at the downstream market of Activision Blizzard, a top video game developer. The FTC worried that

> Microsoft would have both the means and motive to harm competition by manipulating Activision's pricing, degrading Activision's game quality or player experience on rival consoles and gaming services, changing the terms and timing of access to Activision's content, or withholding content from competitors entirely, resulting in harm to consumers.[80]

Apparently, the FTC's concerns—Microsoft had the incentive and ability to foreclose its rivals, like Sony's PlayStation and Nintendo, or other nascent cloud-based streaming platforms to access the Activision's products, so the competition was lessened—seems similar to that of SAMR.

However, the District Court of the Northern District of California denied the FTC's request for a preliminary injunction in the Microsoft/Activision Blizzard merger.[81] The court ruled that the FTC has not presented sufficient evidence to prove the merger may substantially lessen competition. To the contrary, Microsoft committed

> to keep Call of Duty on Play Station for 10 years on parity with Xbox . . . [and] made an agreement with Nintendo to bring Call of Duty to Switch. And it entered several agreements to for the first time bring Activision's content to several cloud gaming services.[82]

Further, the court held that 'the record evidence points to more consumer access to Call on Duty and other Activision content'.[83]

In short, the US federal court's reasonings in Microsoft/Activision Blizzard merger may provide a reference for China's competition authority in Huya/DouYu case. My point of view is that the SAMR's blocking decision need to be backed up by solider evidence and sounder analysis. I doubt whether the merger should be blocked since the potential anti-competitive effects may be offset or reduced through Tencent's commitments or accepting certain restrictive conditions. Interestingly, Microsoft acquisition of Activision Blizzard has been approved unconditionally by the SAMR on 18 May 2023,[84] although this merger

80 FTC, "FTC Seeks to Block Microsoft Corp.'s Acquisition of Activision Blizzard Inc.," *ftc.gov*, December 8, 2022, https://www.ftc.gov/news-events/news/press-releases/2022/12/ftc-seeks-block-microsoft-corps-acquisition-activision-blizzard-inc

81 *Federal Trade Commission v. Microsoft Corporation and Activision Blizzard, Inc.*, 681 F.Supp.3d 1069 (N. D. Cal. 2023).

82 *Ibid.*, at 1101.

83 *Ibid.*

84 SAMR, "2023 Nian 5 Yue 15 Ri—5 Yue 21 Ri Wutiaojian Pizhun Jingyingzhe Jizhong Anjian Liebiao" (2023年5月15日—5月21日无条件批准经营者集中案件列表) [List of Unconditional Approval of Merger Cases (15 May–21 May 2023)], *samr.gov.cn*, May 30, 2023, https://www.samr.gov.cn/fldes/ajgs/wtjjz/art/2023/art_933bfb33968d4799a91c65ac15c9e507.html

faced difficulties and challenges for obtaining US and EU competition authorities' approvals.[85]

3.4.2 Tencent/China music

Tencent Holding Co., Ltd. ('Tencent'), incorporated in 1999 and was initially known as an instant messenger company but later had the ambition of expanding into the fields of entertainment, finance, and information technology and finally of establishing its own business ecosystem.[86] The acquisition of China Music Corporation ('China Music') was a crucial step for Tencent to 'march' into the field of popular music. China Music had 230 million active users in July 2016 (when the acquisition happened), controlling a 49.07% share of the online music platform market on the Chinese mainland.[87]

On 12 July 2016, Tencent acquired sole control of China Music by purchasing a 61.64% stake in the company.[88] Soon after the acquisition, Tencent Music Entertainment Group ('TME') was set up and listed on the New York Stock Exchange in 2018, showing that Tencent has largely completed its commercial expansion into the field of music.

However, Tencent did not file a pre-merger notification with the SAMR for that acquisition. That may have been because the two companies were incorporated overseas and operated their businesses under a VIE structure: Tencent was incorporated in the British Virgin Islands, and China Music was incorporated in the Cayman Islands. The company thought it had found a loophole for bypassing the AML's merger control system but paid a high price for that attempt. After Platform Guidelines was issued in 2021, it stated that all mergers involving VIEs are subject to the AML's merger control.

On 24 July 2021, the SAMR imposed a penalty of RMB 500,000 on Tencent for its failure to provide notification and required Tencent to restore competition by following several orders.[89]

85 UK's competition authority blocked this merger, and the European Commission approved the merger with conditions. See Mack Wilowski, "EU Clears Microsoft's $69 Billion Takeover of Activision Blizzard With Caveats," *investopedia.com*, May 15, 2023, https://www.investopedia.com/eu-approves-microsoft-activision-blizzard-deal−7498231

86 See Chenyang Sun, "Tencent's Acquisition of China Music Corporation: A Case Study," *Advances in Economics Management and Political Sciences* 35 (2023): 14.

87 SAMR, "Shichang Jianguan Zongju Fabu Tengxun Konggu Youxian Gongsi Shougou Zhongguo Yinyue Jituan Guquan Weifa Shishi Jingyingzhe Jizhong An Xingzheng Chufa Juedingshu" (市场监管总局发布腾讯控股有限公司收购中国音乐集团股权违法实施经营者集中案行政处罚决定书) [SAMR Administrative Penalties on Illegal Implementation of Concentration of Tencent Holdings Ltd. and China Music Group], *samr.gov.cn*, July 24, 2021, https://www.samr.gov.cn/zt/qhfldzf/art/2021/art_eb9ea87c21394236bcda4736b0015698.html, at 4. [Hereinafter *Tencent/China Music Group*].

88 Weishan Chen (陈惟杉), "Fanlongduan Zhongjie 'Dujia Banquan', Weihe Meiyou Chaifen Tengxun Yinyue?" (反垄断终结”独家版权”，为何没有拆分腾讯音乐？) [Antimonopoly Enforcement Ended 'Exclusive Copyright License', Why the Agency Did Not Break Up Tencent Music?], *inewsweek.cn*, September 15, 2021, https://www.inewsweek.cn/society/2021-09-15/13857.shtml

89 *Tencent/China Music Group*, note 87.

The SAMR concluded in its decision that the Tencent/China Music acquisition had the effect of eliminating and restricting competition. It provided three reasons to support that conclusion. First, after the acquisition, the relevant market was highly concentrated, with an original HHI index of 6,950 points increasing by 3,350 points.[90] Second, the acquisition involved the top two market players in the relevant market, so the acquisition removed Tencent's major rival and substantially lessened the competition.[91] Third, the SAMR stated that the post-merger company would raise market entry barriers by signing exclusive agreements to lock up a large amount of recorded music copyrights and by fully exercising network effects to hinder competitors from achieving economies of scale, among other issues.

Besides imposing a monetary penalty on Tencent in this decision, the SAMR took the unprecedented step of imposing behavioural remedies in a failure-to-notify case. Tencent was given three orders to restore competition in the relevant market. First, Tencent was ordered to terminate all exclusive music copyright licensing with upstream copyright owners within 30 days of the decision.[92] (Exclusive copyright licensing agreements with independent musicians for a period of up to three years and exclusive agreements for new music releases for up to 30 days were exempted from the ban.[93]) Second, Tencent was forbidden, without justifiable reasons, from requiring upstream copyright owners to grant the most favourable terms, compared to its competitors, for matters including but not limited to the scope of licensing, licensing fees, and licensing period.[94] Third, Tencent was forbidden from indirectly raising its rivals' costs by taking such measures as paying excessive down payments to upstream copyright owners.[95]

These behavioural remedies, however, proved controversial, especially the order to terminate exclusive copyright licensing agreements. Just after the decision was made, TME's share price plummeted, with its market value evaporating by 60%.[96]

The backstory of exclusive copyright licensing agreements can be traced back to 2015. Prior to 2015, music piracy was rampant during the rapid growth of digital music platforms, raising serious concerns from domestic and international observers.[97] On 9 July 2015, the National Copyright Administration (NCA) issued the Notice Ordering Online Music Service Providers to Stop Unlicensed Music Streaming, which is regarded as the strictest order ever given for copyright

90 *Ibid.*, at 4.
91 *Ibid.*, at 5.
92 *Ibid.*, at 7.
93 *Ibid.*, at 7.
94 *Ibid.*, at 7.
95 *Ibid.*, at 7.
96 Dan Wu (吴丹), "Tengxun Yinyue Dujia Banquan Beichufa, Shuzi Yinyue Pingtai Guaidian Daolai" (腾讯音乐独家版权被处罚，数字音乐平台拐点到来) [Tencent Music Be Penalized for Exclusive Copyright Agreements, Turning Point of Digital Music Platform], *yicai.com*, August 2, 2021, https://www.yicai.com/news/101127678.html
97 Xinhua News Agency (新华社), "China Copyright Watchdog Bans Unlicensed Music Streaming," *chinadaily.com.cn*, July 9, 2015, https://www.chinadaily.com.cn/china/2015-07/09/content_21239767.htm

protection.[98] Soon after, more than 2.2 million unlicensed songs were removed from online platforms; Baidu alone removed about 600,000 songs from its platform.[99]

The NCA's order fundamentally destroyed music platforms' previous business model. In order to survive under the new conditions, platforms vied for market share by signing exclusive licensing agreements with upstream copyright owners. Competition for more exclusive licenses, especially from famous singers or musicians, has gradually become cutthroat. Xiami, a music streaming platform known to attract diverse listeners who were keen to discover new musical talent, was squeezed out of the market in 2021, largely because it could not bear the financial burden of obtaining enough exclusive licenses.[100] NetEase CloudMusic spent RMB 5.36 billion on copyright licenses but only earned RMB 2.6 billion in revenue from online music service in 2020.[101] Thus, these losses can be directly linked to competition for exclusive copyright licensing. To gain an exclusive license for the songs of Jay Chuo, a top pop singer in China, Alibaba and Tencent engaged in a fierce bidding war that Tencent finally won by paying RBM 570 million for a three years' exclusive license.[102] In the end, Tencent's 'deep financial pockets' brought it to victory in this battle of 'enclosure movement'.

The NCA, which had sought to protect copyright and curb music piracy, did not predict its order would set off bloodthirsty competition and ultimately create an oligopoly market. That also reignites the debate regarding conflict between the AML and intellectual property law.[103] The value of the copyright mechanism is to encourage creation. But what happened in the online music market demonstrates how large platforms have managed to squeeze rivals out of the market through the copyright mechanism, which has ultimately damaged creation.

Although the SAMR intended to restore competition in the market by halting exclusive agreements for music copyright licensing, the effectiveness of this measure remains to be seen. The SAMR's order is only binding on Tencent, rather than the upstream copyright holders. After the SAMR issued its decision, Tencent

98 National Copyright Administration, "Guanyu Zeling Wangluo Yinyue Fuwushang Tingzhi Weijing Shouquan Chuanbo Yinyue Zuopin De Tongzhi" (关于责令网络音乐服务商停止未经授权传播音乐作品的通知) [Notice on Ordering Online Music Providers to Stop Distributing Unauthorized Musical Works], *cac.gov.cn*, July 9, 2015, https://www.ncac.gov.cn/xxfb/tzgg/201507/t20150709_50373.html

99 Xiuxiu Lu (鲁修修), "Yinyue Banquan 'Qu Dujia' Weihe Reng Yaoyao Wuqi?" (音乐版权'去独家'为何仍遥遥无期？) [Why Is It Hard to Stop Entering Exclusive Agreements for Music Works?], *thepaper.cn*, November 3, 2021, https://www.thepaper.cn/newsDetail_forward_15183734

100 Rebecca Davis, "Alibaba to Shutter Its Xiami Music App Next Month," *variety.com*, January 5, 2021, https://variety.com/2021/music/news/alibaba-xiami-music-closure-tencent-netease-1234878679/

101 Wu, note 96.

102 *Ibid.*

103 See Haitao Jiao (焦海涛), "Shuzi Yinyue Dujia Banquan Xieyi De 'Fanlongduan Fa' Jianguan" (数字音乐独家版权协议的《反垄断法》监管) [Regulation of the Anti-Monopoly Law Over Exclusive Copyright Agreements of Digital Music], *China Copyright* 5 (2021): 14; see also Taixuan Wu and Yu Tan (吴太轩，谭羽), "Shuzi Yinyue Banquan Dujia Shouquan Xieyi De Fanlongduan Fa Fenxi" (数字音乐版权独家授权协议的反垄断法分析) [An Analysis of Anti-Monopoly Law of the Exclusive Copyright Agreement of Digital Music], *Competition Policy Research* 4 (2019): 38.

did not immediately terminate exclusive agreements because all but one upstream copyright holder delayed announcing their termination.[104] And considering the cross-shareholding between Tencent and the world's three biggest music publishers (Sony Music Publishing, Universal Music Publishing Group, and Warner Chappell Music), terminating exclusive licence agreements may not be enough to shake Tencent's dominance in the online music streaming market.[105]

3.5 Conclusion

In the 15 years since the AML's enactment, China's competition authority has improved both the procedural and the substantial rules for its merger control regime. Like most competition authorities in other antitrust jurisdictions, however, China's competition authority is also 'wading across the river by feeling the stones' when it comes to enforcing anti-monopoly law in the digital sector.

As to SAMR's future movements, three facets deserve the notice of overseas observers. First, the current pre-merger notification framework and review process are still in rough shape, which leaves plenty to be normalised and refined. On the one hand, it would increase undertakings' uncertainty about setting business strategies and predicting their behaviours' potential legal risks. On the other hand, it motivates China to look at and learn from advanced competition regimes' approaches and mechanisms to improve its system and solve specific problems. Overseas observers, especially academics and officials, may see this as a good opportunity to influence China with their own antitrust regimes or ideas. In any case, frequent inter-governmental communications and contacts would accelerate China's entry into the landscape of global antitrust enforcement and shape the global order with Chinese influence as well.

Second, 'killer acquisitions' have been a key concern for SAMR, and devising customised criteria for super platforms has always been an important matter on China's legislative agenda. *Guidelines for Internet Platform Classification and Grading (Draft)* and *Guidelines for Internet Platforms' Responsibilities (Draft)*[106] are pending enactments, and the 'gatekeeper' mechanism may be ready for adoption after intensive discussion in recent years. At the end of 2022, the annual Central Economic Work Conference—the most important Party-led annual economic meeting that sets the economic policy agenda for the year ahead—proposed to 'vigorously develop the digital economy' and to encourage platform companies to

104 Guofeng Ding (丁国峰), "Pingtai Jingji Shiyuxia Shuzi Yinyue Dujia Banquan Shichang Lanyong De Guizhi Kunjing Yu Chulu" (平台经济视域下数字音乐独家版权市场滥用的规制困境与出路) [Regulatory Dilemma and Solutions of the Abuse of Digital Music Exclusive Copyright t Under the Perspective of Platform Economy], *Social Science Journal* 268 (2023): 68, 73.

105 *Ibid*., at 73.

106 SAMR, "Guanyu Dui 'Hulianwang Pingtai Fenlei Fenji Zhinan (Zhengqiu Yijiangao)' 'Hulianwang Pingtai Luoshi Zhuti Zeren Zhinan (Zhengqiu Yijiangao)' Gongkai Zhengqiu Yijian De Gonggao" (关于对《互联网平台分类分级指南（征求意见稿）》《互联网平台落实主体责任指南（征求意见稿）》公开征求意见的公告) [Announcement on Solicitating Public Opinions for Guidelines for Internet Platform Classification and Grading (Draft) and Guidelines for Internet Platform Responsibilities (Draft)], *samr.gov.cn*, October 29, 2021, https://www.samr.gov.cn/hd/zjdc/art/2023/art_c0086d02fcc544ea9506c997b3ac93c1.html

create more jobs and participate in global competition'. That proposal signalled a change of regulatory policy toward platforms and may have ramifications for current policies regarding large platforms. It could lead, for example, to alleviating the previously harsh attitude toward large platforms and winding down active investigations against them. But that remains to be seen.

Third, recent reforms that decentralised the merger review authority may facilitate setting up the merger *ex-post* evaluation mechanism. In July 2022, SAMR entrusted five provincial-level local agencies to review nationwide merger cases,[107] which may greatly alleviate SAMR's problem with being understaffed and overloaded.[108] I argue that mergers in the digital market (especially those involving large platforms) should be regularly *ex-post* evaluated. An EU report in 2015 states that, if the *ex-post* evaluation is done correctly, lessons can be learned that would benefit future policy-making.[109] In addition, using retrospective evidence can help develop a more efficient, objective, and accurate merger review process.[110] Unfortunately, empirical data show that competition authorities are reluctant to do *ex-post* evaluations due to the significant increase in enforcement cost.[111] *China's Provisions on the Examination of Concentrations of Undertakings* also provides that SAMR may re-examine restrictive conditions on merger decisions, either on its own initiative or when requested, when a merger transaction or the relevant market has undergone significant change.[112] But in the digital market, such significant changes tend to only turn up when the authorities carry out an *ex-post* evaluation, rather than *vice versa*. Therefore, decentralising the merger review authority opens up the possibility of China's competition authority and its local agencies conducting extensive and regular *ex-post* evaluations of all digital mergers in the future.

107 SAMR, "Shichang Jianguan Zongju Guanyu Shidian Weituo Kaizhan Bufen Jingyingzhe Jizhong Anjian Fanlongduan Shencha De Gonggao" (市场监管总局关于试点委托开展部分经营者集中案件反垄断审查的公告) [Announcement of Trial to Entrust Pilot Agencies to Review Some Merger Cases], *samr.gov.cn*, July 15, 2022, https://www.samr.gov.cn/fldes/sjdt/tpxw/art/2023/art_f239901206cf43c08c649db06578fba4.html

108 The director of the SAMR's Antimonopoly Bureau, Mr. Wu Zhenguo, stated in an interview that as of 30 June 2021, the Antimonopoly Bureau had reviewed 1,705 mergers and closed 304 monopolistic cases. However, there are only about 50 personnel at the Antimonopoly Bureau to deal with national cases related to monopolistic behaviors. The continuing shortfall of personnel greatly limits AML enforcement in the digital market.See China Market Regulation News, "Shichang Jianguan Zongju Fanlongduan Ju Zhuyao Fuze Tongzhi Jieshou Meiguo Lvshi Xiehui Fanlongduan Zaixian Qikan The Antitrust Source" (市场监管总局反垄断局主要负责同志接受美国律师协会反垄断在线期刊 The Antitrust Source专访) [Person in Charge of SAMR's Antimonopoly Bureau Was Interviewed by The Antitrust Source], *thepaper.cn*, July 7, 2021, https://www.thepaper.cn/newsDetail_forward_13496957; also see Lihua Wu (吴丽华), "Pingtai Jingzheng 'Neijuanhua', Bianzhi Buju 50 Ren De Fanlongduan Ju Dasuan Zenmegan?" (平台竞争"内卷化"，编制不足50人的反垄断局打算怎么干？) [Intensive Platform Competition, How Should the Antimonopoly Bureau Deal With It With Fewer Than 50 Personnel?], *thepaper.cn*, February 20, 2021, https://www.thepaper.cn/newsDetail_forward_11389201

109 Peter Ormosi, Richard Havell, and Franco Mariuzzo, *A Review of Merger Decisions in the EU: What Can We Learn From Ex-post Evaluations?* (European Commission, 2015), 1.

110 *Ibid.*

111 Stucke & Grunes, note 37 above, at 220–22.

112 Provisions on the Examination of Concentrations of Undertakings (promulgated by the SAMR on February 20, 2023, effective April 15, 2023), CLI.4.5160993(EN) (Lawinfochina), Art. 55.

Appendix: partially selected merger review decisions involving China's digital giants (2021–2024)

Digital Platform	*Case Name*	*Dates*	*Involved Market*	*Review Decision*
Alibaba				
1	Alibaba (China) Network Technology Co., Ltd. and Guiyang Xingli Department Store Group Co., Ltd. established a joint venture[113]	• M/A completion: 20 March 2018 • Decision issued: 31 December 2021	retailing, supermarket	• Failure of notification before implementing the concentration; • The concentration without effects of eliminating and restricting competition; • A penalty of RMB 500,000 on the two involved parties respectively.
2	Hangzhou Alibaba Venture Capital Co., Ltd., Zhengzhou Xunjie Trading Co., Ltd., and Guiyang Radio and Television Media Group Co., Ltd. ('the three merging parties') acquired equities of Guizhou Fanya ssXintong Network Technology Co., Ltd.[114]	• M/A completion: 24 July 2015 • Decision issued: 31 December 2021	public WIFI construction and operation services	• Failure of notification before implementing the concentration; • The concentration without effects of eliminating and restricting competition; • A penalty of RMB 500,000 on the three merging parties respectively.
3	Alibaba (China) Network Technology Co., Ltd. and Tencent Holdings Limited acquired equities of Yongyang Anfeng (Beijing) Technology Co., Ltd.[115]	• M/A completion: 15 January 2014 • Decision issued: 15 November 2021	internet security technology and products development	• Failure of notification before implementing the concentration; • The concentration without effects of eliminating and restricting competition; • A penalty of RMB 500,000 on Alibaba Network and Tencent respectively.

113 "SAMR Administrative Penalty Decision (2021) SAMR's Decision No. 126," *www.samr.gov.cn*, January 5, 2022, https://www.samr.gov.cn/zt/qhfldzf/art/2022/art_e078a10b161947a2a8dc8a2e62108250.html

114 "SAMR Administrative Penalty Decision (2021) SAMR's Decision No. 121," *www.samr.gov.cn*, January 5, 2022, https://www.samr.gov.cn/fldes/tzgg/xzcf/art/2023/art_fccc9489d8e546f493bbbb083d86dab4.html

115 "SAMR Administrative Penalty Decision (2021) SAMR's Decision No. 103," *www.samr.gov.cn*, November 20, 2021, https://www.samr.gov.cn/fldes/tzgg/xzcf/art/2023/art_d487366ab57d42c7b739e3f89ad536fe.html

Digital Platform	*Case Name*	*Dates*	*Involved Market*	*Review Decision*
4	Alibaba Investment Limited acquired equities of Amap Software Co., Ltd.[116]	• M/A completion: 17 July 2014 • Decision issued: 13 November 2021	digital map	• Failure of notification before implementing the concentration; • The concentration without effects of eliminating and restricting competition; • A penalty of RMB 500,000 on Alibaba Investment.
5	Alibaba Investment Limited acquired equities of Meizu Technology Corporation Limited[117]	• M/A completion: 16 February 2015 • Decision issued: 15 November 2021	smartphone's R&D, producing, and selling	• Failure of notification before implementing the concentration; • The concentration without effects of eliminating and restricting competition; • A penalty of RMB 500,000 on Alibaba Investment.
6	Nanjing Suning.com Investment Co., Ltd. and Alibaba (China) Network Technology Co., Ltd. established a joint venture[118]	• M/A completion: 30 November 2016 • Decision issued: 13 November 2021	e-commerce	• Failure of notification before implementing the concentration; • The concentration without effects of eliminating and restricting competition; • A penalty of RMB 500,000 on the two involved parties respectively.
7	Alibaba Investment Limited acquired equities of Souche Holdings Ltd.[119]	• M/A completion: 26 October 2017 • Decision issued: 17 November 2021	automotive financial leasing & used car trading platform	• Failure of notification before implementing the concentration; • The concentration without effects of eliminating and restricting competition; • A penalty of RMB 500,000 on Alibaba Investment.

116 "SAMR Administrative Penalty Decision (2021) SAMR's Decision No. 102," *www.samr.gov.cn*, November 20, 2021, https://www.samr.gov.cn/fldes/tzgg/xzcf/art/2021/art_0dc36fbdc7644062a34f4af80aa492f0.html

117 "SAMR Administrative Penalty Decision (2021) SAMR's Decision No. 107," *www.samr.gov.cn*, November 20, 2021, https://www.samr.gov.cn/fldes/tzgg/xzcf/art/2023/art_48c6d9ede85c4f538bd9696c5a559678.html

118 "SAMR Administrative Penalty Decision (2021) SAMR's Decision No. 101," *www.samr.gov.cn*, November 20, 2021, https://www.samr.gov.cn/fldes/tzgg/xzcf/art/2023/art_f6d5191ee13f4dd296e6687b14f666e7.html

119 "SAMR Administrative Penalty Decision (2021) SAMR's Decision No. 109," *www.samr.gov.cn*, November 20, 2021, https://www.samr.gov.cn/fldes/tzgg/xzcf/art/2021/art_d8876fbe7e2a4267baa56c78667bae6a.html

Digital Platform	*Case Name*	*Dates*	*Involved Market*	*Review Decision*
8	Alibaba Health Technology (China) Co., Ltd acquired equities of Guizhou Yishu Chain Pharmaceutical Co., Ltd.[120]	• M/A completion: 29 September 2018 • Decision issued: 16 November 2021	pharmaceutical retail	• Failure of notification before implementing the concentration; • The concentration without effects of eliminating and restricting competition; • A penalty of RMB 500,000 on Alibaba Health.
9	Alibaba (China) Network Technology Co., Ltd. acquired equities of Shenzhen Recycling Treasure Technology Co., Ltd.[121]	• M/A completion: 7 September 2018 • Decision issued: 16 November 2021	digital products' recycling	• Failure of notification before implementing the concentration; • The concentration without effects of eliminating and restricting competition; • A penalty of RMB 500,000 on Alibaba (China) Network.
10	Alibaba Venture Capital and Zhejiang Innovation Investment established a joint venture[122]	• M/A completion: 26 July 2016 • Decision issued: 6 July 2021	cloud computing and other internet services	• Failure of notification before implementing the concentration; • The concentration without effects of eliminating and restricting competition; • A penalty of RMB 500,000 on the two involved parties respectively.
11	Alibaba (China) Network Co., Ltd. acquired equities of Tian Xian Pei (Shanghai) Technology Co., Ltd.[123]	• M/A completion: 15 November 2019 • Decision issued: 6 July 2021	pasteurised and low temperature dairy products	• Failure of notification before implementing the concentration; • The concentration without effects of eliminating and restricting competition; • A penalty of RMB 500,000 on Alibaba Network.

120 "SAMR Administrative Penalty Decision (2021) SAMR's Decision No. 104," *www.samr.gov.cn*, November 20, 2021, https://www.samr.gov.cn/fldes/tzgg/xzcf/art/2023/art_5f379dff66a946b1a01f5bd6a56ad147.html

121 "SAMR Administrative Penalty Decision (2021) SAMR's Decision No. 105," *www.samr.gov.cn*, November 20, 2021, https://www.samr.gov.cn/fldes/tzgg/xzcf/art/2023/art_a3ba0dd71f1140898bb08445d27ba83f.html

122 "SAMR Administrative Penalty Decision (2021) SAMR's Decision No. 57," *www.samr.gov.cn*, July 7, 2021, https://www.samr.gov.cn/fldes/tzgg/xzcf/art/2023/art_29cc2e6cbcaf4c4983c1f1c5e01bb55d.html

123 "SAMR Administrative Penalty Decision (2021) SAMR's Decision No. 52," *www.samr.gov.cn*, July 7, 2021, https://www.samr.gov.cn/fldes/tzgg/xzcf/art/2023/art_5cc6909c5e9d4facae195883cd341945.html

Digital Platform	*Case Name*	*Dates*	*Involved Market*	*Review Decision*
12	Alibaba Venture Capital Co., Ltd. and Shanghai Commercial Investment Group established a joint venture[124]	• M/A completion: 28 November 2018 • Decision issued: 6 July 2021	retailing	• Failure of notification before implementing the concentration; • The concentration without effects of eliminating and restricting competition; • A penalty of RMB 500,000 on the two involved parties respectively.
13	Alibaba (China) Network acquired equities of Theland New Cloud (Shanghai) Digimart Ltd.[125]	• M/A completion: 26 December 2017 • Decision issued: 6 July 2021	liquid milk and adult milk powder	• Failure of notification before implementing the concentration; • The concentration without effects of eliminating and restricting competition; • A penalty of RMB 500,000 on Alibaba Network.
14	Alibaba (China) Network acquired equities of Guangzhou Evergrande Football Club[126]	• M/A completion: 4 July 2014 • Decision issued: 6 July 2021	football professionals club	• Failure of notification before implementing the concentration; • The concentration without effects of eliminating and restricting competition; • A penalty of RMB 500,000 on Alibaba Network.
15	Alibaba Venture Capital acquired equities of Wukuang Electronic Commerce Ltd.[127]	• M/A completion: 24 May 2016 • Decision issued: 6 July 2021	digital platform of metallurgical raw materials or steel supply	• Failure of notification before implementing the concentration; • The concentration without effects of eliminating and restricting competition; • A penalty of RMB 500,000 on Alibaba Venture Capital.

124 "SAMR Administrative Penalty Decision (2021) SAMR's Decision No. 53," *www.samr.gov.cn*, July 7, 2021, https://www.samr.gov.cn/fldes/tzgg/xzcf/art/2023/art_ae3ce89a099241968b8270438cbc4edd.html

125 "SAMR Administrative Penalty Decision (2021) SAMR's Decision No. 54," *www.samr.gov.cn*, July7,2021,https://www.samr.gov.cn/fldes/tzgg/xzcf/art/2023/art_deef3d6467c7450c97c34978fd2e19c0.html

126 "SAMR Administrative Penalty Decision (2021) SAMR's Decision No. 55," *www.samr.gov.cn*, July7,2021,https://www.samr.gov.cn/fldes/tzgg/xzcf/art/2023/art_fe3121dbc5d0458d8ee221b2474fb81f.html

127 "SAMR Administrative Penalty Decision (2021) SAMR's Decision No. 56," *www.samr.gov.cn*, July 7, 2021, https://www.samr.gov.cn/fldes/tzgg/xzcf/art/2023/art_32232a821bbe42e3a20b97f9ca5883f3.html

Digital Platform	*Case Name*	*Dates*	*Involved Market*	*Review Decision*
16	Alibaba Investment Limited acquired equities of Intime Retail (Group) Company Limited[128]	• M/A completion: June 2017 • Decision issued: 14 December 2020	retailing, shopping centres	• Failure of notification before implementing the concentration; • The concentration without effects of eliminating and restricting competition; • A penalty of RMB 500,000 on Alibaba Investment.
17	Alibaba (China) Network Technology Co., Ltd. acquired equities of 1919 Wines & Spirits Platform Technology Co. Ltd.[129]	• M/A completion:11 February 2019 • Decision issued:17 November 2021	liquor retail	• Failure of notification before implementing the concentration; • The concentration without effects of eliminating and restricting competition; • A penalty of RMB 500,000 on Alibaba (China) Network.
18	Alibaba Travel Holdings Limited and Marriott International, Inc. established a joint venture[130]	• M/A completion:1 August 2017 • Decision issued:18 November 2021	management of hotel, travel and hospitality	• Failure of notification before implementing the concentration; • The concentration without effects of eliminating and restricting competition; • A penalty of RMB 500,000 on the two involved parties respectively.
19	Hema (China) Co., Ltd. acquired equities of Guizhou Xinghe Zongheng Network Technology Co., Ltd.[131]	• Decision issued:27 April 2022	fresh produce retail and life services	• Unconditional approval.

128 "SAMR Administrative Penalty Decision (2020) SAMR's Decision No. 26," *www.samr.gov.cn*, December 14, 2020, https://www.samr.gov.cn/fldes/tzgg/xzcf/art/2020/art_6e098fe1404541d99eb4b6e2a58901cf.html

129 "SAMR Administrative Penalty Decision (2021) SAMR's Decision No. 110," *www.samr.gov.cn*, November20,2021,https://www.samr.gov.cn/fldes/tzgg/xzcf/art/2021/art_7b35cff57ecb4de8907042ea54e06f19.html

130 "SAMR Administrative Penalty Decision (2021) SAMR's Decision No. 106," *www.samr.gov.cn*, November 20, 2021, https://www.samr.gov.cn/fldes/tzgg/xzcf/art/2021/art_a9cd722b577845169dbdad51ae2f5521.html

131 "List of Cases of Concentrations of Undertakings Unconditionally Approved from 25th April 2022 to 1st May 2022," *www.samr.gov.cn*, May 6, 2022, https://www.samr.gov.cn/fldes/ajgs/wtjjz/art/2023/art_530ca39abddc40068bbe8c5604b53304.html

Digital Platform	*Case Name*	*Dates*	*Involved Market*	*Review Decision*
20	Taobao China Holding Limited acquired equities of Ele.me (owned by Rajax Holding)[132]	• M/A completion:8 May 2018 • Decision issued:15 November 2021	online takeout ordering services	• Failure of notification before implementing the concentration; • The concentration without effects of eliminating and restricting competition; • A penalty of RMB 500,000 on Taobao China Holding.
Tencent				
1	Tencent Holdings Limited acquired equities of Tianjin Animation Hall Art Development Co., Ltd.[133]	• Decision issued:17 August 2021	animation, film, and related culture and entertain-ment	• Unconditional approval
2	HUYA Inc. and DouYu International Holdings Limited established a joint venture[134]	• Decision issued:10 July 2021	video game livestrea-ming, entertain-ment livestrea-ming, e-commerce livestrea-ming, and short-form video markets	• The concentration having or potentially having effects of eliminating and restricting competition; • Prohibition of the concentration of undertakings.
3	Tencent Holdings Limited and Shenzhen HongShan Yuchen Equity Investment Partnership (L.P.) acquired equities of Guangxi Jiaojiu Network Technology Co., Ltd.[135]	• M/A completion:30 November 2020 • Decision issued:31 December 2021	online liquor retailing	• Failure of notification before implementing the concentration; • The concentration without effects of eliminating and restricting competition; • A penalty of RMB 500,000 on Tencent and Shenzhen HongShan Yuchen respectively.

132 "SAMR Administrative Penalty Decision (2021) SAMR's Decision No. 80," *www.samr.gov.cn*, November 20, 2021, https://www.samr.gov.cn/fldes/tzgg/xzcf/art/2023/art_7a09f57d0ce0439c940c7c327ceff425.html

133 "List of Cases of Concentrations of Undertakings Unconditionally Approved From 16th August 2021 to 22nd August 2021," *www.samr.gov.cn*, August 24, 2021, https://www.samr.gov.cn/fldes/ajgs/wtjjz/art/2023/art_20cb877c9d6f494591402eba74398f75.html

134 "Announcement of the SAMR on the Anti-Monopoly Review Decision Concerning the Prohibition of the Merger Between HUYA Inc. and DouYu International Holdings Limited," *www.samr.gov.cn*, July 10, 2021, https://www.samr.gov.cn/fldes/tzgg/ftj/art/2023/art_47b307e668484e83a598add8793dcdca.html

135 "SAMR Administrative Penalty Decision (2021) SAMR's Decision No. 132," *www.samr.gov.cn*, January 5, 2022, https://www.samr.gov.cn/fldes/tzgg/xzcf/art/2023/art_5fc8318eefb24ec6a9ed92aa54bb0e74.html

Digital Platform	*Case Name*	*Dates*	*Involved Market*	*Review Decision*
4	Qingdao Hisense Network Technology Co., Ltd. and Tencent Holdings Limited established a joint venture[136]	• M/A completion:26 March 2020 • Decision issued:31 December 2021	multimedia, IT intelligent information systems and modern service	• Failure of notification before implementing the concentration; • The concentration without effects of eliminating and restricting competition; • A penalty of RMB 500,000 on the two involved parties respectively.
5	Tencent Holdings Limited acquired equities of Beijing Niannian Sharing Technology Development Co., Ltd.[137]	• M/A completion:27 November 2019 • Decision issued:31 December 2021	instant delivery services	• Failure of notification before implementing the concentration; • The concentration without effects of eliminating and restricting competition; • A penalty of RMB 500,000 on Tencent Holdings.
6	Tencent Holdings Limited acquired equities of VERSA Inc.[138]	• M/A completion:21 November 2018 • Decision issued:31 December 2021	mobile image editing software	• Failure of notification before implementing the concentration; • The concentration without effects of eliminating and restricting competition; • A penalty of RMB 500,000 on Tencent Holdings.
7	Tencent Holdings Limited acquired equities of Yonghui Yunchuang Technology Co., Ltd.[139]	• M/A completion:23 March 2018 • Decision issued: 31 December 2021	fresh food retailing	• Failure of notification before implementing the concentration; • The concentration without effects of eliminating and restricting competition; • A penalty of RMB 500,000 on Tencent Holdings.

136 "SAMR Administrative Penalty Decision (2021) SAMR's Decision No. 131," *www.samr.gov.cn*, January 5, 2022, https://www.samr.gov.cn/fldes/tzgg/xzcf/art/2022/art_9d5d6fc240f14b06919247cfd2b73910.html

137 "SAMR Administrative Penalty Decision (2021) SAMR's Decision No. 129," *www.samr.gov.cn*, January 5, 2022, https://www.samr.gov.cn/fldes/tzgg/xzcf/art/2023/art_f866906138fc4268b46e74e14221d124.html

138 "SAMR Administrative Penalty Decision (2021) SAMR's Decision No. 128," *www.samr.gov.cn*, January 5, 2022, https://www.samr.gov.cn/fldes/tzgg/xzcf/art/2023/art_848539311bfd3420f8b205b448471ab16.html

139 "SAMR Administrative Penalty Decision (2021) SAMR's Decision No. 127," *www.samr.gov.cn*, January5,2022,https://www.samr.gov.cn/fldes/tzgg/xzcf/art/2023/art_059021fd710d4b8084338bb0ce320f55.html

Digital Platform	*Case Name*	*Dates*	*Involved Market*	*Review Decision*
8	Tencent Holdings Limited acquired equities of Beijing Youhu Science and Technology Co., Ltd.[140]	• M/A completion:2 March 2018 • Decision issued:31 December 2021	anime production business	• Failure of notification before implementing the concentration; • The concentration without effects of eliminating and restricting competition; • A penalty of RMB 500,000 on Tencent Holdings.
9	Tencent Holdings Limited and Shanghai Huasheng Lingfei Equity Investment Partnership (L.P.) acquired equities of Beijing Millward Software Systems Co., Ltd.[141]	• M/A completion: 2017 • Decision issued: 31 December 2021	OI service platform, enterprise-level data analysis	• Failure of notification before implementing the concentration; • The concentration without effects of eliminating and restricting competition; • A penalty of RMB 500,000 on Tencent Holdings and Shanghai Huasheng Lingfei respectively.
10	Tencent Holdings Limited acquired equities of IngageApp Global Limited[142]	• M/A completion:12 December 2016 • Decision issued: 31 December 2021	CRM service (Customer relationship management system)	• Failure of notification before implementing the concentration; • The concentration without effects of eliminating and restricting competition; • A penalty of RMB 500,000 on Tencent Holdings.
11	Tencent Holdings Limited and Henan Harmony Automobile Trading Co., Ltd. established a joint venture[143]	• M/A completion:2 July 2015 • Decision issued: 31 December 2021	traditional fuel-powered vehicles' sales and after-sales services	• Failure of notification before implementing the concentration; • The concentration without effects of eliminating and restricting competition; • A penalty of RMB 500,000 on the two involved parties respectively.

140 "SAMR Administrative Penalty Decision (2021) SAMR's Decision No. 125," *www.samr.gov.cn*, January 5, 2022, https://www.samr.gov.cn/fldes/tzgg/xzcf/art/2022/art_8f1d5301d29c4410a2bc8a344e77bd20.html

141 "SAMR Administrative Penalty Decision (2021) SAMR's Decision No. 124," *www.samr.gov.cn*, January 5, 2022, https://www.samr.gov.cn/fldes/tzgg/xzcf/art/2022/art_16662cba0d4c417190ba07b3270ce1da.html

142 "SAMR Administrative Penalty Decision (2021) SAMR's Decision No. 123," *www.samr.gov.cn*, January 5, 2022, https://www.samr.gov.cn/fldes/tzgg/xzcf/art/2023/art_a65374a588284b1f918aeb72eeacac73.html

143 "SAMR Administrative Penalty Decision (2021) SAMR's Decision No. 120," *www.samr.gov.cn*, January 5, 2022, https://www.samr.gov.cn/fldes/tzgg/xzcf/art/2022/art_009b9718802442db898f065002e5c2d2.html

Digital Platform	*Case Name*	*Dates*	*Involved Market*	*Review Decision*
12	Alibaba (China) Network Technology Co., Ltd. and Tencent Holdings Limited acquired equities of Yongyang Anfeng (Beijing) Technology Co., Ltd.[144]	• M/A completion:15 January 2014 • Decision issued: 15 November 2021	internet security tech and products development	• Failure of notification before implementing the concentration; • The concentration without effects of eliminating and restricting competition; • A penalty of RMB 500,000 on Alibaba and Tencent respectively.
13	Tencent Holdings Limited and Jihui Management Consulting (Shanghai) Co., Ltd. acquired equities of Beijing Tengkang Huiyi Medical Technology Co., Ltd.[145]	• M/A completion: December 2016 • Decision issued: 17 November 2021	offline private clinics, and internet healthcare	• Failure of notification before implementing the concentration; • The concentration without effects of eliminating and restricting competition; • A penalty of RMB 500,000 on Tencent and Jihui Management Consulting respectively.
14	Tencent Holdings Limited acquired equities of Zhuan Spirit Holdings Limited[146]	• M/A completion:28 April 2017 • Decision issued: 15 November 2021	online trading platform for second-hand goods	• Failure of notification before implementing the concentration; • The concentration without effects of eliminating and restricting competition; • A penalty of RMB 500,000 on Tencent Holdings.
15	Tencent Holdings Limited acquired equities of China Medonline Inc.[147]	• M/A completion:9 February 2017 • Decision issued: 13 November 2021	internet healthcare services	• Failure of notification before implementing the concentration; • The concentration without effects of eliminating and restricting competition; • A penalty of RMB 500,000 on Tencent Holdings.

144 "SAMR Administrative Penalty Decision (2021) SAMR's Decision No. 103," *www.samr.gov.cn*, November 20, 2021, https://www.samr.gov.cn/fldes/tzgg/xzcf/art/2023/art_d487366ab57d42c7b739e3f89ad536fe.html

145 "SAMR Administrative Penalty Decision (2021) SAMR's Decision No. 82," *www.samr.gov.cn*, November 20, 2021, https://www.samr.gov.cn/fldes/tzgg/xzcf/art/2021/art_bfbfb461105a4111a1ae7eb8852c7933.html

146 "SAMR Administrative Penalty Decision (2021) SAMR's Decision No. 77," *www.samr.gov.cn*, November 20, 2021, https://www.samr.gov.cn/fldes/tzgg/xzcf/art/2023/art_f815698acf0b49c48589fe065dbb6014.html

147 "SAMR Administrative Penalty Decision (2021) SAMR's Decision No. 100," *www.samr.gov.cn*, November 20, 2021, https://www.samr.gov.cn/fldes/tzgg/xzcf/art/2021/art_b7e32ec70fda4d489b42bf369ebbccb7.html

Digital Platform	*Case Name*	*Dates*	*Involved Market*	*Review Decision*
16	Tencent Holdings Limited acquired equities of Beijing Paidian E-commerce Co., Ltd.[148]	• M/A completion:20 November 2017 • Decision issued:15 November 2021	commodity retailing	• Failure of notification before implementing the concentration; • The concentration without effects of eliminating and restricting competition; • A penalty of RMB 500,000 on Tencent Holdings.
17	Tencent Holdings Limited acquired equities of Beijing Yunji Technology Co., Ltd.[149]	• M/A completion:6 December 2017 • Decision issued: 18 November 2021	commercial robots	• Failure of notification before implementing the concentration; • The concentration without effects of eliminating and restricting competition; • A penalty of RMB 500,000 on Tencent Holdings.
18	Tencent Holdings Limited acquired equities of Shenyang Mxnavi Co., Ltd.[150]	• M/A completion:31 May 2018 • Decision issued: 16 November 2021	digital map navigation services	• Failure of notification before implementing the concentration; • The concentration without effects of eliminating and restricting competition; • A penalty of RMB 500,000 on Tencent Holdings.
19	Tencent Holdings Limited acquired equities of Tianjin 58 Financial Services Co., Ltd.[151]	• M/A completion:20 July 2018 • Decision issued: 16 November 2021	financial leasing, internet classified ad and info diversion platforms	• Failure of notification before implementing the concentration; • The concentration without effects of eliminating and restricting competition; • A penalty of RMB 500,000 on Tencent Holdings.

148 "SAMR Administrative Penalty Decision (2021) SAMR's Decision No. 114," *www.samr.gov.cn*, November20,2021,https://www.samr.gov.cn/fldes/tzgg/xzcf/art/2021/art_f00448433c974fa3b031c7f7ca1c2f06.html

149 "SAMR Administrative Penalty Decision (2021) SAMR's Decision No. 97," *www.samr.gov.cn*, November 20, 2021, https://www.samr.gov.cn/fldes/tzgg/xzcf/art/2023/art_48679e55f4a94b39b5d8b5dce238a9fe.html

150 "SAMR Administrative Penalty Decision (2021) SAMR's Decision No. 96," *www.samr.gov.cn*, November 20, 2021, https://www.samr.gov.cn/fldes/tzgg/xzcf/art/2023/art_545c7a44327c41daac435516f4b3a664.html

151 "SAMR Administrative Penalty Decision (2021) SAMR's Decision No. 95," *www.samr.gov.cn*, November 20, 2021, https://www.samr.gov.cn/fldes/tzgg/xzcf/art/2021/art_55beba1083834683bc391bf7c23857c7.html

Digital Platform	*Case Name*	*Dates*	*Involved Market*	*Review Decision*
20	Tencent Holdings Limited acquired equities of Chengdu Superlove Technology Co., Ltd.[152]	• M/A completion:27 August 2018 • Decision issued:16 November 2021	online English education	• Failure of notification before implementing the concentration; • The concentration without effects of eliminating and restricting competition; • A penalty of RMB 500,000 on Tencent Holdings.
21	Tencent Holdings Limited acquired equities of Beijing Oriental Jinxin Technology Co., Ltd.[153]	• M/A completion:18 April 2019 • Decision issued: 16 November 2021	big data platform, and big data solutions business	• Failure of notification before implementing the concentration; • The concentration without effects of eliminating and restricting competition; • A penalty of RMB 500,000 on Tencent Holdings.
22	Tencent Holdings Limited, China Lounge Investments Limited and other operators established a joint venture[154]	• M/A completion:4 July 2019 • Decision issued: 17 November 2021	financial services and investment management	• Failure of notification before implementing the concentration; • The concentration without effects of eliminating and restricting competition; • A penalty of RMB 500,000 on the two involved parties respectively.
23	Tencent Holdings Limited acquired equities of Chongqing Yipin Hong Technology Co., Ltd.[155]	• M/A completion:13 June 2019 • Decision issued: 16 November 2021	offline fresh food retailing	• Failure of notification before implementing the concentration; • The concentration without effects of eliminating and restricting competition; • A penalty of RMB 500,000 on Tencent Holdings.

152 "SAMR Administrative Penalty Decision (2021) SAMR's Decision No. 93," *www.samr.gov.cn*, November 20, 2021, https://www.samr.gov.cn/fldes/tzgg/xzcf/art/2023/art_37d15b4d5aec4ff49f5c843e8bb5911e.html

153 "SAMR Administrative Penalty Decision (2021) SAMR's Decision No. 111," *www.samr.gov.cn*, November 20, 2021, https://www.samr.gov.cn/fldes/tzgg/xzcf/art/2023/art_6b0a6d34ccd7473f87e5754ebc2bd98f.html

154 "SAMR Administrative Penalty Decision (2021) SAMR's Decision No. 85," *www.samr.gov.cn*, November20,2021,https://www.samr.gov.cn/fldes/tzgg/xzcf/art/2023/art_a6824d372e1947ebb87c83fff15195b9.html

155 "SAMR Administrative Penalty Decision (2021) SAMR's Decision No. 117," *www.samr.gov.cn*, November 20, 2021, https://www.samr.gov.cn/fldes/tzgg/xzcf/art/2023/art_6bf23bc4c9aa4656bebf499716f6b93b.html

Digital Platform	*Case Name*	*Dates*	*Involved Market*	*Review Decision*
24	Tencent Holdings Limited acquired equities of Beijing Yijiupi Electronic Commerce Co., Ltd.[156]	• M/A completion:29 August 2019 • Decision issued:18 November 2021	Wholesales of foods and daily necessities	• Failure of notification before implementing the concentration; • The concentration without effects of eliminating and restricting competition; • A penalty of RMB 500,000 on Tencent Holdings.
25	Tencent Holdings Limited acquired equities of China Music Corporation[157]	• M/A completion:6 December 2017 • Decision issued: 24 July 2021	online music platform, record publishing, and copyright agency services	• Failure of notification before implementing the concentration; • A penalty of RMB 500,000 on Tencent; • Ordering Tencent to terminate all exclusive music copyright licensing; • Prohibiting Tencent from requiring copyright owners to grant it the most favourable terms; • Prohibiting Tencent from indirectly raising its rivals' costs.
26	Tencent Holdings Limited acquired equities of Sogou Inc.[158]	• M/A completion:16 September 2013 • Decision issued: 6 July 2021	internet search, input method and browser services	• Failure of notification before implementing the concentration; • The concentration without effects of eliminating and restricting competition; • A penalty of RMB 500,000 on Tencent Holdings.
27	Tencent Holdings Limited acquired equities of Xingin International Holding Limited[159]	• M/A completion:21 August 2020 • Decision issued: 6 July 2021	internet retail platform operation	• Failure of notification before implementing the concentration; • The concentration without effects of eliminating and restricting competition; • A penalty of RMB 500,000 on Tencent Holdings.

156 "SAMR Administrative Penalty Decision (2021) SAMR's Decision No. 90," *www.samr.gov.cn*, November 20, 2021, https://www.samr.gov.cn/fldes/tzgg/xzcf/art/2023/art_601c708292814f1ea9d337c8621efa72.html

157 "SAMR Administrative Penalty Decision (2021) SAMR's Decision No. 67," *www.samr.gov.cn*, July 24, 2021, https://www.samr.gov.cn/fldes/tzgg/xzcf/art/2021/art_0cb8e8f0b7854199adbff80da40c1133.html

158 "SAMR Administrative Penalty Decision (2021) SAMR's Decision No. 65," *www.samr.gov.cn*, July 7, 2021, https://www.samr.gov.cn/fldes/tzgg/xzcf/art/2023/art_14c730063da64c9b905385c393734ecf.html

159 "SAMR Administrative Penalty Decision (2021) SAMR's Decision No. 59," *www.samr.gov.cn*, July 7, 2021, https://www.samr.gov.cn/fldes/tzgg/xzcf/art/2023/art_a76b6321cb874e9f9496c8fd78017243.html

Digital Platform	*Case Name*	*Dates*	*Involved Market*	*Review Decision*
28	Tencent Mobility Limited acquired equities of 58.COM INC.[160]	• M/A completion:17 September 2020 • Decision issued: 6 July 2021	real estate, recruitment and local life information services	• Failure of notification before implementing the concentration; • The concentration without effects of eliminating and restricting competition; • A penalty of RMB 500,000 on Tencent Mobility.
29	Tencent Holdings Limited acquired equities of Kingsoft Internet Security Software Holdings Limited[161]	• M/A completion:7 July 2011 • Decision issued: 6 July 2021	R&D of online games, internet security, dictionaries, and office software	• Failure of notification before implementing the concentration; • The concentration without effects of eliminating and restricting competition; • A penalty of RMB 500,000 on Tencent Holdings.
30	Tencent Holdings Limited acquired equities of Mogu Inc.[162]	• M/A completion:3 February 2016 • Decision issued: 6 July 2021	internet retail platform	• Failure of notification before implementing the concentration; • The concentration without effects of eliminating and restricting competition; • A penalty of RMB 500,000 on Tencent Holdings.
31	Tencent Holdings Limited acquired equities of Shanghai Lantu Information Technology Co., Ltd.[163]	• M/A completion:18 November 2019 • Decision issued: 28 April 2021	vehicle maintenance	• Failure of notification before implementing the concentration; • The concentration without effects of eliminating and restricting competition; • A penalty of RMB 500,000 on Tencent Holdings.

160 "SAMR Administrative Penalty Decision (2021) SAMR's Decision No. 58," *www.samr.gov.cn*, July7,2021,https://www.samr.gov.cn/fldes/tzgg/xzcf/art/2021/art_ea108f49deef4b41ac311b222bfa46f1.html

161 "SAMR Administrative Penalty Decision (2021) SAMR's Decision No. 60," *www.samr.gov.cn*, July7,2021,https://www.samr.gov.cn/fldes/tzgg/xzcf/art/2023/art_056dc475fff747219de6735246bba7fd.html

162 "SAMR Administrative Penalty Decision (2021) SAMR's Decision No. 61," *www.samr.gov.cn*, July7,2021,https://www.samr.gov.cn/fldes/tzgg/xzcf/art/2023/art_dff71c9a0b69439d85a1063eeac64326.html

163 "SAMR Administrative Penalty Decision (2021) SAMR's Decision No. 31," *www.samr.gov.cn*, April 30, 2021, https://www.samr.gov.cn/fldes/tzgg/xzcf/art/2021/art_dbc5e2cbde2940ae8f13c27f80339889.html

Digital Platform	*Case Name*	*Dates*	*Involved Market*	*Review Decision*
32	Tencent Holdings Limited acquired equities of Bitauto Holdings Limited[164]	• M/A completion:4 November 2020 • Decision issued: 28 April 2021	internet car advertising and automobile financial services	• Failure of notification before implementing the concentration; • The concentration without effects of eliminating and restricting competition; • A penalty of RMB 500,000 on Tencent Holdings.
33	Tencent Holdings Limited acquired equities of YUAN INC[165]	• M/A completion:29 November 2018 • Decision issued: 12 March 2021	online education	• Failure of notification before Failure of notification before implementing the concentration; • The concentration without effects of eliminating and restricting competition; • A penalty of RMB 500,000 on Tencent Holdings.
Baidu				
1	Baidu Yunzhi (Beijing) Technology Co., Ltd., Tongxiang Yijin Technology Co., Ltd. and other operators established a joint venture[166]	• Decision issued: 29 December 2022	internet data, and AI	• Unconditional approval.
2	Baidu Online Network Technology (Beijing) Co., Ltd. and Nanjing Net Code Technology Co., Ltd. acquired equities of Nanjing XinFeng Network Technology Co., Ltd.[167]	• M/A completion:12 March 2013 • Decision issued: 15 November 2021	software development	• Failure of notification before implementing the concentration; • The concentration without effects of eliminating and restricting competition; • A penalty of RMB 500,000 on Baidu and Nanjing Net Code respectively.

164 "SAMR Administrative Penalty Decision (2021) SAMR's Decision No. 30," *www.samr.gov.cn*, April30,2021,https://www.samr.gov.cn/fldes/tzgg/xzcf/art/2023/art_f1df1f6bb5534cd0a639896753ca3bc3.html

165 "SAMR Administrative Penalty Decision (2021) SAMR's Decision No. 13," *www.samr.gov.cn*, March 12, 2021, https://www.samr.gov.cn/fldes/tzgg/xzcf/art/2023/art_717632bc70a44bee944419135153e4bf.html

166 "List of Cases of Concentrations of Undertakings Unconditionally Approved From 26th December 2022 to 1st January 2023," *www.samr.gov.cn*, January 10, 2023, https://www.samr.gov.cn/fldes/ajgs/wtjjz/art/2023/art_caaa20de724d4ab69496a464a8fab212.html

167 "SAMR Administrative Penalty Decision (2021) SAMR's Decision No. 75," *www.samr.gov.cn*, November20,2021,https://www.samr.gov.cn/fldes/tzgg/xzcf/art/2021/art_f15228ef3cab46d5a9dfc5285890f88e.html

Digital Platform	*Case Name*	*Dates*	*Involved Market*	*Review Decision*
3	Fujian Baidu Borui Websoft Technology Ltd. and China CITIC Bank Corporation Limited established a joint venture[168]	• M/A completion:5 September 2017 • Decision issued: 15 November 2021	digital finance and fintech	• Failure of notification before implementing the concentration; • The concentration without effects of eliminating and restricting competition; • A penalty of RMB 500,000 on the two involved parties respectively.
4	Baidu Online Network Technology (Beijing) Co., Ltd. and Zhejiang Geely Holding Group Co., Ltd. established a joint venture[169]	• M/A completion:2 March 2021 • Decision issued: 13 November 2021	R&D of automobile tech and M&S of automobiles	• Failure of notification before implementing the concentration; • The concentration without effects of eliminating and restricting competition; • A penalty of RMB 500,000 on the two involved parties respectively.
5	Baidu Holdings Limited acquired equities of Ainemo Inc.[170]	• M/A completion:16 July 2020 • Decision issued: 12 March 2021	R&D and manufac-turing of smart home & its software	• Failure of notification before implementing the concentration; • The concentration without effects of eliminating and restricting competition; • A penalty of RMB 500,000 on Baidu Holdings.
JD.com				
1	China Merchants Bank Co., Ltd. and JD Digits Technology Holding Co., Ltd. established a joint venture[171]	• Decision issued: 31 March 2021	digital finance and fintech	• Unconditional approval.

168 "SAMR Administrative Penalty Decision (2021) SAMR's Decision No. 79," *www.samr.gov.cn*, November 20, 2021, https://www.samr.gov.cn/fldes/tzgg/xzcf/art/2023/art_d4b424266d60419ea2b1406d95b0673e.html

169 "SAMR Administrative Penalty Decision (2021) SAMR's Decision No. 116," *www.samr.gov.cn*, November20,2021,https://www.samr.gov.cn/fldes/tzgg/xzcf/art/2021/art_83451745dc8840148edd3b0d676544ec.html

170 "SAMR Administrative Penalty Decision (2021) SAMR's Decision No. 16," *www.samr.gov.cn*, March12,2021,https://www.samr.gov.cn/fldes/tzgg/xzcf/art/2023/art_604dc439b2a1457681e052457b8098ab.html

171 "List of Cases of Concentrations of Undertakings Unconditionally Approved From 22nd March 2021 to 31st March 2021," *www.samr.gov.cn*, April 1, 2021, https://www.samr.gov.cn/fldes/ajgs/wtjjz/art/2023/art_9e844a6bf36544aa8095a8bb75d9c169.html

Digital Platform	*Case Name*	*Dates*	*Involved Market*	*Review Decision*
2	Beijing Jingdong Shangke Information Technology Co., Ltd. and iFLYTEK Co., Ltd. established a joint venture[172]	• M/A completion:24 April 2015 • Decision issued: 17 November 2021	R&D, production and services of intelligent voice tech	• Failure of notification before implementing the concentration; • The concentration without effects of eliminating and restricting competition; • A penalty of RMB 500,000 on the two involved parties respectively.
Others				
1	ELong Net Information Technology (Beijing) Co., Ltd. acquired equities of Beijing Tongcheng Tourism Investment Group Co., Ltd.[173]	Decision issued: 8 August 2023	tourism and its related services	Unconditional approval.
2	China Unicom Digital Technology Co., Ltd., Chang'an Huitong Investment Management Co., Ltd. and other operators acquired equities of Yunshang Shaanxi Technology Operation Co., Ltd.[174]	Decision issued: 30 May 2023	cloud computing, data services and telecom	Unconditional approval.
3	Microsoft Corporation acquired equities of Activision Blizzard, Inc.[175]	Decision issued: 18 May 2023	AI, cloud computing, gaming and entertain-ment	Unconditional approval.
4	Huawei Device Co., Ltd., China International Television Corporation and other operators established a joint venture[176]	Decision issued: 27 July 2021	digital media and infotech	Unconditional approval.

172 "SAMR Administrative Penalty Decision (2021) SAMR's Decision No. 112," *www.samr.gov.cn*, November20,2021,https://www.samr.gov.cn/fldes/tzgg/xzcf/art/2021/art_e3af7adfe92244e9b7dfb3079bd94218.html

173 "List of Cases of Concentrations of Undertakings Unconditionally Approved From 7th August 2023 to 13rd August 2023," *www.samr.gov.cn*, August 21, 2023, https://www.samr.gov.cn/fldes/ajgs/wtjjz/art/2023/art_5f5ce79af38445bfab995b9992087b7a.html

174 "List of Cases of Concentrations of Undertakings Unconditionally Approved From 29th May 2023 to 4th June 2023," *www.samr.gov.cn*, June 12, 2023, https://www.samr.gov.cn/fldes/ajgs/wtjjz/art/2023/art_d2a6fefa9963403689e6f044335edfb0.html

175 "List of Cases of Concentrations of Undertakings Unconditionally Approved From 15th May 2023 to 21st May 2023," *www.samr.gov.cn*, May 30, 2023, https://www.samr.gov.cn/fldes/ajgs/wtjjz/art/2023/art_933bfb33968d4799a91c65ac15c9e507.html

176 "List of Cases of Concentrations of Undertakings Unconditionally Approved From 26th July 2021 to 1st August 2021," *www.samr.gov.cn*, August 3, 2021, https://www.samr.gov.cn/fldes/ajgs/wtjjz/art/2023/art_78ae9350ff4a4faf9115b846aae6ba9b.html

Digital Platform	*Case Name*	*Dates*	*Involved Market*	*Review Decision*
5	Reliance Industries Limited and Viacom18 Media Private Limited acquired equities of Star India Private Limited[177]	Decision issued: 6 September 2024	television media and entertainment	Unconditional approval.
6	Rajax Holding acquired equities of Baidu Life Technology Co., Ltd.[178]	• M/A completion:24 August 2017 • Decision issued: 15 November 2021	takeout food ordering business	• Failure of notification before implementing the concentration; • The concentration without effects of eliminating and restricting competition; • A penalty of RMB 500,000 on Rajax Holding.
7	Suning.com Co., Ltd. and Mitsubishi Heavy Industries, Ltd. established a joint venture[179]	• M/A completion:28 September 2011 • Decision issued: 6 July 2021	household air conditioning system	• Failure of notification before implementing the concentration; • The concentration without effects of eliminating and restricting competition; • A penalty of RMB 500,000 on the two involved parties respectively.
8	Didi Mobility Pte. Ltd. and SoftBank Corp. established a joint venture[180]	• M/A completion:29 June 2018 • Decision issued: 12 March 2021	telecommunications and internet	• Failure of notification before implementing the concentration; • The concentration without effects of eliminating and restricting competition; • A penalty of RMB 500,000 on the two involved parties respectively.

177 "Public Notice Form for Simple Cases of Concentrations of Undertakings," *scjgj.cq.gov.cn*, September 6, 2024, http://scjgj.cq.gov.cn/zt_225/jyzjzfldsc/ajgs/jyzjzjyajgs/202409/t20240906_13604988.html

178 "SAMR Administrative Penalty Decision (2021) SAMR's Decision No. 78," *www.samr.gov.cn*, November20,2021,https://www.samr.gov.cn/fldes/tzgg/xzcf/art/2023/art_00f9b115f27040a89837c5da52faadeb.html

179 "SAMR Administrative Penalty Decision (2021) SAMR's Decision No. 63," *www.samr.gov.cn*, July 7, 2021, https://www.samr.gov.cn/fldes/tzgg/xzcf/art/2023/art_c44bf729e3b6496cbc0373f6488082a4.html

180 "SAMR Administrative Penalty Decision (2021) SAMR's Decision No. 18," *www.samr.gov.cn*, March 12, 2021, https://www.samr.gov.cn/fldes/tzgg/xzcf/art/2023/art_780ff8cca62e4cc2807974dae489f377.html

4 Monopoly agreements in the digital market

4.1 Confusion and controversy about monopoly agreements: transplantation vs localisation

US and EU competition law were the two most influential references during the long gestation period of China's AML.[1] Given that China had no experience with a general competition law before 2007, US antitrust law, which includes a large number of reported cases and an extensive academic and practical literature, naturally became a valuable source of information and subject of study for Chinese scholars and officials.[2] Besides US law, EU competition law was also influential. The textual structure of the AML was modelled on EU competition law. In particular, the laws of Germany and other EU countries have substantially shaped the AML.[3]

On the one hand, enforcers in advanced antitrust jurisdictions as well as international organisations, such as the OECD, made a great effort to exert pressure and sought to influence the AML from general legal concepts to specific provisions.[4] On the other hand, Chinese scholars and officials were willing to learn from their overseas counterparts and wanted a panacea to apply the antitrust law efficiently and quickly in China. To offer a personal anecdote, I had an internship at the US Federal Trade Commission (FTC) in 2009, just one year after the AML took effect. Almost every week, I could see Chinese delegations at all levels (both national and provincial) visiting the FTC and studying US antitrust law.

Implementing such a massive legal transplantation in a relatively short time, however, would inevitably cause confusion. How well would Chinese enforcers comprehend the relevant terminologies and theories? How would the Chinese market and domestic factors colour and tone the perception of foreign law? AML enforcement of monopolistic agreements is the most prominent area that has

1 Anti-monopoly Law of the People's Republic of China (promulgated by Standing Comm. Nat'l People's Cong., August 30, 2007, effective August 1, 2008, amended August 1, 2022), CLI.1.5128034(EN) (Lawinfochina) [Hereinafter the AML].

2 David Gerber, *Global Competition: Law, Markets, and Globalization* (Oxford University Press, 2010), 228–29.

3 Xiaoye Wang, "Issues Surrounding the Drafting of China's Anti-Monopoly Law," *Washington University Global Studies Law Review* 3 (2004): 285, 286.

4 Gerber, note 2, at 232.

DOI: 10.4324/ 9781003654452-4

revealed such confusion, which mainly results from the application of the rule of reason and the application of the *per se* rule for analysing monopolistic agreements.

'The rule of reason' and '*per se* illegality' are extraordinary creations of US antitrust law over the past century that play a key role in determining the legality of a monopolistic agreement. Article 1 of the Sherman Act prohibits 'every contract, combination in the form of trust or otherwise, or conspiracy, in restraint of trade or commerce among the several States, or with foreign nations'. More than a hundred years ago, as described in *United States v. Trans-Missouri Freight Assn.*,[5] 18 railroads created an association to fix freight rates for all railroads west of the Mississippi River. When they were sued by the government for restricting interstate commerce, the defendants argued that Article 1 of the Sherman Act prohibited only unreasonable restraints on trade, rather than 'every contract' in a literal sense. Although the Court rejected the defendants' argument, Justice Edward White wrote in a dissenting opinion that the statute should be interpreted, in the course of common law, such that 'the words "restraint of trade" embrace only contracts which unreasonably restrain trade'.[6] That is the origin of the rule of reason. In *Chicago Bd. of Trade v. United States*,[7] the Court elaborated on the rule of reason, stating that the legality of a restraint depends on whether it promotes or suppresses competition. Thereafter, the rule of reason has been widely accepted and applied in antitrust cases involving monopoly agreements.

Although the rule of reason, on a case-by-case basis, can be a good fit for complicated and volatile competition and markets, it inevitably has drawbacks: namely, the lack of foreseeability, the high cost of enforcement, and the risk of false negatives.[8] Thus, the *per se* rule is applied to particular practices for which no exculpatory justification should ever be considered based on enforcers' previous experience. Thus, considering the obvious anti-competitive effects of horizontal agreements, a consensus has been reached in the US antitrust community, and even by advocates of the Chicago School, that horizontal price fixing is *per se* illegal.

The AML and its supporting regulations, however, have never used the terms 'rule of reason' or '*per se* rule', even though they are frequently mentioned and discussed by academics and are taught in law schools' lectures. Meanwhile, provisions involving monopoly agreements (Article 13, 14, and 15)[9] under the AML

5 *United States v. Trans-Missouri Freight Assn.*, 166 U.S. 290 (1897).

6 *Ibid.*, at 346.

7 *Chicago Bd. of Trade v. United States*, 246 U.S. 231 (1918).

8 False negative refers to business conduct that is anti-competitive but not properly punished. On the contrary, false positive occurs when a business conduct is pro-competitive but wrongfully considered illegal.

9 The AML (2008), Article 13: The competing business operators are prohibited from reaching any of the following monopoly agreements with each other:

1. Fixing or changing the price of commodities;
2. Restricting the production quantity or sales volume of commodities;
3. Dividing the sales market or the raw material supply market;
4. Restricting the purchase of new technology or new facilities or the development of new technology or new products;

(2008) were patterned on Article 101 (1) to (3) of the Treaty on Functioning of the European Union (TFEU). Thus, it seems that the AML also accepted the concept of 'hardcore restriction' under EU competition law[10] and categorised agreements into horizontal and vertical ones.

However, the adoption of those concepts and approaches from various antitrust regimes has caused chaos in the enforcement of the AML, especially in the early stages.

Section 4.1 introduces the status quo of AML enforcement over monopoly agreements and then explores the reasons behind such enforcement traits and patterns. The cases addressed in this section include fields beyond the digital market since that was not the enforcement focus of AML, especially in its early stage. However, the conclusions and problems arising in those cases can generally be applied to the digital market.

---

5. Jointly boycotting transactions; or
6. Other monopoly agreements as determined by the Anti-monopoly Law Enforcement Agency under the State Council.

The term "monopoly agreements" as mentioned in this Law refers to the agreements, decisions or other concerted behaviors that may eliminate or restrict competition.

Article 14: Business operators are prohibited from reaching any of the following monopoly agreements with their trading parties:

1. Fixing the price of commodities for resale to a third party;
2. Restricting the minimum price of commodities for resale to a third party; or
3. Other monopoly agreements as determined by the Anti-monopoly Law Enforcement Agency under the State Council.

Article 15: Where the business operators can prove that a monopoly agreement reached by them falls under any of the following circumstances, the monopoly agreement shall be exempt from Articles 13 and 14 of this Law:

1. For the purpose of improving technologies, researching, and developing new products;
2. For the purpose of upgrading product quality, reducing costs, improving efficiency, unifying product specifications or standards, or carrying out professional labor division;
3. For the purpose of enhancing operational efficiency and reinforcing the competitiveness of small and medium-sized business operators;
4. For the purpose of realizing public interests such as conserving energy, protecting the environment and providing disaster relief, etc.
5. For the purpose of mitigating the severe decrease of sales volume or obviously excessive production during economic recessions;
6. For the purpose of protecting the justifiable interests of the foreign trade or foreign economic cooperation; or
7. Other circumstances prescribed by the law or the State Council.

Where a monopoly agreement falls under any of the circumstances prescribed in Items 1–5 and is exempt from Articles 13 and 14 of this Law, the business operators shall also prove that the reached such an agreement shall not substantially restrict competition in the relevant market and can enable the consumers to share the benefits from the agreement.

10 Jian Li (李剑), *Zhongguo Fanlongduan Fa De Yizhi Yu Bentu Hua* (中国反垄断法的移植与本土化) [*Transplantation and Localization of China Anti-Monopoly Law*] (Law Press China, 2022), 121–22.

4.1.1 Horizontal agreements

As stated earlier, the terms 'rule of reason' and '*per se* rule' have never appeared in China's antitrust legislative texts. Surprisingly, the first explicit citation of 'rule of reason' in a court judgement was a case involving horizonal price fixing,[11] which exemplifies the confusion arising from the application of foreign legal concepts to Chinese anti-monopoly enforcement.

The case in question concerned the Shenzhen Pest Control Association, which organised its members to sign 'self-discipline pacts' to set the price of pest control services. In a lawsuit against the association, the plaintiff claimed that it had suffered losses due to the price fixing agreement. The case was heard by the Intermediate Court of Shenzhen City, Guangdong Province, for the first trial.[12] The trial court stated that since a monopolistic agreement is one that restricts or eliminates competition, the rule of reason should be applied here; if there were reasons to justify the agreement, it could be exempted despite involving a horizontal restriction.[13] The trial court held in favour of the defendant with the reasoning that pest control services involved the public interest, so price fixing was justified and reasonable in order to avoid vicious price competition at the cost of worse service.[14]

The plaintiff appealed to the High People's Court of Guangdong Province, which stated that there were two major issues in this case: (1) whether the 'self-discipline pact' was a price fixing agreement and (2) whether reaching such an agreement could be justified.[15] As to the first issue, the appellate court asserted that it was necessary to define the relevant market and then determine whether the behaviour had an anti-competitive effect on the relevant market. Regarding the second issue, the appellate court affirmed the trial court's reasoning, holding that the self-discipline pact did not substantially reduce competition and endorsing the defendant's claim that its behaviour could be justified in terms of protecting the public interest.[16] Thus, the price fixing agreement was held to be legal, and the plaintiff lost the case.

Obviously, both the trial court and the appellate court misread the rule of reason. Horizontal price fixing (a price cartel) is the least controversial area in the international antitrust community. A majority of antitrust jurisdictions hold price cartels to be *per se* illegal since they have obviously anti-competitive effects. That eliminates the need to evaluate such cartels' competitive effects on a case-by-case basis, saving the enforcement cost and reducing the risk of false negatives.

11 *Ibid.*, at 112.

12 *Huierxun Technology Co., Ltd. v. Shenzhen Pest Control Association* (深圳市惠尔讯科技有限公司与深圳市有害生物防治协会横向垄断协议纠纷案), (2011) Min Chu Zi Di 67 Hao [(2011) Shenzhen Intermediate People's Ct. First Instance Decision No. 67] (China).

13 *Ibid.*

14 *Ibid.*

15 *Huierxun Technology Co., Ltd. v. Shenzhen Pest Control Association* (深圳市惠尔讯科技有限公司与深圳市有害生物防治协会横向垄断协议纠纷案), (2012) Yue Gao Fa Min San Zhong Zi Di 155 Hao [(2012) Guangdong Province Higher People's Court Final Decision No. 155] (China).

16 *Ibid.*, at 12–16.

The courts in the *Shenzhen Pest Control Association* case mistakenly applied the rule of reason to a price fixing agreement. Nevertheless, their error becomes more explicable when we consider the ambiguity of the AML (2008) provisions. Chapter 2, which regulates monopolistic agreements, includes four articles. Article 13 prohibits horizontal monopolistic agreements; Article 14 addresses vertical monopolistic agreements; Article 15 provides exemptions; and Article 16 prohibits industrial associations from organising undertakings to reach monopolistic agreements.

A close look at Article 13 reveals the source of ambiguity.

> Article 13: The competing business operators are prohibited from reaching any of the following monopoly agreements with each other:
>
> 1. Fixing or changing the price of commodities;
> 2. Restricting the production quantity or sales volume of commodities;
> 3. Dividing the sales market or the raw material supply market;
> 4. Restricting the purchase of new technology or new facilities or the development of new technology or new products;
> 5. Jointly boycotting transactions; or
> 6. Other monopoly agreements as determined by the Anti-monopoly Law Enforcement Agency under the State Council.
>
> The term 'monopoly agreements' as mentioned in this Law refers to the agreements, decisions or other concerted behaviours that may eliminate or restrict competition.[17]

From a literal reading, Article 13 lists and prohibits six kinds of horizontal monopoly agreements. This is akin to the 'hardcore restrictions' under the EU competition law. These 'hardcore restrictions' apply to behaviours that are unlikely to have pro-competitive effects, such as enhancing efficiency, creating objective economic benefits, or benefiting consumers, which are restrictions of competition 'by object'. Thus, it imposes '*de facto* a regime very close to a per se prohibition for such hardcore restrictions'.[18] We may therefore conclude that Article 13 intends to treat the five typical horizontal agreements (the sixth is a catch-all clause) as *per se* illegal. However, the second section of Article 13 defines monopoly agreements as 'the agreements, decisions or other concerted behaviours that may eliminate or restrict competition'. This causes a logical problem and an equivocal reading. Some may read the provision as definitely regarding all the listed horizontal agreements

17 The AML (2008), note 1, Art. 13.

18 Massimo Motta, Patrick Rey, Frank Verboven, and Nikos Vettas, "Hardcore Restrictions Under the Block Exemption Regulation on Vertical Agreements: An Economic View," *commission.europa.eu*, July 6, 2021, https://competition-policy.ec.europa.eu/system/files/2021-07/eagcp-opinion_hardcore_restrictions_under_BER_vertical-agreements.pdf

as 'monopoly agreements', with anti-competitive effects of eliminating or restricting competition, so the plaintiff need not prove anti-competitive effects. But others may understand Article 13 as only prohibiting 'monopoly agreements', requiring the plaintiff to first prove that the alleged agreement is one of the six kinds of listed monopoly agreements. In other words, the plaintiff would have to prove the agreement's anti-competitive effects of eliminating or restricting competition. Clearly, the courts in *Shenzhen Pest Control Association* adopted the second reading.

During the same period, however, a series of cases of public enforcement demonstrated that administrative enforcers treated horizontal agreements as *per se* illegal. For example, at the end of 2010, a building material industry association in Liaoning province (a province located in northeast China known as the centre of China's heavy industry) organised 13 cement producers to restrict output and set prices.[19] The administrative agency concluded that the industry association's price fixing and output restriction violated Article 13, and the association failed to justify its behaviours under the exemption in Article 15.[20] Besides that case, public enforcers launched a series of investigations against insurance industry associations, second-hand vehicle dealers, marine sand producers, and others for fixing prices, dividing geographic markets and restricting outputs.[21] Although the administrative agency did not use the term '*per se* rule', all these horizontal agreements were ruled as directly violating Article 13 without analysing these agreements' anti-competitive effects.

Although horizontal agreements can resort to exemption under Article 15, very few companies can simultaneously satisfy the three stringent conditions: (1) the agreement is reached to achieve certain justified purposes, such as developing new products, improving efficiency, or protecting public interests; (2) the agreement would not substantially injure competition; and (3) consumers can enjoy benefits generated from the agreement.

19 "Liaoning Sheng Gongshang Xingzheng Guanli Ju Xingzheng Chufa Jueding Shu" (辽宁省工商行政管理局行政处罚决定书) [Liaoning Province Administration for Industry and Commerce's Administrative Penalty Decision], Liao Gong Shang Chu Zi [2012] No. 2, *samr.gov.cn*, June 6, 2012, https://www.samr.gov.cn/cms_files/filemanager/samr/www/samrnew/fldys/tzgg/xzcf/202204/t20220424_341963.html

20 *Ibid*.

21 See "Hunan Sheng Gongshang Xingzheng Guanli Ju Xingzheng Chufa Jueding Shu" (湖南省工商行政管理局行政处罚决定书) [Hunan Province Administration for Industry and Commerce's Administrative Penalty Decision], Xiang Gong Shang Jing Chu Zi [2012] No. 1, *samr.gov.cn*, November30,2012,https://www.samr.gov.cn/jzxts/tzgg/xzcf/art/2023/art_f3edd50475ca4c87aaeb445fd7e26154.html; see also "Henan Sheng Gongshang Xingzheng Guanli Ju Xingzheng Chufa Jueding Shu" (河南省工商行政管理局行政处罚决定书) [Henan Province Administration for Industry and Commerce's Administrative Penalty Decision], Yu Gong Shang Chu Zi [2012] No. 1, *samr.gov.cn*, January 4, 2012, https://www.samr.gov.cn/jzxts/tzgg/xzcf/art/2023/art_66dfa889c2394c928237e27c167dbdc2.html; see also An Li (李岸), "Fanlongduan Fa Shishi 8 Zhounian: Jizhe Jiemi Fanlongduan 'Zhan Yi'" (《反垄断法》实施8周年 记者揭秘反垄断"战役") [On the 8th Anniversary of the AML Enforcement: Journalists Reveal the 'Battle' During the AML Enforcement], *finance.cnr.cn*, August 25, 2016, https://finance.cnr.cn/txcj/20160825/t20160825_523079023.shtml

Fortunately, such equivocality did not last long. Scholars wrote articles to criticise the courts' opinion in *Shenzhen Pest Control Association* for contradicting widely accepted antitrust theory and practice.[22] The Judicial Interpretation was revised in 2020 to clarify that defendants take the burden of proof to show that their agreement does not have the effect of eliminating or restricting competition, when the agreement is one of the horizontal agreements listed under Article 13. Therefore, a consensus has already been reached in China's antitrust community that competitors reaching agreements about fixing prices, restricting output, dividing markets, restricting technological development, and boycotting inherently violate the AML, despite the fact that the terms '*per se* rule' or 'hardcore restrictions' do not appear in legislation. This is consistent with global antirust practice. Nevertheless, equivocality involving vertical agreements is still the most contentious issue today.

4.1.2 Vertical agreements

Compared to horizontal agreements, vertical agreements are reached among undertakings that are not competitors with each other. Normally, they are independent undertakings at various levels of vertical markets, such as producers, wholesalers, retailers, and consumers. Vertical restraints can be divided into several categories according to different standards. Depending on whether a restraint involves price restrictions, vertical restraints can be classified as price restraints or nonprice restraints (e.g., territorial restrictions).[23] Resale price maintenance ('RPM'), for example, is a price restraint because it requires dealers to sell products at certain prices. A territorial restriction, however, is a nonprice restraint because it insulates appointed dealers from competition from sellers of the same products but does not directly restrict prices.[24]

Article 14 of the AML (2008) only lists two types of vertical agreements: (1) fixing the price of commodities for resale to a third party and (2) restricting the minimum price of commodities for resale to a third party. Thus, lawmakers distinguished RPM from other vertical restraints and treated it separately. RPM remains one of the most controversial areas of the global antitrust community since legal and economic experts lock horns about RPM's pro- and anti-competitive effects. Such controversy would become even more thorny in China, which is still a fledgling antitrust jurisdiction with a jumble of foreign influences and domestic factors.

A major task of amending the AML in 2022 was to solve the conflicts and contentions arising when applying the AML to RPM. Therefore, I take the AML's

22 Jian Li (李剑), "Hengxiang Longduan Xieyi Falv Shiyong de Wudu yu Chengqing—Ping 'Shenzhen Youhai Shengwu Fangzhi Xiehui Longduan An'" (横向垄断协议法律适用的误读与澄清—评'深圳有害生物防治协会垄断案') [Misunderstanding and Clarification of the Legal Application of Horizontal Monopoly Agreements: A Review of the 'Shenzhen Pest Control Association Monopoly Case'], *Law Science* 3 (2014): 128.

23 Herbert Hovenkamp, *The Antitrust Enterprise: Principle and Execution* (Harvard University Press, 2008), 186–90.

24 Ernest Gellhorn, William E. Kovacic, and Stephen Calkins, *Antitrust Law and Economics in a Nutshell* (West Academic Publishing, 2004), 359.

amendment in 2022 as the fulcrum for this section's discussion, which will centre on RPM.

4.1.2.1 Before the AML's amendment in 2022

4.1.2.1.1 PUBLIC ENFORCEMENT[25]

Historically speaking, many Chinese companies have used RPM.[26] An increasing number of high-profile investigations and decisions between August 2008 and March 2016 by the NDRC, however, have alerted companies to be cautious about using RPM.

In 2013, the NDRC imposed penalties on two of the most famous state-owned Chinese producers of premium liquor for using RPM. This marked the first time the NDRC penalised RPM under the AML. According to statistics issued by the China Alcoholic Drinks Association in 2006, the sales volume of premium white spirits was merely 0.48% of the whole white spirits industry, but its sales revenue accounted for 15% of the industry.[27] As leading producers of high-priced white spirits, Moutai and Wuliangye hold roughly 75% of the market share in the high-priced white spirits market.[28]

The popularity of Moutai's and Wuliangye's products could be explained by the importance of white spirits in Chinese culture. White spirits are traditionally served during special occasions, such as weddings, family gatherings, reunions, and business or official banquets. White spirits are also popular choices in the tradition of Chinese gift-giving. Because of their price, the white spirits produced by Moutai and Wuliangye are usually chosen as gifts for official or business purposes. Therefore, this preference of picking white spirits as gifts further increases their price, which has soared since 2009.

On 5 February 2012, however, President Xi Jinping issued his 'eight-point principles' for government officials, which imposed a form of austerity on civil servants.[29] President Xi hoped to end extravagant taxpayer-financed banquets and

25 Section 4.1.2.1.1 is excerpted from part of my previous published article: Jingmeng Cai, "Public Antitrust Enforcement of Resale Price Maintenance in China: A Crusade or Discrimination?" *Brooklyn Journal of International Law* 42 (2016): 1.

26 Rui Zhou (周锐), "Moutai Chufa Jiangjia Jingxiao Shang, Zhuanjia Cheng Huojiang Zhaozhi Fanlongduan Diaocha" (茅台处罚降价经销商专家称或将招致反垄断调查) [Moutai Punished Distributors Who Giving Discounts, Experts Claimed It May Cause Antitrust Probe], *chinanews.com*, January 11, 2013, https://www.chinanews.com.cn/cj/2013/01-11/4481529.shtml

27 Juan Zhang and Liyong Tan (张娟，谭立永), "Woguo Baijiu Hangye De Xianzhuang Yu Fazhan Qushi" (我国白酒行业的现状与发展趋势) [Current Situation and Developing Trend of White Spirits Industry in China], *Shidai Jingmao [Economic & Trade Update]* 5 (2007): 57, 58.

28 *Ibid*., at 58.

29 "Zhonggong Zhongyang Zhengzhiju Guanyu Gaijin Gongzuo Zuofeng, Miqie Lianxi Qunzhong De Ba Xiang Guiding" (中共中央政治局关于改进工作作风、密切联系群众的“八项规定”) [The Eight-point Regulations of the Political Bureau of the Communist Party of China Central Committee on Improving Work Style and Maintaining Close Ties with the People], *www. gov.cn*, December 4, 2012, https://www.ccdi.gov.cn/bxgdzlb/ssxzbxgdzlb/202504/t20250408_415765.html

bribes that are typically associated with the giving of gift-wrapped luxuries, such as premium white spirits.[30] This political incident was one of the major reasons why this best-selling period of premium white spirits ended.

As a result, the sale of Moutai's and Wuliangye's white spirits plummeted before the 2013 Chinese New Year, which used to be a peak selling season.[31] In response, Moutai and Wuliangye required their dealers to strictly implement RPM in order to prevent the retail price from decreasing. According to information disclosed by provincial agencies, beginning in 2009, Wuliangye entered into more than 3,200 RPM agreements with independent distributors.[32]

The NDRC authorised provincial agencies in Sichuan province and Guizhou province to investigate Wuliangye and Moutai, respectively,[33] and the agencies started investigating them around January 2013.[34] In response to the Guizhou agency's investigation, Moutai declared on its official website that (1) all the company's marketing policies that violated the AML would be terminated immediately,

30 As the first point, President Xi emphasizes that no banquet or reception should be held or arranged for civil servants, as gifts and premium wines are traditionally given and served in such banquets and receptions. See *Ibid.*

31 Xin Zhang and Jingyi Liu (张鑫&刘靖宜), "Kong "Sangong" Chang Jiejian Chengxiao Mingxian, Canting Shou Moutai, Jieqian Po Liangqian" (控 '三公' 倡节俭成效明显餐厅售茅台节前破两千) [Remarkable Effects of Imposing Austerity, the Price of Moutai Dropped Below 2,000 RMB Per Bottle Before the Spring Festival], *Legal Evening News*, January 28, 2013, http://www.ce.cn/cysc/sp/info/201301/28/t20130128_21327998.shtml

32 Rui Zhou (周锐), "Sichuan Sheng Fagaiwei Gongbu Fadan, Wuliangye Jiage Longduan Shoufa 2.02 Yi" (四川发改委公布罚单，五粮液价格垄断受罚2.02亿) [Sichuan Provincial Development and Reform Commission Issued Administrative Penalty of RMB 202 Million on Wuliangye], *people.cn*, February 22, 2013, http://politics.people.com.cn/n/2013/0222/c70731–20572752.html [Hereinafter 'Sichuan Provincial Agency's Decision on Wuliangye'].

33 This is because Wuliangye is headquartered in Sichuan Province and Moutai is headquartered in Guizhou Province.

34 In the end of December 2012 Wuliangye and Moutai punished their dealers for violating the RPM agreements. See Sichuan Provincial Agency's Decision on Wuliangye, see note 32 above; see also "Guizhou Sheng Wujia Ju Guanyu 'Moutai Jiage Longduan Fakuan' Gonggao" (贵州物价局关于'茅台价格垄断罚款'公告) [Guizhou Provincial Price Bureau's Administrative Penalty Decision on Moutai's Price Monopoly], February 23, 2013, https://www.chinanews.com.cn/cj/2013/02-22/4588648.shtml [Hereinafter Guizhou Provincial Agency's Decision on Moutai]. Shortly thereafter, on 16 January 2013, Moutai made an announcement on its official website claiming that it would stop implementing RPM agreements because of the Provincial Agency's investigation. One day after, Wuliangye made a similar announcement. Unfortunately, these two announcement have been removed from their official website when the author checked on 11 February 11 2025. But there is some news about these announcements. See "Wuliangye Fabu Gonggao Cheng Jiang Yiju 'Fanlongduan Fa' Jinxing Chedi Zhenggai" (五粮液发布公告称将依据《反垄断法》进行彻底整改) [Wuliangye Announced to Thoroughly Rectify Its Behaviours According to the AML], January 18, 2013, http://www.cinic.org.cn/xy/sc/127656.html [Wuliangye Announcement]; see also "Guizhou Moutai Fa Gonggao Cheng Quxiao 'Xianjia Ling' Jiang Jingxing Chedi Zhenggai" (贵州茅台发公告称取消'限价令'将进行彻底整改) [Kweichow Moutai Announced to Abolish Price Restriction, Thoroughly Rectify Its Behaviours], January 15, 2013, https://finance.huanqiu.com/article/9CaKrnJyG4E [Hereinafter "Moutai Announcement"]. Therefore, it is reasonable to infer that the agencies conducted their investigations between the end of December 2012 and 16 January 2013. Because, normally, companies respond quickly after the agencies launch their investigations, it is likely that the agencies started the probes only one or two days before the companies made their announcements.

(2) punishments for distributors would be revoked, and (3) all confiscated deposits would be returned to distributors.[35] One day later, Wuliangye made a similar announcement on its website.

Despite the two companies' 'confessions', however, the provincial agencies imposed on Moutai and Wuliangye fines calculated as 1% of each company's sales revenue from the previous year. Both companies paid the penalties in full in less than a month.[36] While each of the provincial agencies issued their respective decisions, their decisions were brief with insufficient analysis. Compared to the Guizhou agency's one paragraph decision regarding Moutai, the Sichuan regulators disclosed relatively more information. The Sichuan regulators stated that by entering into price-restricting agreements and dividing geographical markets, Wuliangye set a price floor for products through vertical monopoly agreements that violated Article 14 of the AML (2008). Such behaviours thus restricted and eliminated competition and harmed consumers' welfare.

The infant formula case is another example of public concern driving enforcement. In 2008, China's infant formula industry was involved in a food safety scandal.[37] Several domestic brands of infant formula were found to be adulterated with melamine, a toxic chemical.[38] As a result of safety concerns, the scandal ruined the reputation of infant formula producers in China, and Chinese parents resorted to purchasing foreign brands instead.[39] Prior to the milk scandals in 2008, domestic milk producers accounted for more than 60% of the market share. After the scandal, however, their market share dropped to 48% in 2013.[40] Due to Chinese parents' obsession with foreign infant formula and their growing distrust in domestic brands, prices of foreign-brand infant formula had increased by at least 30% since 2008.[41]

On 7 August 2013, approximately five months after launching the investigation, the NDRC imposed fines totalling RMB 668.73 million (about USD 102.88 million) on six manufacturers of infant formula—five foreign producers and one Chinese Hong Kong company—for restricting the minimum resale price with distributors in violation of Article 14 of the AML (2008).[42]

35 Moutai Announcement, *Ibid.*

36 Xiaosong Zhang and Cheng Qian (张晓松，钱成), "Moutai Wuliangye Yi Quan'e Jiaona 4.49 Yiyuan Jiage Longduan Fadan" (茅台五粮液已全额缴纳4.49亿元价格垄断罚单) [Moutai and Wuliangye Paid the Penalty of RMB 449 Million in Full], *xinhuanet.com*, March 15, 2013, http://www.ce.cn/cysc/sp/info/201303/15/t20130315_21446781.shtml

37 Fan Yang (杨帆), "Zhongguo Ruye Zhe Wunian" (中国乳业这五年) [Five Years of China's Dairy Industry], *people.com.cn*, October 1, 2013, https://paper.people.com.cn/xaq/html/2013-10/01/content_1324677.htm

38 *Ibid.*

39 *Ibid.*

40 *Ibid.*

41 Edward Wong, "Chinese Search for Infant Formula Goes Global," *cnbc.com*, July 26, 2013, https://www.cnbc.com/2013/07/26/chinese-search-for-infant-formula-goes-global.html

42 NDRC, "Heshengyuan Deng Rufen Shengchan Qiye Weifan Fanlongduan Fa Xianzhi Jingzheng Xingwei Gongbei Chufa 6.6873 Yiyuan" (合生元等乳粉生产企业违反《反垄断法》限制竞争行为共被处罚6.6873亿元) [Penalty on Milk Powder Producers of Restricting Competition and Fined RMB 668.73 Million], *ndrc.gov.cn*, August 7, 2013, https://www.ndrc.gov.cn/xwdt/xwfb/201308/t20130807_956179.html [Hereinafter NDRC Decision on Infant Formula Milk Producers].

According to the NDRC's decision, the involved companies fixed their products' resale prices or restricted the minimum resale prices and punished violators through various methods, such as imposing fines, deducting rebates, and limiting or stopping supply.[43] The NDRC further claimed that infant formula producers had restricted resale prices, boosted prices, eliminated inter-brand competition and damaged consumers' welfare.[44] Furthermore, the decision also disclosed that all the companies involved admitted that their conduct had constituted RPM and that they had failed to prove that their conduct could satisfy the exemption requirements under Article 15 of the AML.[45]

Notably, the NDRC investigated nine companies in total, but only imposed penalties against six companies.[46] The NDRC did not penalise three companies because they voluntarily reported their RPM to the NDRC. Among the six companies, the NDRC gave mitigated penalties to five of them that had proactively cooperated with the investigation and/or carried out self-corrective measures.[47]

Besides those two cases, in that period of time, the NDRC has also investigated and issued fines for cases of RPM in various industries, such as corrective lens[48] and automobiles.[49] In the corrective lens case, eyeglasses business associations in several cities had organised their members to squeeze discounters out of the market. Notably, the NDRC used the term RPM for the first time in the headline of a decision. Previously, in the liquor case, the NDRC used the term 'price monopoly', while in the infant formula case it used the phrase 'behaviours restricting competition' in the headline of the decision to refer to such arrangements.

Before discussing this issue further, it is worth taking a close look at the legislative text first, which helps us understand the origin of the problem. Articles 14 and 15 of the AML (2008) were designed and drafted based on the framework of EU competition law. Article 14 of the AML outlines provisions regarding vertical

43 *Ibid.*
44 *Ibid.*
45 *Ibid.*
46 *Ibid.*
47 *Ibid.*
48 NDRC, "BuFen YanJing Jingpian Shengchan Qiye Weichi Zhuanshou Jiage Xingwei Bei Yifa Chachu" (部分眼镜镜片生产商维持转售价格行为被依法查处) [Imposed Penalty on Part Corrective Lenses Producers' RPM], *www.gov.cn*, May 29, 2014, https://www.gov.cn/xinwen/2014-05/29/content_2689910.htm [Hereinafter NDRC Decision on Corrective Lenses Producers].
49 See Ye Pan (潘晔), "Benchi Gongsi Zai Jiangsu 'Jiage Longduan' Bei Fakuan 3.5 Yi Yuan" (奔驰公司在江苏实施"价格垄断"被罚款3.5亿元) [Mercedes Benz in Jiangsu Province Been Penalized of RMB 350 Million for 'Price Monopoly'], *www.gov.cn*, April 23, 2015, https://www.gov.cn/xinwen/2015-04/23/content_2852076.htm; also see, Weiwei Chen and Chao Zhao (陈炜伟，赵超), "Yiqi Dazhong Xiaoshou Gongsi Shishi Jiage Longduan Bei Chufa Kuan 2.4 Yiyuan" (一汽大众销售公司实施价格垄断被处罚款2.4亿元) [FAW Volkswagen Sales Company Been Fined RMB 240 Million for Price Monopoly], *www.gov.cn*, September 11, 2014, https://www.gov.cn/xinwen/2014-09/11/content_2749003.htm; also see Yuan Lin (林远), "Kelai Sile, Yiqi Dazhong Yin Jiage Longduan Beifa Jukuan" (克莱斯勒一汽大众因价格垄断被罚巨款) [Chrysler and FAW Volkswagen Been Imposed Huge Amount of Fines for Price Monopoly], *rmzxw.com.cn*, September 12, 2014, https://www.rmzxw.com.cn/c/2014-09-12/375923.shtml

monopoly agreements, and Article 15 of the AML provides exemptions when certain conditions are satisfied. In practice, however, Chinese antitrust practitioners and academics alike have interpreted Articles 14 and 15 differently. There is a major divergence between the understanding and interpretation of EU and US antitrust laws' analytical methods and their influences on the AML regarding the RPM. Some scholars even claim that the influence of such foreign concepts has led to a strange phenomenon in China: The AML uses the content of US antitrust law to fill in the framework of EU competition law.[50] Here I will briefly describe the US and EU approaches to analysing RPM agreements and how this led to confusion in China.

Antitrust statutes in the United States, which have expansive and open-ended language, do not provide clear or applicable guidance for analysing RPM. In contrast, common law decisions gradually developed a body of law in regard to RPM, which has helped to flesh out the meaning of the statutory language. In *Dr Miles Medical Co. v. John D. Park & Sons Co.*,[51] the US Supreme Court established the *per se* rule for RPM.[52]

Thereafter, RPM was treated as *per se* illegal for nearly a century. In 1997, the US Supreme Court ruled in *State Oil Co. v. Khan*[53] that the price ceiling (maximum RPM) set by an oil producer for its dealers should be treated with the rule of reason.[54] It was not until 2007 that the *per se* rule for minimum RPM was overruled by the US Supreme Court in *Leegin Creative Leather Products, Inc. v. PSKS, Inc.*[55]

50 Yingying Hong (洪莹莹), "Woguo Xianzhi Zhuanshou Jiage Zhidu de Tixihua Jieshi Jiqi Wanshan" (我国限制转售价格制度的体系化解释及其完善) [The Systematic Explanation and Improvement of RPM in China], *ECUPL Journal* 4 (2015): 49, 57.

51 See *Dr. Miles Medical Co. v. John D. Park & Sons Co.*, 220 U.S.373 (1911). In *Dr. Miles*, a proprietary medicines producer sued one of its wholesalers, who resold its medicine at discounted prices, refused to enter into an RPM contract with the producer, and induced others to violate the producer's price restrictions. The US Supreme Court relied on the common law doctrine and decided that a 'general restraint upon alienation is ordinarily invalid'. The court reasoned that the complainant's RPM agreement was used as a means to limit freedom of trade and prevent price competition among dealers and to harm the public interest, which would be *per se* illegal.

52 *Ibid.*

53 *State Oil Co. v. Khan*, 522 U.S.3, 9 (1997).

54 Under the rule of reason, RPM agreements are not *per se* illegal, but agencies or courts should analyze and balance both anti-competitive and procompetitive effects of RPM agreements on competition and consumers. The agreements are only illegal under the rule of reason if their anti-competitive outweigh their procompetitive effects.

55 See *Leegin Creative Leather Prods., v. PSKS, Inc.*, 551 U.S. 877 (2007). Leegin was a manufacturer of handbags, belts, jewelry, and other products under the 'Brighton' brand. Leegin distributed its products through its own stores as well as independent retailers. The plaintiff, PSKS, an independent women's clothing and accessories store, carried the 'Brighton' brand. Leegin imposed a minimum RPM on its distributors. When PSKS sold discounted 'Brighton' products, Leegin terminated PSKS's distributorship. Then PSKS sued Leegin alleging that Leegin violated the antitrust laws by entering into minimum RPM agreements with retailers. Leegin did not deny carrying out RPM agreements, but instead it challenged the *per se* rule for minimum RPM itself. Finally, the US Supreme Court held that the minimum RPM had procompetitive effects, which enhanced inter-brand competition, facilitated market entry for new firms and brands, and encouraged dealers to offer services. As a result, the court concluded that minimum RPM should not be regarded as *per se* illegal.

As the purposes of antitrust law began to change, the rules governing RPM began to evolve similarly. When the *per se* rule was first established, antitrust law in the United States was associated with several purposes, such as keeping the common law tradition[56] and protecting small and medium-sized companies.[57] A relatively clear, simple, and predictable goal of antitrust law was not formed until the economic revolution of the 1970s, with the emergence of the Chicago School. The Chicago School refers to an ideological movement that initially began at the University of Chicago in the 1950s and reached its peak in the 1970s and 1980s.[58] The Chicago School advocates that efficiency should be the sole purpose of antitrust law.[59] It focuses on the efficiency and effects of conduct on market prices rather than the forms of conduct itself.[60] Therefore, the Chicago School challenges the *per se* rule for RPM by claiming that the *Dr. Miles* rule is formalistic and that the courts have ignored RPM's economic purpose and its effects on consumer welfare.[61] The Chicago School believes that nearly all vertical practices, such as RPM, '[a]re rarely or never anticompetitive'.[62]

Notably, there are two preconditions for US antitrust law changing from *per se* rule to the rule of reason for RPM. First, a large body of economic literature enables US courts and antitrust agencies to conduct comprehensive economic analyses on RPM. Second, US courts play a central role in the antitrust system, allowing them to create relatively flexible rules for RPM to meet the rapidly changing nature of business.

Although EU competition law is based on the common law tradition, rules about RPM agreements highlight prominent features of the civil law system because the European Commission, as a bureaucracy, has sole authority to assess anti-competitive and pro-competitive effects of RPM agreements in accordance with Article 101(3) of TFEU.[63] Unlike US antitrust law, therefore, the enforcement of EU competition law is administratively driven. Article 101(1) of the TFEU generally prohibits RPM,[64] which is categorised as a 'hardcore restriction'[65] and

56 For example, in *Dr. Miles*, the US Supreme Court ruled that the right of alienation was the essential right of property in movables, and restraints on that would be 'obnoxious to public policy'. See *Dr. Miles v. John D. Park & Sons*, note 51, at 404.

57 For example, the Robinson-Patman Act was a product of populism during the Great Depression, the purpose of which was to protect small and independent merchants from the chain stores' price competition. Although the Robinson-Patman Act has been criticized extensively, it has not been repealed because of the advocacy of populism. See Robinson-Patman Act, 15 U.S.C.§13 (2012).

58 See Richard A. Posner, "The Chicago School of Antitrust Analysis," *Penn Carey Law Journals* 127 (1979): 925, 925–28.

59 John J. Gibbons, "Antitrust, Law & Economics, and Politics," *Law and Contemporary Problems* 4 (1987): 217, 218.

60 See Gerber, note 2, at 141; see also William E. Kovasic and Carl Shapiro, "Antitrust Policy: A Century of Economic and Legal Thinking," *The Journal of Economic Perspectives* 14 (2000): 43, 53.

61 Gellhorn, et al., note 24, at 341.

62 Hovenkamp, *The Antitrust Enterprise*, note 23, 32.

63 Marsela Maci, "The Assessment of RPM Under EU Competition Rules: Certain Inconsistencies Based on a Non-Substantive Analysis," *European Competition Law Review* 35 (2014): 103, 103–4.

64 See Consolidated Version of the Treaty on Functioning of the European Union Art. 101 (1), October 26, 2012, 2012 O.J. (C 326) 47 [Hereinafter TFEU].

65 See Commission Guidelines on Vertical Restraints, 2010 O.J. (C 130) (EC), para. 48.

cannot be applied to a block exemption.[66] The block exemption provides virtually all vertical agreements with exemptions if the market share of both suppliers and buyers of the agreements are below 30%;[67] however, RPM is excluded from the block exemption, which can only be applied on a case-by-case basis. The US Supreme Court's ruling in *Leegin* also impacted the way the European Union views RPM agreements. In response, the European Commission issued the *Guidelines on Vertical Restraints* in 2010 ('Vertical Guidelines').[68] Although the Vertical Guidelines still classify RPM agreements as a hardcore restriction,[69] they emphasise economic analysis in the need for a more open-minded approach to RPM.[70] The Guidelines note that 'undertakings may demonstrate pro-competitive effects under Article 101(3) in an individual case',[71] which would exempt an RPM agreement. The impact of US antitrust law on the European Union's view of RPM, however, is still limited. It is theoretically possible for companies in Europe to claim that RPM agreements create efficiencies and thus should be exempt under Article 101(3) of the TFEU; in practice, however, this is always difficult and almost impossible.[72] Dereck Ridyard, a European lawyer specialising in competition law, noted in his article that

> the current treatment of RPM in EU competition law is and seems destined to remain very hostile, [and it] is highly unlikely that the EU competition law or the authorities that enforce it will move away from its instinctive dislike of RPM.[73]

66 See Commission Regulation 330/2010, April 23, 2010, O.J. (L 102), 1 (EU). [Hereinafter Regulation 330/2010] Article 4 provides: '[T]he exemption . . . shall not apply to vertical agreements which, directly or indirectly, in isolation or in combination with other factors under the control of the parties, have as their object: (a) the restriction of the buyer's ability to determine its sale price, without prejudice to the possibility of the supplier to impose a maximum sale price or recommend a sale price, provided that they do not amount to a fixed or minimum sale price as a result of pressure from, or incentives offered by, any of the parties'.

67 See Commission Guidelines on Vertical Restraints, note 65, sec. III. The block exemption provides a safe harbor for most vertical agreements. The block exemption requires three conditions that must be fulfilled in order to exempt a vertical agreement from the prohibition of Article 101 (1) of TFEU. First, the agreement shall not contain any hardcore restrictions. Second, both suppliers and buyers need to have a market share cap of 30%. Third, the block exemption needs to impose specific conditions on three vertical restraints, specifically noncompete obligations during the contract, non-compete obligations after termination of the contract, and the exclusion of specific brands in a selective distribution system.

68 See Commission Guidelines on Vertical Restraints, note 65 above, para. 48.

69 *Ibid.*

70 See generally Commission Guidelines on Vertical Restraints, note 65 above, para. 5 ("Article 101 provides a legal framework for the assessment of vertical restraints, which takes into consideration the distinction between anti-competitive and pro-competitive effects.")

71 Commission Guidelines on Vertical Restraints, note 65 above, para. 47.

72 Filippo Amato, "RPM in the European Union: Any Developments Since Leegin?" *jonesday.com*, November 14, 2013, https://competitionpolicyinternational.com/assets/Uploads/AmatoNOV-131.pdf

73 Dereck Ridyard, "Resale Price Maintenance: An Overview of EU and National Case Law," Art. No. 41915, *Concurrences* 1 (January 24, 2012): 10, https://www.concurrences.com/en/bulletin/special-issues/Resale-Price-Maintenance/

In short, there are two main characteristics of the approaches to RPM under EU competition law. First, RPM is presumed to be anti-competitive, and overturning such a presumption is difficult. Second, unlike US antitrust law, the enforcement of EU competition law is administratively driven. The European Commission is the dominant authority for assessing whether RPM agreements are anti-competitive, and EU courts only conduct limited judicial review because they usually defer to the European Commission's decisions.[74]

As mentioned earlier, the design of the AML was based on the TFEU framework. Article 14 of the AML, which is similar to Article 101(1) of the TFEU, prohibits three categories of vertical restraints: fixing resale prices, setting minimum RPM, and other vertical monopoly agreements identified by antitrust agencies. In addition, similar to Article 101(3) of the TFEU, Article 15 of the AML lists conditions for exemption. In practice, the method of analysing RPM remains one of the most controversial issues in China today. In the liquor case, the NDRC did not explicitly state which analytical approach of RPM it had adopted; it simply ruled that the RPM agreement directly violated the AML. In the infant formula case, the decision stated that the RPM agreement violated the AML generally and that the involved companies failed to prove that the RPM agreements were exempt under Article 15. This train of thought is similar to the methods used under EU competition law. In the corrective lens case, the NDRC seemed hesitant to follow the EU approach to RPM agreements. The NDRC's decision was the first to use the term 'resale price maintenance', a term transplanted from the United States. Moreover, if the NDRC follows the EU approach, it should first apply Article 14 to generally ban RPM and then discuss whether an alleged RPM can be exempted according to Article 15. The NDRC, however, did not mention whether Article 15 could be applied in the corrective lens case, which would not appear to follow the EU approach in this case. In its automotive industry decisions, however, the NDRC returned to the EU approach.

Kunlin Xu, the former leader of the NDRC's Antitrust Bureau, summarised the approach toward RPM as 'Prohibition + Exemption'.[75] Xu explained that, under the AML, RPM agreements are generally prohibited but may be exempted if listed conditions are satisfied in accordance with Article 15.[76] Based on Xu's comments, we can conclude that the NDRC has accepted EU methodology with respect to RPM agreements. The state of RPM agreements under the AML, however, is still in flux because agencies and courts have not yet reached a consensus.

74 Maci, note 63, at 106.

75 Kunlin Xu (徐昆林), "Kuanda Zhengce Shiyong Yu Zongxiang Longduan Xieyi" (宽大政策适用于纵向垄断协议) [Leniency Policy Applying to Vertical Monopoly Agreements], *ceh.com.cn*, October 31, 2013, https://www.ceh.com.cn/epaper/uniflows/html/2013/10/31/A03/A03_48.htm

76 *Ibid.*

4.1.2.1.2 PRIVATE ENFORCEMENT[77]

Compared to public enforcers, the judicial system seems more deeply affected by US antitrust law. In the *Rainbow v. Johnson & Johnson* case,[78] the court's reasoning was akin to that of *Leegin*, in contrast with public enforcement.

Beijing Ruibang Yonghe Equipment Technology & Trading Co., Ltd. ('Rainbow'), a medical equipment distributor, filed a lawsuit in the Shanghai Intermediate Court ('Intermediate Court') in August 2010, claiming that its 15-year partners—Johnson & Johnson (Shanghai) Medical Equipment Co., Ltd. and Johnson & Johnson (China) Medical Equipment Co., Ltd. (collectively referred to as 'Johnson & Johnson')—enforced RPM with their distributors, which violated Article 14 of the AML.[79] In January 2008, Johnson & Johnson entered into a distribution agreement with Rainbow. According to the agreement, Rainbow could sell products neither outside the designated territory nor at a lower price than the retail price set by Johnson & Johnson.[80] In March 2008, Rainbow bid for a project outside the designated territory at a lower price. Johnson & Johnson terminated Rainbow's distributorship, stopped supplying all products (not only the suturing products involved in the alleged RPM agreement, but also other products, like surgical staplers) and confiscated the bond Rainbow had deposited.[81] The Intermediate Court held in favour of the defendant (Johnson & Johnson) with the reasoning that the plaintiff (Rainbow) could not prove that the agreement was a 'monopoly agreement' with the effect of eliminating or restricting competition.[82] The case was appealed before the Shanghai High People's Court ('High Court'). The High Court reversed the Intermediate Court's judgement.[83] As the final judgement, the High Court upheld parts of Rainbow's claims and ordered Johnson & Johnson to compensate Rainbow with RMB 530,000 (about USD 85,483).[84]

Compared to the analytical approach for RPM adopted by the NDRC, the High Court used an analytical method like the rule of reason in US antitrust law. The High

77 Section 4.1.2.1.2 is excerpted from part of my previous published article: Jingmeng Cai, "Private Antitrust Enforcement of Resale Price Maintenance in China: What Lessons Can China Learn From the United States?" *Asian-Pacific Law and Policy Journal* 18 (2017): 1.

78 *Beijing Ruibang Yonghe Equipment Technology & Trading Co., Ltd v. Johnson & Johnson (Shanghai) Medical Equipment Co., Ltd. and Johnson & Johnson (China) Medical Equipment Co., Ltd.* (北京锐邦涌和科贸有限公司诉强生（上海）医疗器材有限公司&强生（中国）医疗器材有限公司纵向垄断协议纠纷案), (2010) Hu Yi Zhong Min Wu (Zhi) Chu Zi Di 169 Hao [(2010) Civil Judgment of Shanghai No. 1 Intermediate People's Court No. 169] (China), Wolters Kluwer.

79 *Ibid.*

80 *Ibid.*

81 *Ibid.*

82 *Ibid.*

83 *Beijing Ruibang Yonghe Equipment Technology & Trading Co. Ltd. ("Rainbow") v. Johnson & Johnson (Shanghai) Medical Equipment Co. Ltd., and Johnson & Johnson (China) Medical Equipment Co., Ltd.* (2012) (北京锐邦涌和科贸有限公司诉强生（上海）医疗器材有限公司&强生（中国）医疗器材有限公司纵向垄断协议纠纷案), Hu Gao Min San (Zhi) Zhong Zi Di 63 Hao [(2012) Shanghai High People's Court Final Decision No. 63] (China), Wolters Kluwer. [Hereinafter *Rainbow v. Johnson & Johnson*].

84 *Ibid.*

Court asserted that RPM was not '*per se* illegal' according to Article 14 of the AML but that the AML defines monopoly agreements as agreements with the effect of eliminating or restricting competition. Therefore, the plaintiff had to provide *prima facie* evidence that the alleged agreement was a monopoly agreement. As to this point, the High Court affirmed the lower court's finding. However, compared to the Intermediate Court's reasoning, the High Court conducted a relatively comprehensive analysis to conclude that the plaintiff had already satisfied its burden of proof.

First, the High Court rejected Johnson & Johnson's argument that Rainbow was not eligible to bring a private antitrust lawsuit because Rainbow was a party to the agreement. According to Article 50 of the AML (2008), any party that has suffered loss from a monopoly agreement is a qualified plaintiff. Furthermore, the High Court observed that a party involved in an alleged monopoly agreement could access more evidence and information about the agreement than consumers or outsiders.[85]

Second, the High Court held that the plaintiff had to prove that the alleged RPM agreement was a 'monopoly agreement' with the effect of eliminating or restricting competition. The High Court stated that Article 7 of the Judicial Interpretation provided that

> if a behaviour is alleged to violate Article 13 of the AML (regulations about horizontal monopoly agreements), the defendant bears the burden of proving that her conduct does not have the effect of eliminating or restricting competition in order to avoid a penalty.[86]

Therefore, the High Court stated that the Judicial Interpretation (2012) provided that such a reversed burden of proof can only be applied to horizontal monopoly agreements, rather than vertical monopoly agreements, such as RPM. Since such a reversed burden of proof should be explicitly provided by law, plaintiffs in RPM litigation cannot be exempted from the responsibility of proving the alleged RPM to be a monopoly agreement.

Third, the highlight of the High Court's judgement was that the Court listed four factors for evaluating RPM's economic effects on competition: (1) whether the relevant market was highly competitive; (2) whether the defendant had strong market power; (3) the motivation of the defendant to conduct RPM; and (4) whether anti-competitive effects of the RPM could be offset by its pro-competitive effects.

In sum, the High Court found that the demand elasticity of the relevant market was low, that Johnson & Johnson had strong market power to control prices and the motivation to restrict resale prices, and that Johnson & Johnson could not prove that anti-competitive effects of the RPM could be offset by its pro-competitive

85 *Ibid.*

86 Provisions of the Supreme People's Court on Several Issues Concerning the Application of Law in the Trial of Civil Dispute Cases Arising From Monopolistic Conduct (promulgated by Sup. People's Ct. May 3, 2012, effective June 1, 2012, expired July 1, 2024) CLI.3.173345(EN) (Lawinfochina) [Hereinafter Judicial Interpretation on AML Lawsuits], Art. 7.

effects. Therefore, the High Court held that the RPM agreement implemented by Johnson & Johnson had the effect of eliminating and restricting competition and was therefore a monopoly agreement prohibited by Article 14 of the AML (2008).

Although *Rainbow v. Johnson & Johnson* is the first RPM private lawsuit that the plaintiff (Rainbow) won, even Rainbow's attorney expressed his concerns about the heavy burden of proof that may easily allow RPMs with anti-competitive effects to escape penalties.[87]

The distinctly contradictory approaches toward RPM taken by public enforcers and judges buried a landmine for AML enforcement. That landmine finally exploded with the *Hainan Yutai Fish Feed* case,[88] which forced enforcers and lawmakers to face the problem and devise a solution.

Hainan Yutai, a little-known fish feed producer, had signed a price fixing agreement with its distributors, but that agreement had not yet been carried out. Then the Price Bureau of Hainan Province ruled the agreement to be a RPM, which violated the AML, and imposed a fine of RMB 300,000. Hainan Yutai brought a lawsuit in the Intermediate Court of Haikou City, requesting the court to review and dismiss the administrative penalty decision. The Intermediate Court followed the reasoning pattern in *Rainbow v. Johnson & Johnson* and found that the administrative decision had applied the law in error and dismissed it.[89] The defendant, the Price Bureau of Hainan Province, appealed to the High Court of Hainan Province. The High Court, however, respected the agency's analytical approach toward RPM and held in the defendant's favour.[90]

This case was ultimately presented to the Supreme People's Court for a retrial, which put the SPC in a dilemma. If it upheld the administrative decision, that would mean the rule of reason for RPM used by the judicial system was wrong. But if it dismissed the administrative decision, the SPC would have to provide a rationale sufficient to persuade public enforcers to follow the judicial system's approach. However, that might break the subtle balance and mutual constraining relationship between public and private enforcement, not to mention that the AML enforcement system was centred on public enforcement.

87 Bin Dai and Fanyu Zeng (戴宾，曾凡宇), "Zongxiang Jiage Longduan Xieyi Minshi Susong Falv Wenti Yanjiu—Yi Qiangsheng An Wei Shijiao Zhankai" (纵向价格垄断协议民事诉讼法律问题研究——以强生案为视角展开) [Research on Private Enforcement of Vertical Price Restraints: From the Perspective of Rainbow v. Johnson & Johnson], *Journal of Law Application* 3 (2016): 97, 101.

88 Supreme People's Court Final Decision: Hainan Yutai Science and Technology Feed Co., Ltd. v. Hainan Province Price Bureau (海南省物价局与海南裕泰科技饲料有限公司行政处罚纠纷案), (2018) Zui Gao Fa Xing Shen 4675 Hao [(2018) Sup. People's Ct. Administrative Ruling No. 4675] (China), Wolters Kluwer.

89 The Trial Court's Decision: *Hainan Yutai Science and Technology Feed Co., Ltd. v. Hainan Province Price Bureau* (海南省物价局与海南裕泰科技饲料有限公司行政处罚纠纷案), (2017) Qiong 01 Xing Chu 681 Hao [(2017) Haikou City Intermediate People's Court Administrative Judgement No. 68] (China), Wolters Kluwer.

90 The Appellate Court's Decision: *Hainan Province Price Bureau v. Hainan Yutai Science and Technology Feed Co., Ltd.* (海南省物价局与海南裕泰科技饲料有限公司行政处罚纠纷案), (2017) Qiong Xing Zhong 1180 Hao [(2017) Hainan Province High People's Court Administrative Judgement No. 1180] (China), Wolters Kluwer.

Therefore, the SPC shrewdly sought to smooth things over while giving offense to neither side. The reasoning of the SPC's judgement mainly consisted of four parts. First, the SPC concluded that certain horizontal agreements (fixing prices, restricting output, and dividing markets) were *per se* illegal, but other agreements, like RPM, generated both anti- and pro-competitive effects and should be analysed on a case-by-case basis. Thus, the SPC affirmed that the judicial system applying the rule of reason to RPM was appropriate. The Court further stated, however, that considering the fledgling state of the AML and the current development of the market, requiring public enforcers to conduct comprehensive and in-depth analysis on every RPM case would be a heavy burden that would tremendously increase the cost and reduce the efficiency of public enforcement.

Moreover, the SPC underlined the difference between public enforcement and private lawsuit in regard to their purpose and function. The Court noticed that it was reasonable to let plaintiffs prove the PRM's anti-competitive effects since a private lawsuit's major purpose was to compensate the plaintiffs. On the contrary, a major goal of public enforcement was to prevent and deter monopolistic behaviours, so the criteria for determining RPM's illegality could be different from private lawsuits. As the SPC stated, it was also appropriate that public enforcers do not have to prove the anti-competitive effects of RPM but simply rule it as *per se* illegal.

Nevertheless, the SPC admitted that the inconsistency of the AML application should be soon resolved and called for lawmakers to clarify and unify the analytical approach to RPM. Thus, solving that inconsistency became a major task for amending the AML in 2022, which will be discussed in the next section.

4.1.2.2 The AML amendment in 2022

Unifying the approaches toward monopoly agreements was a major part of amending the AML in 2022.

First, in the amended law, the definition of monopoly agreement is provided separately in Article 16 to illustrate that this definition applies equally to both horizontal and vertical monopoly agreements. Second, Article 17 lists and prohibits five types of horizontal agreements, just like the original law. That makes clear that these five kinds of horizontal agreements are *per se* illegal unless they satisfy the exemption set by Article 20.

The main changes concern vertical agreements. Article 18 explicitly prohibits undertakings from fixing resale prices or setting minimum resale prices (collectively referred to as RPM). Otherwise, the second section of Article 18 provides that 'if undertakings can prove that RPM lacks the anti-competitive effects of eliminating or restricting competition, RPM shall not be prohibited'. This newly added provision is designed to resolve the conflicts and inconsistency between public and private enforcement. According to the provision, RPM is not *per se* illegal as horizontal agreements are, but it seems that the approach applied to RPM is not the rule of reason either. Under this new rule, RPM is presumed to be illegal unless the undertaking, rather than the administrative agency or plaintiffs, can prove RPM lacking anti-competitive effects. Thus, the new AML seems to take the middle way, treating RPM neither as harshly as the *per se* rule nor as leniently as the rule of reason. It imposes the burden of proof regarding competitive effects on the defendant. It is easier for administrative agencies and private plaintiffs to win an RPM case under the amended AML than when the rule of reason was applied.

One highlight of this amendment is importing the 'safe harbour' mechanism from EU competition law. Section 3 of Article 18 provides that 'if the undertaking can prove that its market share is lower than the threshold provided by the antimonopoly agency under the State Council and satisfies other conditions specified by the agency, the agreement shall not be prohibited'. This provision has prompted much controversy and discussion.[91] Even though I use the phrase 'importing from EU law' to refer to the origin of this new provision, it may be more accurate to say the EU 'safe harbour' mechanism was borrowed to serve as a shell for holding China's own material.

There are two types of safe harbours in EU competition law. First, the safe harbour gives block exemptions to certain agreements. For example, the Vertical Block Exemption Regulation (VBER), under Article 101(3) TFEU, sets a safe harbour from antitrust investigation for vertical agreements, which is designed to afford legal certainty to businesses and save the agency's enforcement costs. RPM, however, as a 'hardcore restriction', cannot be protected by the safe harbour. Moreover, the newly revised VBER[92] and Vertical Guidelines[93] further narrow the scope of safe harbour. For example, dual distribution cannot be exempted where there are hardcore restrictions (e.g., RPM).[94] Besides VBER, the block exemptions given to certain research and development agreements,[95] and certain specialisation agreements[96] can also be categorised as this type of safe harbour.

91 See Haitao Jiao (焦海涛), "Longduan Xieyi 'Anquan Gang' Zhidu De Xingzhi Dingwei Yu Guifan Xiufu" (垄断协议'安全港'制度的性质定位与规范修复) [The Nature and Normative Restoration of the "Safe Harbor" System for Monopoly Agreements], *Global Law Review* 6 (2023): 63; see also Huiqun Wang (王慧群), "Zhongguo Longduan Xieyi Anquan Gang Guize De Lifa Luoji: Xinxi Chengben De Shijiao" (中国垄断协议安全港规则的立法逻辑：信息成本的视角) [Chinese Legislative Logic for Safe Harbor Rule for Vertical and Horizontal Agreements Under Antitrust Law: The Information Cost Approach], *The Jurist* 1 (2023): 57; see also Jifeng Liu (刘继峰), "Woguo Fanlongduan Fa Zongxiang Longduan Xieyi AnquanGang Zhidu De Wanshan" (我国反垄断法纵向垄断协议安全港制度的完善) [Perfection of the Safe Harbor System of Vertical Monopoly Agreement in China's Anti-Monopoly Law], *Academic Journal of Zhongzhou* 2 (2023): 64.

92 Vertical Block Exemption Regulation (VBER), (EU) 2022/720, https://eur-lex.europa.eu/legal-content/EN/TXT/PDF/?uri=CELEX:32022R0720

93 Guidelines on Vertical Restraints (EU) 2022/C 248/01, https://eur-lex.europa.eu/legal-content/EN/TXT/PDF/?uri=CELEX:52022XC0630(01)

94 VBER, note 92, para. 12.

95 Commission Regulation (EU) 2023/1066 of June 1, 2023 on the Application of Article 101(3) of the TFEU to Certain Categories of Research and Development Agreements, OJ [2023] L 143/9.

96 Commission Regulation (EU) 2023/1067 of June 1, 2023 on the Application of Article 101(3) of the TFEU to Certain Categories of Specialisation Agreements, OJ [2023] L 143/20.

Second, the EU Notice on Agreements of Minor Importance[97] creates the other type of safe harbour (the so-called *De Minimis* safe harbour). The *De Minimis* safe harbour can apply to both vertical and horizontal agreements, but only if businesses' market share is below 15% (in agreements entered into between non-competitors) or 10% (in agreements between competitors). Just as before, hardcore restrictions such as RPM are excluded from the protection scope of the *De Minimis* safe harbour.

Obviously, the safe harbour instrument under the AML (2022) resembles neither of the two types of safe harbours in EU law. The drafters of the AML (2022) put the safe harbour in Article 18, the provision regarding vertical agreements. Thus, it is not an equivalent to the *De Minimis* safe harbour, which applies equally to all agreements. Nevertheless, from a literal reading, the safe harbour does not exclude RPM, so it differs from the safe harbour under the VBER as well.

Haitao Jiao, a professor at the China University of Political Science and Law, opines that this phenomenon arises from the Chinese academic community's superficial understanding of the EU's safe harbour instrument.[98] However, I would submit a different opinion. This provision may actually be a compromise between various voices that is very likely influenced by certain scholars who have insisted on adopting an approach close to the rule of reason under US antitrust law.

Actually, even before the AML amendment in 2022, lawmakers had already submitted the safe harbour instrument to a practical test. The potential contentions and inconsistent viewpoints emerged then.

The Anti-Monopoly Committee of the State Council issued the *Antimonopoly Guidelines in the Field of Intellectual Property* (the 'IP Guidelines') on 4 January 2019.[99] Article 13 of the IP Guidelines explicitly stipulates the safe harbour rules. This article is modelled after the *De Minimis* safe harbour of the European Union, although the thresholds of market share are higher than that of the EU law and RPM is not excluded. The article provides that horizontal and vertical agreements involving IP can be exempted under the following conditions: (1) when the agreement is entered between competitors and the aggregate market share in the relevant market does not exceed 20%; (2) when the agreement is entered between non-competitors and the aggregate market share in the relevant market does not exceed 30%; or (3) when the market share is difficult to ascertain or cannot accurately reflect businesses' market power and there are at least four technological substitutes that can be obtained at reasonable costs and are controlled by independent third parties for the technology controlled by the parties to the agreement.

Interestingly, the Anti-Monopoly Committee of the State Council issued the *Antimonopoly Guidelines for the Automobile Industry* (the 'Automobile

97 Communication from the Commission Notice on agreements of minor importance which do not appreciably restrict competition under Article 101(1) of the TFEU (De Minimis Notice), OJ [2014] L 291/1.

98 Jiao, see note 91.

99 Guide of the Anti-Monopoly Committee of the State Council for Countering Monopolization in the Field of Intellectual Property Rights (promulgated by Antimonopoly Comm, State Council, issued January 4, 2019, effective January 4, 2014), CLI.4.345983(EN) (Lawinfochina).

Guidelines') on the same day as the IP Guidelines. The safe harbour in the Automobile Guidelines, however, is different from that in the IP Guidelines. It only applies to two types of vertical agreements—the territorial market restriction and customer restriction—as long as the businesses' aggregate market share in the relevant market does not exceed 30%. Clearly, the safe harbour in the Automobile Guidelines is alike that of the EU VBER, which also excludes RPM.

In sum, even before the AML's amendment, the State Council had already realised the two kinds of safe harbour and tried to incorporate both into China's anti-monopoly regime. However, the safe harbour in the amended AML does not follow either of those two patterns. Moreover, the public draft of the *Provisions for Prohibiting Monopoly Agreements* set the threshold of market share at 15%, but the final version of the Provisions taking effect in 2023 has deleted that market share and did not provide any specifics due to the difficulty of reaching a consensus among the various competing opinions.[100] Some leading scholars have criticised the safe harbour provision in the AML (2022). Professor Xiaoye Wang, for example, stated that the safe harbour is not safe anymore since businesses have to satisfy 'other conditions' required by the agency rather than merely relying on a low market share.[101] Professor Jifeng Liu also criticised the AML (2022) for confusing the safe harbour with the general exemption instrument.[102] All in all, the amended AML makes the conflicts more salient and the legal application more complex, rather than solving the problem.

The previous discussion sketched a picture of AML regulation and enforcement over the monopoly agreement. It covers the current legal texts, confusion and conflicts in practice, and controversies in the academic community. Although the discussion in this section does not directly address the digital market, businesses in the digital market and the AML's enforcement of that market inevitably operate within the same framework. Thus, all this discussion generally fits the digital market as well. The next section will address issues that are more specific to the digital market.

4.2 Monopoly agreements in the digital market: a trickier issue?

Due to the harsh punishments given to cartels in most antitrust jurisdictions, very few undertakings engage in 'explicit collusion'. Instead, market participants tend to collude with each other implicitly to fake regulators out. A concentrated market with homogeneous products tends to be more transparent, making collusion more likely to succeed. In short, implicit collusion relies heavily on market structure. The emerging technique of algorithms can significantly increase market transparency by reacting faster to competitors' pricing behaviours and customer requests, even when the market has plenty of competitors and products are heterogeneous.

100 Jiao, note 91, at 64.

101 Xiaoye Wang (王晓晔), "Fanlongduan Fa (Xiuzheng Caoan) De Pingxi" (反垄断法（修正草案）的评析) [An Analysis of the Anti-Monopoly Law (Draft Amendment)], *Contemporary Law Review* 3 (2022): 36, 45–46.

102 Liu, note 91, at 66–67.

Therefore, the use of algorithms can be an independent and intelligent business strategy by market participants that circumvents the AML.

Since the fundamental analytical approaches for monopoly agreements under the AML are still contentious as discussed in Section 4.1, monopoly agreements, and particularly algorithmic collusion, in the digital market make the problem more complicated. Two prominent questions for lawmakers and enforcers are (1) what are the rules to assess such collusion, and (2) what can the competition authorities do about it?[103]

Therefore, the topic of algorithmic collusion is being heatedly debated by academics and businesspeople all over the world at this very moment. There is a major divide between legal experts on this question.[104] Some scholars opine that algorithmic collusion is a task for competition law; others argue there is a need to re-interpret existing concepts; and some even propose creating a new regulatory instrument to deal with this new business model.[105]

Although there has been abundant research about algorithmic collusion, the paucity of direct empirical evidence is a salient difficulty for scholars seeking to determine whether and how algorithms lead to collusion. European Commissioner Margrethe Vestager 'alleges that the collusion between machines without any involvement of human beings is still "science fiction"'.[106] Nicolas Petit calls for 'evidence-based antitrust policy'.[107] Thus, at present it is unclear what role algorithms play in collusion because there is not enough available empirical evidence, especially in the pricing scenario.[108]

Therefore, in this section, I will discuss Chinese anecdotes in an attempt to enrich the global research literature about this legal issue. At the same time, this discussion can help overseas observers and businesses better understand and foresee the attitudes of China's competition authorities and their potential approach toward the use of algorithms. Although no cases of algorithmic collusion have been disclosed to the public yet in China, Chinese legislators and scholars are paying keen attention to this issue. A series of laws and regulations have been issued, and abundant academic research has centred on this topic. I will discuss the work of legislators and scholars separately in the following parts.

4.2.1 Work on policies and legislation

China held the Central Economic Work Conference in December 2023 to set the plan for the next year. At the conference, President Jinping Xi stated that 'sci-tech innovation should lead the development of a modern industrial system: we must

103 Steven Van Uytsel, Salil K. Mehra, and Yoshiteru Uemura, *Algorithm, Collusion and Competition Law: A Comparative Approach* (Edward Elgar Publishing, 2023), 41.

104 *Ibid.*, at 3.

105 *Ibid.*, at 3.

106 Recite from Uytsel, et al., note 103, at 10.

107 Nicola Petit, "Antitrust and Artificial Intelligence: A Research Agenda," *Journal of European Competition Law and Practice* 6 (2017): 361, 362.

108 Uytsel, et al., note 103, at 41.

vigorously promote new industrialization, develop the digital economy and accelerate the development of artificial intelligence'.[109] Thereafter, in early 2024, at the second session of the 14th NPC, the Government Work Report set promoting innovative development of the digital economy as one of the government's major tasks for 2024. Furthermore, it asserted that the government would 'set up R&D and application of big data and AI, launch an "AI Plus" (so-called "AI+") initiative, and build digital industry clusters with international competitiveness'.[110] This was the first time the 'AI+' initiative was written into the central government's work report.

Hence, China's top leaders value the role that the digital economy, and especially AI technology, are playing in the development of the national economy. For a long time to come, policymakers seek to encourage and normalise regulation over the digital market. For example, the State Council has just issued the *Guidelines for Setting a National Standardisation System for the AI Industry* (2024), which plans to set over 50 national and industrial standards and over 20 international standards about AI technology to improve the high-quality development of AI industry by 2026.[111]

In May 2021, the Cyberspace Administration of China announced the Clean and Healthy Cyberspace Initiative, which included a series of campaigns to fight fake information online, abuse of algorithms, unhealthy obsessions with celebrities among the youth, and cyber violence.[112] That reflects regulators' determination to create a healthy and dynamic environment for the development of digital industry.

To achieve the aforementioned national policies, algorithms, as the core element of artificial intelligence and related digital technology, have become the focus for regulators. A series of laws and regulations have thus been issued in the past two years to realise this policy goal.

The AML (2022) adds a new provision to regulate hub-and-spoke collusion,[113] considering that algorithms would be used by businesses, and especially platforms, to facilitate that kind of collusion. The *Guidelines for Anti-Monopoly in the Field of Platform Economy* (2021)[114] enacted by the State Council defines 'concerted

109 Xinhua News Agency (新华社), "Zhongyang Jinji Gongzuo Huiyi Zai Beijing Juxing, Xi Jing Ping Fabiao Zhongyao Jianghua" (中央经济工作会议在北京举行，习近平发表重要讲话) [Xi Jinping Delivers Important Speech at the Central Economic Work Conference Held in Beijing], *www.gov.cn*, December 12, 2023, https://www.gov.cn/yaowen/liebiao/202312/content_6919834.htm

110 "2024 Nian Zhengfu Gongzuo Baogao" (2024年政府工作报告) [Government Work Report of 2024], *www.gov.cn*, March 12, 2024, https://www.gov.cn/yaowen/liebiao/202403/content_6939153.htm

111 "Guojia Rengong Zhineng Chanye Zonghe Biaozhun Hua Tixi Jianshe Zhinan (2024 Ban)" (国家人工智能产业综合标准化体系建设指南) [Guideline for Setting a National Standardization System for AI Industry (2024 Version)], *www.gov.cn*, June 5, 2024, https://www.gov.cn/zhengce/zhengceku/202407/content_6960720.htm

112 Cao Yin, "Efforts Made to Monitor, Regulate Cyberspace," *Chinadaily.com.cn*, September 15, 2021, https://www.chinadaily.com.cn/a/202109/15/WS6141364aa310e0e3a6821963.html

113 The AML (2022), note 1, Art. 19.

114 Guidelines of the Anti-Monopoly Commission of the State Council for Anti-monopoly in the Field of Platform Economy (promulgated by Anti-monopoly Comm, State Council, February 7, 2021, effective February 7, 2021), CLI.4.352590(EN) (Lawinfochina) [Hereinafter the Platform Guidelines].

conducts' as monopoly agreements in which substantive coordination and consensus are mediated by algorithms.[115] The *Prohibition on Monopoly Agreements* issued by the SAMR in 2023 notably prohibits undertakings from utilising 'data and algorithms, technology, and platform rules' to reach agreements or concerted conducts.[116] Apparently, the antitrust lawmakers have foreseen the substantial impacts of algorithms on the market and attempts to harness this nascent technology that will inevitably grow into a behemoth in the future.

Legislative activity targeting algorithms has not only been launched in the antitrust field but has also manifested in other legal areas. One example is the *Provisions on the Administration of Algorithm-Generated Recommendations for Internet Information Service*[117] (the 'Provisions on Algorithm-Generated Recommendations'), which were issued by the CAC along with three other national ministries on the last day of 2021. For the purpose of protecting consumers' interests, the Provisions on Algorithm-Generated Recommendations require the algorithm service provider to (1) notify users of the basic principles, purposes, and main operating mechanics of the algorithm (the right to know);[118] (2) offer users services that are not tailored to their personal profiles and the option to turn off the algorithm-recommended services (the right to decline);[119] and (3) follow specific rules to protect the legal interests of juveniles, the elderly, and labourers relying on the algorithms for work assignments.[120]

More importantly, the Provisions on Algorithm-Generated Recommendations provide a filing system. If the algorithm-recommended service involves public opinion or is capable of social mobilisation, the algorithm service provider must file information about the algorithm with the Internet Information Service Algorithm Filing System within 10 working days of the algorithm service entering use.[121] The same filing system is adopted by the *Provisions on the Administration of Deep Synthesis of Internet-Based Information Service*,[122] which was adopted later. Also, the *Personal Information Protection Law*, which took effect in 2021, grants individuals the right to ask companies handling their personal information

115 *Ibid.*, Art. 5.

116 Provisions on Prohibiting Monopoly Agreements (promulgated by SAMR, March 10, 2023, effective April 15, 2023), CLI.4.5160995(EN) (Lawinfochina), Art. 13.

117 CAC, Ministry of Industry and Information Technology, Ministry of Public Security, and SAMR, "Hulian Wang Xinxi Fuwu Suanfa Tuijian Guanli Guiding" (互联网信息服务算法推荐管理规定) [Provisions on the Administration of Algorithm-generated Recommendations for Internet Information Service] (Issued January 4, 2022, effective March 1, 2022), *www.gov.cn*, January 4, 2022, https://www.gov.cn/zhengce/2022-11/26/content_5728941.htm

118 *Ibid.*, Art. 16.

119 *Ibid.*, Art. 17.

120 *Ibid.*, Art. 18–20.

121 *Ibid.*, Art. 24.

122 CAC, Ministry of Industry and Information Technology, and Ministry of Public Security, "Hulian Wang Xinxi Fuwu Shendu Hecheng Guanli Guiding" (互联网信息服务深度合成管理规定) [Provisions on the Administration of Deep Synthesis of Internet-Based Information Service] (Issued November 25, 2022, effective January 10, 2023), *www.gov.cn*, November 25, 2022, https://www.gov.cn/zhengce/zhengceku/2022-12/12/content_5731431.htm

to explain algorithms (as a method of automated decision-making) when they have a major impact on individual's rights.

In short, the rapid growth of the internet market in China has driven a flurry of related legislative activity. At present, the laws and regulations regarding algorithms, aside from the laws in competition law area, emphasise the protection of consumer welfare, rather than the protection of competition.[123] These laws require algorithm providers to make algorithmic operations more transparent by disclosing or explaining the fundamental principles, operating mechanisms and nature of algorithms to regulators or users. However, it is uncertain how lawmakers and regulators can determine the authenticity and extent of such information disclosure considering that algorithms are a black box. Furthermore, the obligation of information disclosure may conflict with the purpose of the AML under certain circumstances. Algorithms can usually be regarded as commercial secrets and intellectual property of undertakings, so a heavy burden of disclosure risks undermining algorithm providers' motivation for innovation and reducing the dynamic of market competition. That may also run counter to the national policy of relying on sci-tech innovation to lead the modern industrial system.

4.2.2 Status quo of academic research and major scholars' arguments in China

Over the past five years, there has been prolific research and debate about algorithmic collusion and related issues in the Chinese academic community. A search using the keywords 'antimonopoly' and 'algorithm' in the China National Knowledge Infrastructure, China's largest academic database, turns up more than 170 academic journal articles and over 250 master's theses and doctoral dissertations about this topic. As an 'imported' good, the AML has been (and will continue to be) affected by scholars' interpretations, explanations, and in-depth studies of the terminologies and traditional theories of antitrust laws, as well as foreign legislative texts and precedents. The debate over the RPM, as discussed in Section 4.1.2, reflects the significant impact of academic research and scholars' opinions on China's anti-monopoly development.

Articles published in major Chinese law journals over the past five years can be categorised into three groups as follows.

Group 1: Scholars in this group argue that the current anti-monopoly regime cannot regulate all problems of algorithmic collusion and propose that new regulatory instruments be set up to assist to deal with this issue. Generally, this group of scholars advocates active interference and regulation by China's competition authorities. Bing Chen advocates setting up a filing system, explanatory mechanism, and auditing system to improve the transparency of algorithmic

123 Chunfeng Shi (施春风), "Dingjia Suanfa Zai Wangluo Jiaoyi Zhong De Fanlongduan Falv Guizhi" (定价算法在网络交易中的反垄断法律规制) [Antitrust Legal Regulation of Pricing Algorithms in Internet Transactions], *Hebei Law Science* 36 (2018): 111, 113.

operations.[124] Jiguo Yin and others propose that the competition authorities use algorithms to regulate algorithms by setting up an automated enforcement system to monitor and detect any collusion.[125] They also agree that algorithm providers should be obliged to make regular reports to the competition authorities about their algorithmic operations and encouraged to disclose algorithms to consumers.[126] Moreover, they propose that the competition authorities adopt structural remedies to dismantle market structures that facilitate algorithmic collusion, such as prohibiting undertakings from disclosing price information to competitors.[127] Chunfeng Shi argues that when algorithms are commercial secrets that should not be disclosed to the public, they should still be disclosed to the competition authorities.[128] Moreover, he suggests that the competition authorities could create basic algorithms that are imbedded into businesses' pricing algorithms.[129]

Group 2: Compared to the first group of academics, scholars in this group advise that algorithms be regulated under the current AML regime, with a moderate and prudent regulatory model. Jiayao Tang and Yufeng Yin stress the principle of neutrality of competition, so they oppose the competition authorities' frequent use of structural remedies.[130] He also opines that the competition authorities should not require businesses to refrain from disclosing price information, collecting data, reducing the frequency of price adjustment, or setting up a data pool,[131] in opposition to the proposals made by some scholars in the first group. Guofeng Ding also stands for modest regulation, following the proportionality principle and adopting a cost-benefit analysis as the approach for evaluating algorithmic collusion.[132]

124 Bing Chen (陈兵), "Shuzi Jingji Xia Suanfa Gongmou Fengxian Ji Fanlongduan Fa Guizhi Jinlu" (数字经济下算法共谋风险及反垄断法规制进路) [Risk and Antitrust Law Regulation of Algorithm Conspiracy and in Digital Economy], *Legal Forum* 39 (2024): 80, 88. In Chen's article, he argues that the algorithms explanatory mechanism requires algorithm providers to account for the algorithms and/or offer ways to correct errors arising from data or algorithms, as competition authorities or entities affected by algorithms require. The algorithm auditing system includes company's internal auditing and external auditing by independent third parties.

125 Jiguo Yin, Hongyi Shen, and Ziqi Yue (殷继国，沈鸿艺，岳子祺), "Rengong Zhineng Shidai Suanfa Gongmou De Guizhi Kunjing Jiqi Pojie Lujing" (人工智能时代算法共谋的规制困境及其破解路径) [The Regulation Dilemmas and Solutions of Algorithmic Collusion in the Era of Artificial Intelligence], *Journal of South China University of Technology (Social Science Edition)* 22 (2020): 33, 39.

126 *Ibid.*

127 *Ibid.*

128 Shi, note 123, at 118.

129 *Ibid.*, at 118.

130 Jiayao Tang and Yufeng Yin (唐家要，尹钰锋), "Suanfa Gongmou De Fanlongduan Guizhi Ji Gongju Chuangxin Yanjiu" (算法合谋的反垄断规制及工具创新研究) [Antitrust Regulation and Tools Innovation on Algorithmic Collusion], *Industrial Economic Review* 2 (2020): 5, 14.

131 *Ibid.*, at 14.

132 Guofeng Ding (丁国峰), "Dashu Ju Shidai Xia Suanfa Gongmou Xingwei De Falv Guizhi" (大数据时代下算法共谋行为的法律规制) [Legal Regulation of Algorithmic Conspiracy in the Age of Big Data], *Social Science Journal* 254 (2021): 127.

Group 3: Scholars in this group find the middle path. They suggest re-interpreting existing concepts and improving the present regulatory mechanisms. Wei Zhou calls for expanding the applicable scope of concepts such as 'monopoly agreements' and 'undertakings' when determining algorithmic collusion.[133] Also, he suggests further expanding the leniency programme and studying how to break away from the 'human-centred' stereotype when applying the leniency programme to algorithmic collusion.[134] Jianzhong Shi expresses concern that the use of algorithms would aggravate the anti-competitive effects of oligopolistic market, so he suggests learning from EU competition law to create the concept of 'collective dominance'.[135]

In sum, these academic works show two salient traits as follows:

First, the overwhelming majority of scholars, to various extents, have been affected by EU competition law and US antitrust law. Most articles have used the taxonomy about algorithmic collusion ('Messenger, Hub and Spoke, Predicable Agent and Digital Eye') proposed by Ariel Ezrachi and Maurice E. Stucke.[136] This taxonomy seems to have been widely accepted by the Chinese antitrust community.

More importantly, scholars have reached the consensus that determining whether there is anti-competitive collusion using algorithms is one of the trickiest issues that enforcers face. Thus, the factors for determining algorithmic collusion are a focus of their academic papers. However, there are clear traces of how various EU and US theories and enforcement have influenced Chinese scholars and experts. In an article in a top-ranking Chinese law journal, for example, Haitao Jiao articulately points out that the root cause of the confusion and conflicts over monopoly agreements in the Chinese antitrust community is a misunderstanding about 'object restriction' in EU competition law and suggests analysing the

133 Wei Zhou (周围), "Suan Fa Gong Mou De Fan Long Duan Fa Gui Zhi" (算法共谋的反垄断法规制) [Antitrust Regulation of Algorithmic Conspiracies], *Law Science* 458 (2020): 40, 58–59.

134 *Ibid*.

135 Jianzhong Shi (时建中), "Gongtong Shichang Zhipei Diwei Zhidu Tuozhan Shiyong Yu Suanfa Moshi Gongmou Yanjiu" (共同市场支配地位制度拓展适用于算法默示共谋研究) [Expanding the Application of the Collective Dominance Institution to the Tacit Algorithmic Collusion], *China Legal Science* 2 (2020): 89.

136 Ariel Ezrachi and Maurice E. Stucke raised the taxonomy about algorithmic collusion in their book: *Virtual Competition: The Promise and Perils of the Algorithm-Driven Economy* (Harvard University Press, 2016). There are several Chinese scholars have accepted such taxonomy. For example, Yanchuan Wang (王延川), "Suanfa Hemou De Yansheng Luoji Yu Zhili Lujing" (算法合谋的演生逻辑与治理路径) [Evolutionary Logic and Governance Path of Algorithmic Collusion], *ECUPL Journal* 3 (2023): 47. In Wang's article, the discussion to re-interpreted terms of the AML to regulate algorithm collusion is based on the four categories of algorithm collusions; see also Zhengli Li and Yi Li (李振利，李毅), "Lun Suanfa Gongmou De Fanlongduan Guizhi Lujing" (论算法共谋的反垄断规制路径) [Study of the Regulatory Path over Algorithm Collusion], *Academic Exchange* 292 (2018): 73. In this article, authors introduce the four kinds of algorithm collusions in detail and process their discussion based on the taxonomy; see also Ding, note 132. This article is also based on that taxonomy to discuss algorithm collusion under China's legal regime.

'effects' of a monopoly agreement in the AML regime.[137] Jiao is evidently advocating that EU competition law should be a major reference for solving Chinese problems. Also, Sen La introduces several cases from the European Union, such as *VM Remonts* and *Eturas*, to suggest evaluating 'concerted conducts' in the scenario of algorithmic collusion.[138] Meanwhile, others prefer resorting to American approaches to addressing Chinese problems. Wei Zhou suggests relying on circumstantial evidence, developed by US precedents, to detect implicit collusion.[139] Jin Sun and Lan Lan refer to US cases (e.g., *United States v. Airline Tariff Publishing Co*, Case C-836/9; *United States v. Topkins*, Case C-15/201) when discussing the challenge of determining algorithmic collusion.[140]

In China's academic community, EU and US antitrust laws are the two primary models for scholars to explore ways to solve problems in the Chinese digital market. However, compared to US antitrust law, the EU model seems to be a more influential force in China. Even scholars who prefer US law make a point of also mentioning EU approaches. That may be because China shares a similar culture of bureaucratic-centred enforcement with the European Union. It may also be because most primary scholars, especially experts in legislation, have an educational background in EU law.[141] However, I am not sure whether China should follow in the regulatory footsteps of the European Union, which intends to set up a stricter and more comprehensive regulatory regime for the digital market than the United States, or whether it will have a laxer and more modest regulatory environment after achieving national policy targets or under pressure from digital giants.

Second, although academic research in China on algorithmic collusion is still nascent and there have not been any disclosed cases to test scholars' propositions, several suggestions have already been accepted by lawmakers and incorporated in newly enacted laws. For example, the *Provisions on Algorithm-Generated Recommendations* provides the filing system, and the *Personal Information Protection Law* requires algorithm providers to disclose information about algorithms

137 Haitao Jiao (焦海涛), "Woguo Fanlongduan Fazhong Longduan Xieyi Weifa Xing De Fenxi Moshi" (我国反垄断法中垄断协议违法性的分析模式) [Analytical Model of Illegality Determination of the Monopoly Agreement Under Anti-Monopoly Law in China], *Law Science* 507 (2024): 149, 153.

138 Sen La (剌森), "Suanfa Gongmou Zhong Jingying Zhe Zeren De Rending: Jiyu Yisi Lianluo De Jiedu Yu Fenxi" (算法共谋中经营者责任的认定：基于意思联络的解读与分析) [Determination of Undertakings' Responsibilities in Algorithmic Collusion: Interpretation and Analysis Based on Communication], *Modern Finance and Economics-Journal of Tianjin University of Finance and Economics* 386 (2022): 101, 106.

139 Zhou, note 133.

140 Jin Sun and Lan Lan (孙晋，蓝澜), "Shuzi Longduan Xieyi De Fanlongduan Fa Zhenbie Jiqi Guizhi" (数字垄断协议的反垄断法甄别及其规制) [Anti-Monopoly Law Screening and Regulation of Digital Monopoly Agreements], *Science Technology and Law Chinese-English Version* 13 (2023): 1, 2.

141 For example, some leading antitrust scholars in China, such as Xiaoye Wang, Jianzhong Shi, Yong Huang, and Xianlin Wang, have educational background or visiting scholar experience in European universities or research institutes (such as Max Planck Institute). More of them were involved in the AML's drafting and amending.

and explain their operating principles to consumers under certain conditions. Thus, academics have become a force that cannot be underrated in shaping AML enforcement.

4.3 Conclusion

AML enforcement over monopoly agreements, and especially vertical agreements, is a typical example of the conflicts and confusion that accompany legal transplantation. The AML's amendment in 2022 was intended to clarify ambiguity and solve conflicts. However, due to compromises made to various voices and the lack of sufficient practical experience, the amended AML, far from resolving existing problems, seems to have created new ones. As for the digital market, given the critical role that data, algorithms and AI technology play in the development of the national economy, future AML enforcement will be largely affected by national policy.

In addition, a series of laws and regulations have been enacted to address these issues. But these laws, with their various targets and focuses, may overstate the protection of consumer welfare and impose a heavy burden of information disclosure on undertakings. There is a sore need for further study and debate about key issues such as the goals of the AML and the conflicts between the AML and other laws (they will be discussed in Chapter 5).

Algorithmic collusion is a topic that is being heatedly debated in the Chinese academic community, and abundant research centres on this issue. But there is not sufficient practical data to test the academic proposals and hypotheses. Considering the large scale of the Chinese digital market, practical cases and enforcement experience in the near future are expected to enrich global antitrust theory and enforcement.

5 Advancing a research agenda for agencies and academics

Unresolved issues

5.1 Conflicts within the legal system: abuse of superior bargaining position

Amid the exponential growth of China's digital market, lawmakers and enforcers have encountered one new issue after another in short order. The adoption of makeshift solutions to specific problems is likely to cause conflicts and chaos in the competition law system. A typical example of such issues is the debate about the regulation of abuse of superior bargaining position ('ASBP'), especially in the digital sector. Taking ASBP as a research target, this section will discuss these conflicts and note how it aggravates inconsistency within the competition law system, destroys the logic of the regulatory regime, and weakens the AML's role in the regulatory regime. That serves as a call for further research on this topic.

5.1.1 The Anti-Unfair Competition Law *and the AML*

On 21 December 2024, a draft amendment to the *Anti-Unfair Competition Law* was submitted to the Standing Committee of the National People's Congress for review. This is the third time for the AUCL to be revised since it was enacted in 1993. A provision in the draft concerning ASBP has attracted widespread attention and generated fierce debate in China's anti-monopoly community.[1] Since the draft has been submitted to Congress, it is very likely to be passed without substantial changes, so this may be China's first general regulation established to prevent undertakings with superior bargaining position from abusing their market power.

1 See Haitao Jiao (焦海涛), "Lanyong Xiangdui Youshi Diwei De Xingzhi Qufen Yu Guize Tixi" (滥用相对优势地位的性质区分与规则体系) [The Multiple Natures of Abuse of Relative Market Power and a Systematic Regulatory Approach Applicable to It], *SJTU Law Review* 6 (2024): 142; see also Gonghuan Zhu (朱公欢), "Shuzi Pingtai Xiangdui Youshi Lanyong Xingwei De Guizhi Liju Yu Jinlu" (数字平台相对优势滥用行为的规制理据与进路) [The Rationale and Approach of Regulating Digital Platforms' Abusive Behavior of Their Comparative Advantage], *Journal of Henan University of Economics and Law* 205 (2024): 87; see also Bo Yuan (袁波), "Lanyong Xiangdui Youshi Diwei Zhidu Naru Fanbu Zhengdang Jingzheng Fa Zhi Zhiyi" (滥用相对优势地位制度纳入反不正当竞争法之质疑) [The Question on the Abuse of Superior Bargaining Position System into Anti-Unfair Competition Law], *Nanjing University Law Journal* 22 (2023): 28.

DOI: 10.4324/ 9781003654452-5

Incorporating ASBP in the competition regulatory regime, however, would potentially generate systemic conflicts and logical confusion with the AML.

ASBP, as opposed to more familiar abuse of dominance under the AML, generally appears when an undertaking's trading counterparties are heavily dependent on it and rarely switch to others even though the undertaking is not dominant in the relevant market. This usually happens in the retail sector and online platforms market.

Chinese academics started to express concern about the issue of ASBP in the early 2000s, even before the AML's enactment.[2] The debate was generated by the 'admission fee' that large supermarkets charged to independent suppliers. These supermarkets can hardly be regarded dominant market players in the relevant market (imagine a chain supermarket in a regional area), but local suppliers heavily relied on them due to the high cost of transferring to another distributor. Compared to suppliers, therefore, these supermarkets enjoyed superior bargaining power. In an attempt to solve this issue, MOFCOM and NDRC issued *Administrative Measures for Fair Transactions Between Retailers and Suppliers* in 2006.[3]

However, there is major controversy about whether ASBP is a competition law issue and whether it should be governed by competition laws. In the 2000s, the debate centred on whether the AML should regulate such behaviours. For example, some scholars argued that the AML would be an ideal instrument to curb undertakings from abusing their superior market power in order to protect competition and maximise consumer welfare.[4] Others, however, asserted to the contrary that AML regulation of such behaviours would be an improper extension of the AML's scope and would damage the AML's goal of protecting 'competition' rather than 'competitors'.[5]

2 See Yanbei Meng (孟雁北), "Lanyong Xiangdui Jingji Youshi Diwei Xingwei De Fanlongduan Fa Yanjiu" (滥用相对经济优势地位行为的反垄断法研究) [Research on Antitrust Law on the Abuse of Relative Economic Advantage Status], *The Jurist* 6 (2003): 82; see also Lijuan Wang and Lin Mei (王丽娟，梅林), "Xiangdui Youshi Diwei Lanyong De Fanlongduan Fa Yanjiu" (相对优势地位滥用的反垄断法研究) [Research on Antitrust Law on the Abuse of Relative Advantage Position], *Law Science* 7 (2006): 62; see also Guanghua Wang (王广华), "Cong 'Jinchang Fei' Xianxiang Kandui 'Xiangdui Youshi Diwei De Lanyong' De Guizhi" (从" 进场费" 现象看对" 相对优势地位的滥用" 的规制) [Regulation of "Abuse of Relative Advantage Position" from the Perspective of "Entry Fee" Phenomenon], *Sun Yatsen University Forum* 26 (2006): 45.

3 Administrative Measures for Fair Transactions Between Retailers and Suppliers (promulgated by MOFCOM, NDRC, Ministry of Public Security, State Taxation Administration, and SAIC, October 13, 2006, effective November 15, 2006), CLI.4.80561(EN) (Lawinfochina).

4 Meng, note 2, at 85; see also Shiying Xu and Maojun Tang (徐士英，唐茂军), "Lanyong Xiangdui Zhipei Diwei Xingwei De Falv Guizhi Yanjiu" (滥用相对支配地位行为的法律规制研究) [Research on Legal Regulation of Abuse of Relative Dominance Status], *Oriental Law* 3 (2008): 35, 41.

5 See Jian Li (李剑), "Lun Jiegou Xing Yaosu Zai Woguo 'Fanlongduan Fa' Zhongde Jichu Diwei—Xiangdui Youshi Diwei Lanyong Lilun Zhi Fouding" (论结构性要素在我国《反垄断法》中的基础地位——相对优势地位滥用理论之否定) [On the Fundamental Position of Structural Elements in China's Anti-Monopoly Law: Denial of the Theory of Relative Advantage Abuse], *Political Science and Law* 10 (2009): 121; see also Haitao Jiao (焦海涛), "Fanlongduan Fa Guizhi Xiangdui Youshi Diwei De Jichu Yu Xiandu" (反垄断法规制相对优势地位的基础与限度) [Status of the Comparatively Dominant Position in Antimonopoly Law], *Presentday Law Science* 6 (2008): 74.

Since the AML's enactment, more scholars have opined that the AML may not be a proper instrument, at least at the present stage, to provide specific protection to undertakings, especially small- and medium-sized enterprises ('SMEs'), against large counterparties abusing their superior bargaining position, leading some scholars to shift their attention to the AUCL.[6] Some argue that, under the general purpose of protecting 'fair competition', regulating ASBP with the AUCL can not only circumvent the high threshold of proving dominance required by the AML but also curb supermarkets' and online platforms' imposition of unfair trade conditions on their suppliers, an issue that occurs very frequently.[7] Others assert that since the AUCL evolved from tort law as a 'special tort law' that aims to protect individuals' interests, rather than paying more attention to competition and social benefits as the AML does, the AUCL is more suitable to regulate ASBP, considering that ASBP directly causes damages to specific individuals.[8] Also, some argue that the AUCL has been regarded as the appropriate law for regulating online platforms' ASBP because such behaviours violate business ethics and damage the competition order that the AUCL is supposed to preserve.[9]

Given these supporting voices, lawmakers have twice sought to include ASBP in the AUCL's regulatory scope, when the AUCL was amended in 2017 and 2025, respectively.

In 2017, the AUCL was amended for the first time since its enactment in 1993. The draft that was submitted for public review included unprecedented provisions in Article 6: Without justified reasons, undertakings with superior bargaining position were prohibited from (1) requiring their trading counterparties to deal with a certain third party or parties, (2) requiring their trading counterparties to purchase certain commodities, (3) imposing restrictive conditions on their trading counterparties when they trade with other undertakings, (4) charging unreasonable fees or requiring other unjustified economic benefits from trading counterparties, or (5) setting other unjustified trading conditions.

However, Article 6 faced fierce criticisms. For example, a judge of the Supreme People's Court objected that the blurry boundary between ASBP and

6 See Wenlei Xiang (向文磊), "Lanyong Xiangdui Youshi Diwei Guizhi De"Sihui Furan"? —Jianping" Fanbu Zhengdang Jingzheng Fa (Zhengqiu Yijian Gao)" Xiangguan Tiaokuan De Xiugai" (滥用相对优势地位规制的"死灰复燃"？—兼评《反不正当竞争法（征求意见稿）》相关条款的修改) [Regulating the Abuse of Superior Bargaining Position Revisited: A Review of Amendments on the Drafted Anti-Unfair Competition Law], *Competition Policy Research* 6: 60.

7 See Long Dai (戴龙), "Lanyong Xiangdui Youshi Diwei De Falv Guizhi Yanjiu—Jianyi" Fanbu Zhengdang Jingzheng Fa (Xiuding Caoan Songshen Gao) 'Di 6 Tiao De Xiugai' (滥用相对优势地位的法律规制研究—兼议《反不正当竞争法（修订草案送审稿）》第6条的修改) [Research on Legal Regulation of Abuse of Relative Advantage Position—Discussion on the Revision of Article 6 of the Anti-Unfair Competition Law (Draft for Review)], *Journal of CUPL* 58 (2017): 146.

8 Jun Long (龙俊), "Lanyong Xiangdui Youshi Diwei De Fanbu Zhengdang Jingzheng Fa Guizhi Yuanli" (滥用相对优势地位的反不正当竞争法规制原理) [The Regulation Principle of the Anti-Unfair Competition Law on Abuse of Relative Advantage Position], *Science of Law (Journal of Northwest University of Political Science and Law)* 5 (2017): 48, 56–58.

9 Zhu, note 1, at 94.

abuse of dominance might easily cause conflict with the AML and increase the risk of excessive government interference in the market.[10] Similar concerns were raised by Professor Xiaoye Wang, who said that the AML, contract law, tort law, and the enactment of special laws could solve most problems arising from ASBP, but regulation based on the AUCL might lead to logical contradictions and theoretical chaos.[11] Due to opposition from these influential scholars, Article 6 was omitted from the final version of the AUCL amendment that took effect in 2017.

In 2022, the AUCL was revised for the third time. In November of that year, SAMR issued a draft for public opinion and put ASBP back on the table.

The provisions related to ASBP in the SAMR's draft were more specific than those in the 2017 draft:

> Article 13: An undertaking that enjoys a relatively dominant market position shall not engage in the following behaviours without justified reasons. These behaviours would unreasonably restrict trade counterparties' business activities, impose unreasonable trade conditions, affect fair trade, and disturb the fair order of market competition.
>
> (1) Forcing trade counterparties to sign exclusive agreements;
> (2) Unreasonably restricting trade counterparties from dealing with a certain party or imposing trade conditions;
> (3) Tying;
> (4) Unreasonably restricting prices, trade parties, trade regions, sale time, or participation in advertising activities;
> (5) Unreasonably retaining deposits or cutting subsidies, discounts, or site traffic, among others;
> (6) Disturbing normal trade by influencing users' choice, reducing site traffic, blocking [certain products], degrading the rank in search, and removing products from shelves;
> (7) Other behaviours that unreasonably restrict fair trade or impose unreasonable conditions.[12]

10 Li Zhu (朱理), "Lanyong Xiangdui Youshi Diwei Wenti De Falv Guizhi—Xuhuan De Diren Yu Zhenshi De Weixian" (滥用相对优势地位问题的法律规制一虚幻的敌人与真实的危险) [The Legal Regulation on Abuse of Superior Bargaining Position: Illusory Enemies and Real Risks], *Electronics Intellectual Property* 6 (2016): 31, 38–39.

11 Xiaoye Wang (王晓晔), 'Lun Lanyong' Xiangdui Youshi Diwei 'De Falv Guizhi' (论滥用"相对优势地位"的法律规制) [Legal Regulation for the Abuse of Superior Bargaining Position], *Modern Law Science* 38 (2016): 79, 90–91.

12 Announcement of the State Administration for Market Regulation on the Request for Public Comments on the Bill to Revise the Anti-Unfair Competition Law of the People's Republic of China (Exposure Draft) (promulgated by State Administration for Market Regulation, November 22, 2022), CLI.1.21673(EN) (Lawinfochina), Art. 13.

However, the draft eventually submitted to the Standing Committee of the National People's Congress for review on 21 December 2024 had been truncated to the following two brief articles:

> Article 14: Platform operators shall not force intra-platform business operators to set prices according to platform pricing rules or sell commodities at lower than cost, which would disturb the fair competition order.
>
> Article 15: Large-scale undertakings shall not abuse their superior bargaining position on capital, technology, trade channels, influence in the industry, and so on to set obviously unreasonable payment conditions, methods, or periods; provide unreasonable breach liability; coerce their trade partners to enter into exclusive agreements; or engage in other behaviours that would disturb the fair competition order.[13]

The truncated articles probably represent a compromise due to loud criticism. Thus, the 2022 draft amendment of the AUCL uses more general statements to describe scenarios that constitute ASBP, rather than listing specific conditions as the SAMR's draft does.

Before I proceed with discussing the potential conflicts and the risk of the AML's function being weakened if ASBP is regulated under the AUCL, I need to explain the relationship between the AUCL and the AML as well as why lawmakers would regard the AUCL as an ideal option for regulating ASBP. This digression will help readers better understand the issues involved.

Although it is widely accepted that the AUCL and the AML are the two pillars of China's competition law system, the AUCL has long been misunderstood as a law that aims to benefit competitors rather than protect competition. In China's academic community and judicial practice, the AUCL was once commonly treated as a supplement to intellectual property laws. According to this understanding, the AUCL applies when a certain behaviour has not been specifically covered by intellectual property laws[14] in the manner of a catch-all provision. Some have even likened intellectual property laws to icebergs floating in the ocean of the AUCL.

13 Request for Public Comments on the Bill to Revise the Anti-Unfair Competition Law (Exposure Draft) (promulgated by SAMR, December 25, 2024), CLI.1.40417(EN) (Lawinfochina), Art. 14 & 15.

14 Chengsi Zheng (郑成思), "Fanbu Zhengdang Jingzheng—Zhishi Chanquan De Fujia Baohu" (反不正当竞争—知识产权的附加保护) [Anti-Unfair Competition—Additional Protection of Intellectual Property Rights], *Intellectual Property* 13 (2003): 3, 3–4; see also Xiaoyao Xie (谢晓尧), "Lun Fanbu Zhengdang Jingzheng Fa Dui Zhishi Chanquan De Baohu" (论反不正当竞争法对知识产权的保护)[On the Protection of Anti-Unfair Competition Law for Intellectual Property], *Journal of Sun Yat-sen University (Social Science Edition)* 46 (2006): 95, 100; see also Ming Yang (杨明), "Shilun Fanbu Zhengdang Jingzheng Fa Dui Zhishi Chanquan De Doudi Baohu" (试论反不正当竞争法对知识产权的兜底保护) [On the Bottom Line Protection of Intellectual Property Rights by the Anti-Unfair Competition Law], *Studies in Law and Business* 95 (2003): 119, 127.

That conception misled judicial decision makers for a long time. For example, in *Louis Cha v. Jiang Nan*,[15] a well-known copyright infringement case, the court used the AUCL to extend the scope of copyright holder's right. In this case, a college student 'borrowed' character names from the famous novel *The Legend of the Condor Heroes*, written by Louis Cha, the giant of Chinese pop literature, to write a best-selling college romance story. The trial court ruled that, even though characters' names and certain elements of their relationships were beyond the protection of copyright law, that does not mean those elements could be used freely and without compensation. As such, the court found those elements should be protected by the AUCL.[16] Judges' mindset about such matters has been reinforced by the fact that cases related to unfair competition issues are normally tried by intellectual property tribunals.

Some scholars, however, object that the AUCL's supplementary role not only unduly expands the protection of intellectual property laws, but also weakens the AUCL's role in competition law.[17] In recognition of that problem, the SPC began to correct these deviations. In a 2009 case,[18] the Court stated,

> Although the court can apply the general terms[19] of the AUCL to improve fair competition, it should refrain from overusing the general term, causing undue interference in the market. When a plaintiff's legal rights have been exhaustively remedied by other laws through special provisions, the general terms of the AUCL should not be applied to provide extra remedies.[20]

15 Liangyong Cha v. Zhi Yang, Beijing United Publishing Co., Ltd., Beijing Jingdian Bowei Culture Media Co., Ltd., Guangzhou Book Center Co., Ltd. (查良镛与杨治、北京联合出版有限责任公司著作权权属、侵权纠纷、商业贿赂不正当竞争纠纷案), (2016) Yue 0106 Min Chu 12068 Hao [(2016) Guangzhou Tianhe District People's Court First-Instance Decision No. 12068] (China), Wolters Kluwer.

16 *Ibid.*, at 36.

17 Xiangjun Kong (孔祥俊), "Fanbu Zhengdang Jingzheng Fa Buchong Baohu Zhishi Chanquan De Youxian Xing" (反不正当竞争法补充保护知识产权的有限性) [The Limitation of Taking Anti-Unfair Competition Law as the Supplementary Protection to Intellectual Property], *China Law Review* 51 (2023): 19, 22.

18 Shandong Shipin Jinchukou Gongsi, Shandong Shanfu Jituan Youxian Gongsi, and Shandong Shanfu Rishui Youxian Gongsi Su Ma Daqing, Qingdao ShengKe Dacheng Maoyi Youxian Gongsi Buzhengdang Jingzheng Jiufen An (山东省食品进出口公司、山东山孚集团有限公司、山东山孚日水有限公司 与马达庆、青岛圣克达诚贸易有限公司不正当竞争纠纷案) [Shandong Food Import and Export Corp., Shandong Shanfu Group Co., Ltd, and Shandong Shanfu Rishui Co., Ltd. v. Ma Daqing and Qingdao ShengKe Dacheng Trading Co., Ltd., (2009) Min Shen Zi Di 1065 Hao [(2009) Sup. People's Ct. Verdict No. 1065] (China), Wolters Kluwer. [Hereinafter '*Shandong Food Corp. et al. v. Ma Daqing et al.*']

19 Article 2 of AUCL is referred to as 'the general term'. It provides that 'when conducting business, undertakings shall follow the principles of free will, equality, fairness, and good faith and abide by laws and business ethics. The "act of unfair competition" is identified as an undertaking that disrupts the order of market competition and causes damage to the lawful rights and interests of other undertakings or consumers when it is doing business'.Thus, when a behavior cannot be regulated by a specialized law, such as the trademark law, then judges used to apply this general term to provide extra remedy to plaintiffs. It is referred to as 'escaping to the general term'.

20 *Shandong Food Corp. et al. v. Ma Daqing et al.*, note 18, at 17.

As a part of competition law, therefore, the AUCL's condemnation of a behaviour should not be (or should not primarily be) because that behaviour injures a certain competitor's commercial interests, but rather because that behaviour damages competition and disturbs the normal competitive order. In contrast with intellectual property law and tort law, which aim to protect an individual's specific rights, the AUCL, just like the AML, is entrusted with a mission of safeguarding the public interest and consumer welfare. That moves the AUCL out of the category of private law (such as intellectual property law, tort law, and civil law) and reflects traits of public law. That is why China classifies the AUCL and the AML under the category of economic law, rather than civil and commercial law.

Although some scholars and judges have tried to correct misconceptions about the AUCL, the habit of regarding the AUCL as a panacea or catch-all provision for solving all market issues that cannot be regulated by other laws is likely to lead to problems and conflicts in the competition law system. The attempts to write ASBP into the newly revised AUCL mirror that mindset. First of all, the scope of superior bargaining position is hard to define. It can cover abusive behaviours that indeed damage competition, but it may also mistakenly punish normal business activities, considering that 'survival of the fittest' is a fundamental rule of the market mechanism and it is normal for one undertaking to be superior to another. Furthermore, regulating ASBP risks obscuring the AUCL's identity as a competition law. It may turn the AUCL into more of a special tort law that focuses on protecting individual competitors, rather than competition itself.

5.1.2 Other regulation concerning ASBP and the AML

Although regulating ASBP under the AUCL is still being debated, lawmakers have already started experiments in the internet market. The E-commerce Law and the Interim Unfair Competition Regulation are two major laws and regulations that govern ASBP. Discussing them is of practical value because they have realised the concerns and conflicts discussed earlier.

5.1.2.1 Chaos caused by the E-commerce Law

The Standing Committee of the National People's Congress issued the E-commerce Law in 2018, which took effect on 1 January 2019.[21] This was China's first comprehensive statute to regulate the e-commerce sector, after five years' preparation, three rounds of soliciting public opinion, and four rounds of reviewing.[22]

21 E-Commerce Law of the People's Republic of China (promulgated by Standing Comm. Nat'l People's Cong., August 31, 2018, effective January 1, 2019), CLI.1.321035(EN) (Lawinfochina).

22 Cong Zhang (张璁), "Lishi Wunian, Lijing Sishen, Dianzi Shangwu Fa Riqian Huo Quanguo Renda Changwei Hui Biaojue Tongguo, Wei Dianzi Shangwu Jiankang Fazhan Huhang" (历时五年，历经四审，电子商务法日前获全国人大常委会表决通过，为电子商务健康发展护航) [After Five Years Preparation, Four Rounds of Reviewing, the E-Commerce Law Was Passed by the Standing Committee of the National People's Congress to Escort the Healthy Development of E-Commerce], *People's Daily*, September 5, 2018, A18, http://money.people.com.cn/n1/2018/0905/c413544-30274033.html

Although the E-commerce Law does not belong to competition law, the comprehensive regulations for the e-commerce field contained therein do involve certain competition issues. Some provisions, unfortunately, conflict with the AML. Since the two laws enjoy the same position in the legal hierarchy, the problem is even more complicated.

Before addressing ASBP, let us look at the E-commerce Law's provision regarding the abuse of dominant market position. Article 22 prohibits e-commerce operators from abusing market dominance. However, the article disregards the related provisions in the AML and separately stipulates four factors for determining market dominance: technological advantage, number of users, control over the relevant industry, and other undertakings' reliance on the e-commerce operator.

Article 22 causes at least two problems: On the one hand, it does not clarify the applicable relationship between Article 22 of the E-commerce Law and Article 23 of the AML. When decision makers determine whether an e-commerce operator (such as a digital platform) enjoys a dominant market position, which law has priority in application? Should market share and barriers to market entry also be taken into consideration in the e-commerce context, as these two factors are identified as vital factors for determining dominance by the AML but are not mentioned by the E-commerce Law? On the other hand, setting aside inconsistency with the AML, the factors provided by the E-commerce Law could themselves cause ambiguity. For example, the number of users is listed as a factor for determining an e-commerce operator's dominance. But the impact of the number of users varies with the business model when evaluating different e-commerce operators' market power.[23] For example, on an online retailing platform such as Taobao or Amazon, sales volume is a more accurate measure of market power than the number of users. But for an instant messaging service like WeChat or WhatsApp, the number of active users is a more proper indicator of market power than the total number of users since the service is free to sign up and use.

Besides these conflicts with the AML, Article 35 of the E-commerce Law also addresses ASBP, creating more inconsistency and causing more chaos. That article prohibits e-commerce platforms from placing unreasonable restrictions on trade, imposing unreasonable trade conditions, or charging unfair fees on other undertakings through service agreements, platform trading rules, and technologies.

The main issue here is that it can hardly be demonstrated that it is either necessary or reasonable to regulate ASBP beyond the competition law regime. It is generally understood that the AML focuses on free competition to improve economic efficiency and that the AUCL emphasises safeguarding generally accepted business ethics to maintain a fair competition order; together, the two laws constitute the competition law regime.[24] No justification has been made for regulating ASBP,

23 Li Zhu and Youlin Zeng (朱理，曾友林), "Dianzi Shangwu Fa Yu Jingzheng Fa De Xianjie: Tixi Luoji Yu Zhifa Zhanwang" (电子商务法与竞争法的衔接：体系逻辑与执法展望) [The Connection of E-commerce Law and Competition Law: System Logic and Future Enforcement], *Journal of University of Chinese Academy of Social Sciences* 230 (2019): 104, 107.

24 *Ibid.*, at 111.

which is apparently a competition law issue, under the E-commerce Law, which is not part of the competition law system. But even if the E-commerce Law could regulate this behaviour, the necessity of Article 35 is doubtful. If a platform gains market power through network effects[25] and then abuses that power, it may be condemned for abusing its dominant market position, rather than for abusing its superior bargaining position. If a platform has not obtained such market power, the rules it makes and the fees it charges are its own business.

In addition, competition in the e-commerce sector demonstrates the Matthew effect and is multisided, dynamic, and heavily reliant on technological development, which makes it difficult to define a relevant market. Since the boundary of the relevant market is so blurry, the difference between market dominance and superior bargaining position is obscure as well, and sometimes the two abusive behaviours are interchangeable depending on the size of the relevant market. Thus, Article 35 leaves a loophole for administrative enforcers to abuse their discretion to select rules and for undertakings to lobby enforcers to levy lighter penalties on them.[26]

5.1.2.2 Interim unfair competition regulation in the internet industry

The *Interim Unfair Competition Regulation in the Internet Industry* (the 'Interim Regulation') was released by the SAMR and came into effect on 1 September 2024. Being a regulation by a department of the State Council, the Interim Regulation is inferior in the legal hierarchy to the AML and the AUCL. The Interim Regulation, consisting of five chapters and 43 articles, not only elaborates on unfair competition under the AUCL in the field of the internet but also specifies some acts that are covered not by the AUCL but by the E-commerce Law, like ASBP.

The Interim Regulation aims to deal with new types of unfair acts that have continued to emerge during the rapid development of the internet market. Although the AUCL added Article 12 to specifically regulate the internet market in its 2017 revision, lawmakers thought that Article 12 was too general to effectively solve the great variety and complexity of unfair acts online. But since the AUCL is a law enacted by the Standing Committee of the National People's Congress, revising it is a time-consuming and strenuous project. Enacting an interim regulation is a

25 The network effects of platforms refer to the value of a platform increases as more users participate, creating a positive feedback loop. Normally, the network effects involve direct effects and indirect effects. The direct effects occur when the value to a user increases with more users on the same side of the platform, such as WhatsApp or WeChat. The indirect effects arise when growth on one side of the platform enhances value of another side. For example, more passengers hailing rides on Didi Chuxing attract more drivers enrolling in the platform, and vice versa, creating a mutually beneficial cycle. The network effects of platforms well explain why competitors in the digital sector spare no efforts to gain market share. In other words, platforms are inherently prone to monopolize.

26 According to Article 35 of E-commerce Law, when a business operator abuses its superior bargaining position, the penalty is a fine ranging from RMB 5,000 to RMB 50,000. If the violation is serious, a fine ranging from RMB 50,000 to RMB 2 million could be imposed. It is obviously lighter than the liabilities provided by the AML for undertakings abusing their market dominance.

handy way to solve urgent legal issues as well as to avoid pressure and objections from various interest groups.

On the one hand, the Interim Regulation indeed plays a supplemental role to the AUCL and elaborates on unclear provisions. In regard to counterfeiting behaviours on the internet, for example, the AUCL only prohibits the unauthorised use of major parts of another party's domain name, website name, or web page, when such unauthorised use may mislead or confuse ordinary people.[27] But the Interim Regulation goes further by specifying unauthorised use in seven scenarios, including the same or similar webpage designs, business names, icons, or the layout of software or applications, online stores, web clients, mini apps, and game interfaces to cause confusion to the public.[28] Also, the Interim Regulation expands the methods of false publicity. An undertaking, for example, is prohibited from relying on live broadcasting, platform recommendations, hot searches, hot comments, hot reposts, and ranking lists, among other methods of deceiving or misleading others about the quality, function, origins, rewards, or qualifications of its products or related producers.[29] Moreover, the AUCL only prohibits false publicity regarding products, but the Interim Regulation expands the scope of prohibition to include false publicity about producers and business operators.[30] Therefore, the Interim Regulation reflects prevalent unfair competition behaviour emerging in the internet market and responds to agencies' regulatory needs as well as legal issues that need to be clarified by the courts.

On the other hand, some regulations in the Interim Regulation may aggravate conflicts within the competition law system. The Interim Regulation not only elaborates on unfair competition behaviour covered in the AUCL but also expands upon the E-commerce Law. The Interim Regulation was intended to combine provisions in the two laws, but that ignores their different values and functions.

For example, Article 23 of the Interim Regulation provides that a platform operator with competitive advantages shall not use technology, abuse back-end transaction data, site traffic, or platform rules to block a third-party's information, disturb commodities search results, or hinder or destroy other undertakings' normal business. Also, Article 24 prohibits platform operators from imposing unreasonable restrictions or conditions on intra-platform transactions, trading prices, and trade with other business operators through service agreements or trading rules, among other methods. In essence, both Article 23 and Article 24 address ASBP. However, the legal consequences for violating the two articles are different. Violators of Article 23 are to be punished according to the liability stipulated by the AUCL—namely, a fine of RMB 100,000–500,000 (or RMB 500,000–3 million

27 Anti-Unfair Competition Law of the People's Republic of China (promulgated by Standing Comm. Nat'l People's Cong., September 2, 1993, effective December 1, 1993, amended November 4, 2017, and April 23, 2019), CLI.1.331488(EN) (Lawinfochina), Art. 6, item 3.

28 Interim Regulations on Anti-Unfair Competition on the Internet (promulgated by State Administration for Market Regulation, May 6, 2024, effective September 1, 2024), CLI.4.5192963(EN) (Lawinfochina), Art. 7.

29 *Ibid.*, Art. 8.

30 *Ibid.*, Art. 8 and 9.

in the case of a serious violation).[31] However, a violation of Article 24 is to be punished according to the E-commerce Law with a fine of RMB 50,000–500,000 (RMB 500,000–2 million for a serious violation).[32] There is no persuasive reason to justify such a discrepancy.

Moreover, Article 41 of the Interim Regulation mandates the confiscation of illicit proceeds from all unfair competition behaviour that violates the regulation. However, that is inconsistent with the AUCL. For example, according to the AUCL, there is no requirement for confiscating illicit gains for false publicity behaviours or illegal promotional sales with prizes. Since the AUCL is the superior law to the Interim Regulation, the Interim Regulation can only elaborate upon the AUCL, rather than creating liabilities beyond the AUCL. What is the legislative authority for the Interim Regulation to create heavier legal liabilities?

The problems arising from the E-commerce Law and Interim Regulation together are likely to aggravate conflicts and inconsistency within the competition law system, significantly weakening the AML's function and irreparably damaging China's competition regulatory regime.

5.1.3 Risks, supporting voices, and potential solutions

5.1.3.1 Motivations and potential risks

As previously discussed, the digital sector is an experimental field for regulating ASBP since the E-commerce Law and the Interim Regulation have previously addressed such behaviours. The AUCL, as one of the fundamental competition laws, will be lawmakers' next target for regulating ASBP more generally. Various interest groups have different motivations for driving such legislative activities, but the potential risks should not be underrated.

First, public enforcers and private plaintiffs have found a high threshold for using the AML to regulate large platforms. In other words, condemning a digital platform for abusing market dominance involves three steps: defining the relevant market, determining that the platform enjoys market dominance, and providing that it has abused that dominance. However, in most private enforcement cases, plaintiffs are defeated at the first step (as in the cases discussed in Chapter 2). Even public enforcers may find it burdensome to define the accurate relevant market and prove the investigated platform's market dominance. On the contrary, allegations of ASBP require neither defining a relevant market nor proving a platform's market dominance; instead, public enforcers and plaintiffs merely need to attest the behaviour's imputability, such as a platform company restricting other parties' trade freedom or disturbing the fair competition order. Alleviating the burden of proof is one of legislators' primary motivations for regulating ASBP under the AUCL. However, the drawback is obvious: The AML would be significantly weakened and would likely become mere window dressing in the competition regulatory regime.

31 *Ibid.*, Art. 37.
32 *Ibid.*, Art. 38.

Second, local enforcers may also have an incentive to support the use of the AUCL, rather than the AML, to regulate ASBP. Authority for enforcing the AML belongs exclusively to the SAMR, which can authorise its local agencies at the provincial level to enforce the AML within their regions.[33] In other words, agencies lower than the provincial level do not have the power to enforce the AML. On the contrary, the authority for enforcing the AUCL is endowed to county-level agencies, which are two levels lower than the AML's provincial-level local enforcers. If ASBP is regulated by the AUCL, it would mean that most of platforms' abusive behaviours could be investigated and penalised by county-level enforcers. That creates the risk of the AUCL becoming a tool for local governments to protect local enterprises and squeeze out outsiders, due to the allurements of boosting local taxes or boosting the political career for local officials. The potential results are administrative monopoly or corruption.

Third, although large platforms oppose regulating ASBP,[34] small- and medium-sized digital platforms are likely to support those legislative activities and lobby lawmakers to regulate their large trading partners' abuse of their superior bargaining power. Furthermore, even for large platforms, the 2022 draft amendment of the AUCL may sound more tolerable than the 2017 draft. The record-breaking penalty of RMB 18 billion (USD 2.8 billion) on Alibaba is still fresh in the memory of large platforms. The hefty penalty imposed under the AML, ranging from 1% to 10% of sales in the previous year, along with confiscation of illicit gains, has become a sword of Damocles hanging over large platforms. However, condemnation of ASBP such as the 'either-or' strategy under the AUCL obviously carries a much lighter penalty. According to the 2022 draft amendment, the normal penalty is to order violators to rectify their unfair competition behaviour without imposing any pecuniary fines. Even the most severe penalty is still a fine of RMB 5 million, which may be a drop in the ocean for most super-large platforms.

In sum, incorporating ASBP into the competition regulatory regime creates at least three risks: First, the AML would be circumvented when regulating the market, and especially the internet market. It is foreseeable that the AUCL (presuming the 2022 amendment is passed) or the Interim Regulation would be frequently applied by public enforcers and private litigants to deal with abusive behaviours because of the fast investigative process and lighter burden of proof. Thus, less effort and fewer resources would be spent discerning and analysing alleged behaviours' economic effects on the market. That is likely to cause some of large platforms' truly abusive behaviours to escape hefty antitrust penalties, and ASBP could also be utilised as a tool to defeat or disturb competitors' normal business operations.

Second, it would inevitably lead to conflicts within the competition law regime. Using the AUCL or the E-commerce Law to regulate ASBP may be a makeshift

33 The AML, Article 13.

34 See Xuezhong Wan (万学忠), "Fanbu Zhengdang Jingzheng Fa Xiuding Nijin Lanyong Youshi Diwei" (反不正当竞争法修订拟禁滥用优势地位) [Revision of the Anti-Unfair Competition Law Proposes to Prohibit the Abuse of Dominant Positions], *chinacourt.org*, March 26, 2016, https://www.chinacourt.org/article/detail/2016/03/id/1828978.shtml

solution to immediate problems, but it will cause irreparable injuries to the competition law regime in the long run. The aim of regulating abusive behaviours—including both abuse of superior bargaining position and abuse of dominant market position—should be protecting competition, in line with the AML's legislative purpose. If an instance of abusive behaviour damages competition, it should be tackled under the AML. If that abusive behaviour merely damages other competitors' interests, that is a private law issue to be solved under contract law or tort law. Since the AUCL used to be mistakenly treated as a 'special tort law', letting the AUCL regulate ASBP bears the risk of cementing that false impression and obscuring the primary value of competition law.

Third, it may grant enforcers excessive discretion and result in corruption. As discussed earlier, enforcers of the AUCL and E-commerce Law are at lower administrative levels than those of the AML. Moreover, the penalties for abusive behaviours under the AUCL and E-commerce Law are also much lighter than those under the AML. In practice, the line between abuse of superior bargaining position and abuse of dominant market position is not clear. Due to the different ways a relevant market can be defined, the two behaviours can convert into each other as well. That provides a great motivation for undertakings, especially large platforms, to lobby enforcers to apply lighter penalties. Also, local-level enforcers have an incentive to apply the law that serves their best interests. All these factors would lead to rent-seeking behaviour and corruption.

5.1.3.2 Can supporting voices effectively mitigate those risks?

SAMR Director Wen Luo explained the 2022 amendment draft of the AUCL in an appearance before the Standing Committee of the National People's Congress on 21 December 2024. He stated that, given investigations in recent years, there is a need to revise the AUCL to make room for SMEs' development and protect consumer welfare.[35] Xu Liu, an expert in competition law, agreed that incorporating ASBP would help address an enforcement issue that urgently needs to be resolved. Liu said that powerful platforms have continuously encroached upon the operating space of small- and medium-sized platforms, degrading their business environment; the AUCL at least provides them with a tool to seek remedies.[36]

Furthermore, Dong Yang, a law professor who helped draft the 2022 amendment of the AUCL, mentioned that the ASBP provision is drawn from corresponding

35 Ge Ni (倪戈), "Fanbu Zhengdang Jingzheng Fa Xiuding Caoan Tiqing Shenyi, Yingzao Shichang Hua Fazhi Hua Yingshang Huanjing" (反不正当竞争法修订草案提请审议，营造市场化法治化营商环境) [The Amendment Draft of the AUCL is Submitted for Review, Aiming to Create a Market-Oriented and Legalised Business Environment], *npc.gov.cn*, December 23, 2024, http://www.npc.gov.cn/c2/c30834/202412/t20241223_441848.html

36 Geng Shao (绍耕), "Jinzhi Lanyong Youshi Diwei Tiaokuan Huo Rengjiu Wufa Xieru" Fanbu Zhengdang Jingzheng Fa 'Di Sanci Xiuding' (禁止滥用优势地位条款或仍旧无法写入《反不正当竞争法》第三次修订) [Prohibition of Abuse of Dominant Position Clause or Still Unable to be Included in the Third Revision of the Anti-Unfair Competition Law], *zhihu.com*, December 22, 2024, https://zhuanlan.zhihu.com/p/13986587508

instruments under Japanese and German law.[37] Under Japan's Anti-Monopoly Act, punishments for ASBP are much lighter than for abuse of market dominance—mainly a cease-and-desist administrative order without pecuniary penalty before the Anti-Monopoly Act was revised in 2009, and a small fine after 2009—compared to a hefty penalty or even criminal liability for abusing dominant market position.[38] During a conversation with the author, Weisi Wang, a professor at Hitotsubashi University, opined that regulating ASBP provides one more option for undertakings to defeat their powerful trade partners; even a minor fine can be a humiliating punishment that deters future violations.

Thus, the flexible and less severe mode of punishment under Japanese law was adopted by the 2022 amendment draft of the AUCL. Article 30 of the draft describes a punishment system on multiple levels. The agency will first order undertakings to rectify their abusive behaviours; if they refuse, the agency can impose a fine of up to RMB 1 million (up to RMB 5 million for a serious violation). Moreover, Article 31 provides that this punishment can be mitigated or even waived when undertakings actively alleviate or eliminate damage. When unfair competition behaviour does not cause damage and undertakings rectify their behaviour in a timely manner, no administrative punishment can be imposed. The designers of the 2022 draft state that the purpose of this punishment system is to relieve concerns about overenforcement and to urge enterprises to enhance their compliance efforts.[39]

It seems that at present the AUCL is taken as a 'half-measure' for regulating ASBP since it can be applied more easily, and with more flexible and lighter punishments, than the relatively high threshold for launching an anti-monopoly enforcement action and the hefty penalty that can be incurred. The urgent need to deal with the ever-growing list of unfair competition behaviours, especially in the internet market, makes the AUCL a handy tool for warning large platforms to be cautious about their behaviour. Considering the practical needs, therefore, systemic conflicts and logical confusion may be secondary considerations, as supporters claim.

Although supporting voices can justify this legislative revision to some extent, three questions still need to be carefully considered since the aforementioned risks would not be negligible. First, is there solid and sufficient practical data to support the conclusion that ASBP is so prevalent and injures competition to such an extent that it needs to be written into the AUCL? Second, can the existing AML regulate such behaviour to avoid potential conflicts and chaos within the competition law regime? Third, is there an effective mechanism for supervision and information disclosure to constrain rent-seeking behaviour and corruption by enforcers?

37 Dong Yang (杨东), "Jujiao Fanbu Zhengdang Jingzheng Fa Xiuding Caoan Sida Liangdian" (聚焦反不正当竞争法修订草案四大亮点) [Focus on the Four Highlights of the Revised Draft of the Anti-Unfair Competition Law], *npc.gov.cn*, January 7, 2025, http://www.npc.gov.cn/c2/c30834/202501/t20250107_442269.html

38 Danzhou Chen (陈丹舟), "Xiang Dui You Shi Di Wei Li Lun Ji Chu Yan Jiu" (相对优势地位理论基础研究) [The Basic Study on the Theory of Superior Bargaining Position], *Competition Policy Research* 3 (2016): 19, 23.

39 Yang, note 37.

5.1.3.3 Potential solutions

Here I intend to offer several solutions that may not provide perfect answers to all problems but at least provide options for tackling those problems.

First, the AML can solve most problems arising from ASBP. If evidence proves an undertaking's dominant market position, AML regulations about the abuse of dominance should definitely be applied since the manifestation of behaviours of the two kinds of abuse are almost identical. If evidence is not sufficient to establish the undertaking's market dominance, AML provisions regarding vertical restraints can also be applied in most situations. ASBP usually occurs in vertical business relationships, such as a powerful chain supermarket and its suppliers or an influential platform owner and business operators on that platform. Thus, abusive behaviours such as imposing unreasonable trade conditions or charging high distribution fees are typically vertical restraints.

In short, the existing AML already provides a sound regulatory framework. Undertakings with market dominance should be regulated by provisions about the abuse of dominant market position; the 'safe harbour' mechanism exempts 'abusive behaviours' of undertakings with a *de minimis* market share; and regulations about vertical restraints can deal with most 'abusive behaviours' conducted by undertakings with superior bargaining positions. Regulating ASBP under the AML has at least two advantages compared to regulating it under the AUCL or the E-commerce Law. On the one hand, AML-based regulation guarantees that similar behaviours will be analysed following the same fundamental rules and approaches to economic analysis. Namely, only behaviours that damage competition, rather than injuring a special competitor's interests, should be condemned. On the other hand, handling all abusive behaviours under the AML framework guarantees the consistency of enforcement agencies and legal liabilities to avoid enforcement conflicts and corruption that may arise when enforcers at various levels have the authority to choose between different levels of legal liability.

Second, if it is really necessary to regulate ASBP under the AUCL, clear and handy criteria need to be formulated to distinguish application of the AUCL and the AML in order to prevent enforcers' abuse of discretion and other rent-seeking behaviour. The provisions of 'commercial bribery' in the AUCL and the Criminal Law can provide us with a reference: The amount of the bribe is an explicit threshold for generating criminal liability, which also clarifies the boundary between applying the AUCL and applying the Criminal Law. It is true that by now it is not practical to devise criteria for differentiating dominant undertakings in all markets, the digital sector may be used as an experiment. Although the *Internet Platform Classification* and *Grading Guidelines and Guidelines for Internet Platforms' Responsibilities* are still pending at the draft stage,[40] the SAMR's efforts to classify

40 SAMR, "Guanyu Dui 'Hulian Wang Pingtai Fenlei Fenji Zhinan (Zhengqiu Yijian Gao)' 'Hulian Wang Pingtai Luoshi Zhuti Zeren Zhinan (Zhengqiu Yijian Gao)' Gongkai Zhengqiu Yijian De Gonggao" (关于对《互联网平台分类分级指南（征求意见稿）》《互联网平台落实主体责任指南（征求意见稿）》公开征求意见的公告) [Announcement on Publicly Soliciting Comments

and grade digital platforms should be applauded and may suggest a way to deal with the problem. By considering several factors (such as the number of active users, business types, sales volume, and the power to impose restrictions), large and super-large platforms can be distinguished from other platforms. In the case of these large and super-large platforms, abusive behaviours are directly regulated by the AML to prevent them from escaping liability given their ability to hire powerful legal professionals and economic experts to exploit loopholes in the law.

Third, it is necessary to comb the rules and regulations within the competition law regime to avoid systemic conflicts and logical confusion. The AML and the AUCL are two fundamental laws in the competition law regime. Therefore, when it comes to competition law issues, they should not be contravened by subordinate laws (like the Interim Regulation) or laws that are not primarily about competition issues (like the E-commerce Law), except when superior interests, such as national security, are at stake. Moreover, following the basic principles of prudence and modesty in market regulation, lawmakers should take a more integrated and macroscopic view of the competition law system and try to avoid obscure regulations, as well as conflicts and overlaps between different laws. For example, Article 40(2) of the Interim Regulation states that 'when undertakings use the internet to eliminate or restrict competition and their behaviours are monopolistic in nature, the AML applies'. The point of this provision is that the AML should take precedence when it overlaps with the AUCL regarding a specific monopolistic behaviour. That sounds reasonable but may prove tricky in practice: Most enforcers of the AUCL are local agencies at the county level, and Article 40 (2) requires them to determine whether a given issue is monopolistic or not. As discussed earlier, that requires them to define the relevant market, determine whether a company has abused its dominant market position and finally decide whether that is an antitrust issue[41]—all steps that require economic and antitrust analysis. It is difficult (if not impossible) for local agencies to analyse such difficult monopolistic issues, which are likely to result in errors of overenforcement or underenforcement.

This section discusses conflicts within the competition law system and addresses specific examples that are relevant to the discussion. If we shift our attention from specific issues and observe the matter from a macroscopic perspective, we may find that all these issues are related to the goals (one could also say values) of the AML. What are the AML's values? Does the AML have a single antitrust goal or multiple goals? When various goals conflict with each other, is there a paramount goal that takes precedence to resolve that conflict? Has China formed an integrated and widely accepted theory about the AML's goals? All these questions will be discussed in the next section.

on the Guidelines for Classification and Grading of Internet Platforms (Draft for Comments) and the Guidelines for Implementing the Responsibilities of Internet Platforms (Draft for Comments)], *samr.gov.cn*, October 29, 2021, https://www.samr.gov.cn/hd/zjdc/art/2023/art_c0086d02fcc544ea9506c997b3ac93c1.html

41 Jiao, note 1, at 150.

5.2 Goals of the AML: controversies and unresolved issues

Robert H. Bork, in his well-known book *The Antitrust Paradox: A Policy at War with Itself*, made the following observation:

> Antitrust policy cannot be made rational until we are able to give a firm answer to one question: What is the point of the law—what are its goals? Everything else follows from the answer we give. Is the antitrust judge to be guided by one value or by several? If by several, how is he to decide cases where a conflict in values arises? Only when the issue of goals has been settled is it possible to frame a coherent body of substantive rules.[42]

Despite the obvious importance of the goals of the AML, both the pioneers of modern antitrust laws (in the United States and the European Union) and up-and-coming antitrust jurisdictions (such as China) have never settled for long upon a definitive statement of antitrust goals. Debates among the Chicago School, Harvard School, Post-Chicago School, Ordoliberalism of the Freiburg School, and the recent New Brandeis movement have all affected and shaped the formation of the AML's goals. Of course, the contribution of China's domestic factors can never be underestimated.

This section will discuss major controversies about the AML's goals in China and arrange unresolved problems into a research agenda for the future.

5.2.1 The evolution of the AML's goals: the academic perspective

Article 1 of the AML states its goals at the outset: 'The law is enacted for the purposes of preventing and prohibiting monopolistic acts, protecting fair competition, encouraging innovation, enhancing economic efficiency, protecting consumer welfare and public interests, and promoting the sound development of the socialist market economy'. While it is evident that the AML embraces multiple goals, scholars and practitioners in China's anti-monopoly community are nowhere near reaching a consensus about whether there is a core goal that should always supersede the others or how to choose between pairs of conflicting goals. The 2022 revision of the AML has not clarified or resolved those debates; instead, it has internalised these debates in the law.

The AML's goals have always been an important topic for Chinese researchers. I have reviewed 119 academic papers (excluding master's theses and doctoral dissertations) from CNKI, China's largest academic literature database. Although my review may not be exhaustive, it does reflect scholars' main viewpoints and research trends over the past 30 years.

Figure 5.1 shows fluctuations in academic research about the AML's goals. As early as 1998, 10 years before the AML's enactment, scholars had started to

42 Robert Bork, *The Antitrust Paradox: A Policy at War with Itself* (Basic Books, Inc., 1979), 50.

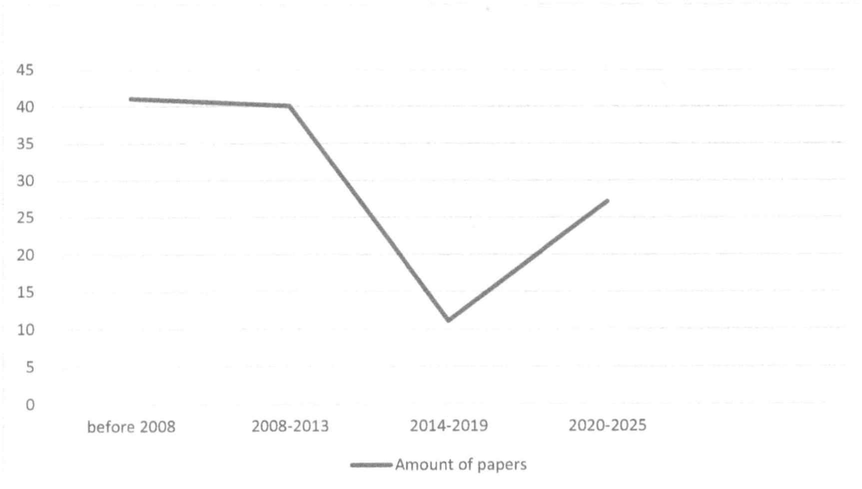

Figure 5.1 Academic papers about AML goals

study antitrust goals. Perhaps with the purpose of influencing antitrust legislation, there was relatively abundant research (41 papers) on this topic. The AML's goals remained a research hotspot even after the law was enacted in 2008: The following five years (2008–2013) also witnessed intense discussion of this issue (40 papers). During the period 2014–2019, the research focus shifted to more specific enforcement issues, with fewer studies concerning the goals issue (only 11 papers). In the next five-year period (2020–2025), the challenges of AML enforcement in the digital sector and the AML's revision in 2022 have drawn academic attention back to the AML's goals (28 papers).

Now let us take a close look at those academic papers and examine their major standpoints, their shifts in focus, and their impact on AML enforcement, especially in the digital sector.

5.2.1.1 Before 2008: scattered and unsystematic research at the early stage

As early as 1998, a Chinese scholar had already proposed a system of goals for the AML, in which goals were individually ranked and rules were set to coordinate conflicts.[43] In this system, the supreme goal was the 'overall social benefit'; protecting the competition order was the fundamental role, ranking in the middle; and the goals of freedom, efficiency, and fairness were specific goals, ranking at the bottom.[44] The claim that overall social benefit was the key antitrust goal was

43 Yu You (游钰), "Fanlongduan Fa Jiazhi Lun" (反垄断法价值论) [Value Theory of Antitrust Law], *Law and Social Development* 6 (1998): 27, 30.

44 *Ibid.*, at 30.

widely accepted at that time.[45] However, these studies did not provide a workable definition of the connotation of 'overall social benefit' or distinguish that from easily conflated concepts such as 'consumer benefit' or 'economic efficiency'.

As more scholars started to study the goals of European, American, and Japanese antitrust laws,[46] the terms 'fair competition', 'substantial justice', 'freedom of competition', 'efficiency', and 'workable competition order' were frequently mentioned in academic papers. As for the goal of efficiency, Xianlin Wang, a well-known Chinese anti-monopoly scholar, stated that efficiency should be understood to be the overall efficiency of society, rather than individual efficiency, and that social efficiency would be realised by protecting workable competition.[47] However, Jiemin Sheng and Weiping Ye were among a handful of scholars who criticised the Chinese academic community's tendency to interpret the AML's goals through the lens of the Harvard School's workable competition theory; instead, they put forward the 'efficiency' advocated by the Chicago School as the ultimate goal of the AML.[48] The 'allocative efficiency' conceived by Robert Bork was also

45 Chundi Wang (王春娣), "Lun Fanlongduan Fa Lifa De Jiazhi Quxiang—Jianxi Weiruan Songan" (论反垄断法立法的价值取向—兼析微软讼案) [The Value of Antimonopoly Law Legislation: An Analysis of the Microsoft Lawsuit], *Contemporary Law Review* 12 (2001): 30; see also Xing Lu (逯星), "Lun Woguo Fanlongduan Fa Ying Caiqu De Yuanze" (论我国反垄断法应采取的原则) [A Study on the Principles of China's Anti-Monopoly Law], *Journal of Political Science and Law* 5 (2003): 44; see also Lei Shi (石磊), "Shilun Woguo Fanlongduan Fa De Jiazhi Quxiang He Yuanze" (试论我国反垄断法的价值取向和原则) [A Study on the Goal and Principles of China's Anti-Monopoly Law], *Journal of the Party School of CPC Jinan Municipal Committee* 3 (2003): 87; see also Wanyi Zhao and Jing Wei (赵万一，魏静), "Lun Woguo Fanlongduan Fa De Jiazhi Mubiao Jieding Ji Zhidu Jiagou" (论我国反垄断法的价值目标界定及制度架构) [A Study on the Definition of Goals and Framework of China's Anti-Monopoly Law], *Social Science Research* 1 (2006): 108; see also Meiling Hu and Peng Zhang (胡枚玲，张鹏), "Lun Fanlongduan Fa De Jiazhi Quxiang" (论反垄断法的价值取向) [A Study on Goals' Choosing forAntimonopoly Law], *Contemporary Manager* 1 (2006): 44; see also Hongwei Wu and Wei Wei (吴宏伟，魏炜), "Lun Fanlongduan Fa De Jiazhi Mubiao" (论反垄断法的价值目标) [A Study on the Goals of Antimonopoly Law], *The Jurist* 3 (2005): 92.

46 Bingyong Liu (刘兵勇), "Meiguo Fanlongduan Fa Jiazhi Mubiao De Bianhua" (美国反垄断法价值目标的变化) [Changes of US Antitrust Law's Goals], *Reality Only* 4 (2003): 43; see also Zongzhang Cheng (程宗璋), "LveLun MeiGuo FanLongDuan Fa JiaZhi QuXiang De YanBian" (略论美国反垄断法价值取向的演变) [On the Evolution of America's Anti-Monopoly Orientation], *Journal of Guizhou University of Technology (Social Science Edition)* 5 (2003): 55; see also Yue Guo (郭跃), "Meiguo Fanlongduan Fa Jiazhi Quxiang De Lishi Yanbian" (美国反垄断法价值取向的历史演变) [The Evolution of Value Orientation of American Antitrust Law], *The Chinese Journal of American Studies* 1 (2005): 77; see also Xianlin Wang (王先林), "Lun Fanlongduan Fa De Jiben Jiazhi" (论反垄断法的基本价值) [A Study on the Basic Value of Antimonopoly Law], *Journal of Anhui University (Philosophy and Social Sciences Edition)* 26 (2002): 15; see also Pengcheng Zheng (郑鹏程), "Oumei Fanlongduan Fa Jiazhi Guan Tantao—Jianping 'Zhonghua Renmin Gonghe Guo Fanlongduan Fa(Caoan)' Di Yitiao"(欧美反垄断法价值观探讨—兼评《中华人民共和国反垄断法（草案）》第一条) [Exploration of the Values of Anti-Monopoly Law in Europe and America: A Review of Article 1 of the Draft Anti-Monopoly Law of the People's Republic of China], *Studies in Law and Business* 117 (2007): 96.

47 Wang, *Ibid.*, at 18.

48 See Jiemin Sheng and Weiping Ye (盛杰民，叶卫平), "Fan Long Duan Fa Jia Zhi Li Lun De Zhong Gou—Yi Jing Zheng Jia Zhi Wei Shi Jiao" (反垄断法价值理论的重构—以竞争价值为视角) [On

introduced to the Chinese academic community and proposed as a way to prevent undue interference by the government.[49]

Besides the goal of efficiency, more scholars advocated that other goals ought to be given greater priority. For example, some argued that 'fairness' and 'justice' should take precedence over efficiency, not only because 'justice' suited the psychological demand of the Chinese public and the demand to maintain social stability, but also because those ideals were consistent with the socialist nature of China's political, legal, and economic systems.[50] Some opined that 'efficiency' should be subordinated to 'protecting interests', which covered public interests and consumer welfare.[51] Others stated that 'freedom' and 'fairness' should be the AML's fundamental goals, echoing the essence of the socialist market economy and dealing with the entrenched problem of the administrative monopoly in China.[52] Unfortunately, these studies did not delve into the question of whether the goals of 'freedom' and 'fairness' would conflict with each other and which should take priority.

In sum, in the early stage of research, the main theories about goals in the international antitrust community were brought to the attention of Chinese scholars and researchers. However, those studies were scattered and had not yet formed systemic theories, let alone a consensus about those concepts' implications or the ranking of those goals. Also, the scholars themselves were likely unsure about those goals' exact implications and scopes, so they normally mentioned several goals in their papers but did not carry out in-depth analysis about their relationships or potential overlaps or conflicts. Some even argued that the ranks of the AML's goals (such as efficiency, fairness, and security) could change along with social demand and economic conditions.[53] Moreover, considering the AML had not yet been enacted during that period, studies still remained at the theoretical level and could not draw upon practical data or enforcement cases.

---

the Reconstruction of the Theory of Legal Values of Anti-Trust Laws—Form the Angle of Values of Competition], *Modern Law Science* 27 (2005): 107.

49 See Weiping Ye (叶卫平), "Lun Fanlongduan Fa Shang De Xiaolv Jiazhi—Jianping Woguo Fanlongduan Fa Caoan Di Ershi Si Tiao" (论反垄断法上的效率价值——兼评我国反垄断法草案第二十四条) [A Study on the Efficiency Value of Anti-Monopoly Law: A Review of Article 24 of the Draft Anti-Monopoly Law of China], *Seeker* 5 (2007): 83.

50 Wang, note 46, at 19.

51 Wei Wang and Junjian Zhang (王巍，张军建), "Lun Woguo Fanlongduan Fa De Lifa Mudi" (论我国反垄断法的立法目的) [On the Legislative Purpose of China's Anti-Monopoly Law], *Social Sciences in Hunan* 1 (2006): 63, 65–66.

52 Zheng, note 46; see also Sijian Qi (漆思剑), "Fan Xingzheng Xing Longduan Shi Woguo Fanlongduan Lifa De Jiazhi Suozai" (反行政性垄断是我国反垄断立法的价值所在) [Anti-Administrative Monopoly is the Value of China's Anti-Monopoly], *Academics* 125 (2007): 207; see also Jian Li (李剑), "Fanlongduan Fa Lifa Jiazhi De Chongtu Yu Xuanze" (反垄断法立法价值的冲突与选择) [Conflicts and Choice of Value of the Antitrust Law in Legislation], *Journal of Harbin Institute of Technology (Social Sciences Edition)* 8 (2006): 42, 44.

53 Lei Yu (喻磊), "Zhongguo Fanlongduan Fa Jiazhilun" (中国反垄断法价值论) [Value Theory of China's Anti-Monopoly Law], *Jiangxi Social Sciences* 3 (2003): 151, 153.

5.2.1.2 The first 10 years of the AML (2008–2019): studies on more concrete issues

Compared to the early stage, a consensus was reached during this period that the AML should have multiple goals. The major debates between researchers during this period reflected the following issues.

First, the goal of 'freedom' was particularly stressed during this period. While the research had remained on a theoretical level in the previous period, AML enforcement now faced actual difficulties such as 'the AML's ineffective regulation of administrative monopolies, preferential treatment of state-owned enterprises (SOEs), excessive expansion of industrial policies, and marginalisation of the competition authority by other administrative authorities'.[54] Thus, weak enforcement actions against SOEs such as China Unicom and China Telecom and feeble deterrence of administrative monopolies led scholars to focus on the goal of freedom. They argued that 'there is no evidence of economic monopolies at present, but major damage is being caused to the market by administrative monopolies'.[55] Since the major problem of AML enforcement exposed at that time was the lack of freedom for competition and economic rationality,[56] the goal of freedom was advocated as the cornerstone of the AML, which was 'substantial freedom' (including the freedoms of capability and control) described by Nobel Prize-winning economist Amartya Sen.[57] Rather than improving economic efficiency, they argued that competition opportunities for SMEs and consumer welfare should be given greater priority in the AML goals system.[58]

Second, more in-depth studies were conducted about US antitrust law, especially the Chicago School's proposition that 'efficiency' should be treated as the single goal. Chinese scholars during this period studied foreign experience more rationally and cautiously than some scholars in early stages who had asserted that 'efficiency' should be the primary goal of the AML, even though they admitted the value of other goals.[59] Some researchers explored the ideological conflicts and political power struggles behind the debate over antitrust goals in the United States,[60] while others studied the evolution of US antitrust goals and revealed the close relationship between changes in those goals and social and economic

54 Weiping Ye (叶卫平), "Fanlongduan Fa De Jiazhi Gouzao" (反垄断法的价值构造) [Value Construction of the Antitrust Law], *China Legal Science* 3 (2012): 135, 136.

55 Zongxiang Xu and Lingfang Zhou (徐宗祥，周灵方), "Ziyou Youxian: Longduan Guizhi De Zhengyi Jiazhi Quxiang" (自由优先：垄断规制的正义价值取向) [Priority of Freedom: the Value of Justice in Monopoly Regulation], *Seeker* 11 (2012): 133, 135.

56 Ye, note 54, at 144.

57 Jian Li (李剑), "Lun Fanlongduan Fa De Jiazhi Quxiang" (论反垄断法的价值取向) [The Value in the Antitrust Law], *Law and Social Development* 79 (2008): 13, 20–21.

58 *Ibid.*

59 See Jiemin Sheng (盛杰民), "Jingzhengfa Zai Zhongguo: Xianzhuang Ji Zhanwang" (竞争法在中国：现状及展望) [Competition Law in China: Status and Prospects], *Economic Law Review* 1 (2000): 265.

60 See Yuling Wu (吴玉岭), "Meiguo Fanlongduan Fa De Jiazhi Zhuiqiu Jiqi Zhengyi beihoude Yishi Xingtai Chongtu" (美国反垄断法的价值追求及其争议背后的意识形态冲突) [The Value Pursuit of U.S. Antitrust Law and the Ideological Conflicts Behind the Controversies], *Journal of Capital Normal University (Social Sciences Edition)* 187 (2009): 57.

development.[61] Thus, Chinese scholars reconsidered the applicability of foreign experience to China and argued that the study of the AML's goals should be based on China's local conditions.[62] Some researchers supported the idea of 'pursing efficiency but also considering the protection of fairness'.[63]

Third, researchers stressed the importance of 'consumer welfare' as an independent goal. Some suggested that the AML and the Consumer Protection Law could be coordinated to effectively increase consumer welfare.[64] It was further argued that, together with the goals of protecting the free competition order and social welfare, protecting consumer welfare should be a core value of the AML that would include consumers' rights to choose commodities and free trade.[65] Others argued that setting consumer welfare as a central goal of the AML not only satisfied the AML's nature as an economic law (namely, a law based on the public interest), but also conformed to booming global consumer activities of the time.[66]

Fourth, these discussions also touched on more abstract conceptions, such as justice and ethics. One paper suggested exploring AML goals beyond the legal and economic fields, including ethical values like the pursuit of competitive justice.[67] Based on an analysis of high-profile cases of that time, such as the penalties on American company Qualcomm and Japanese manufacturer Hitachi, some argued that China's AML should be responsible for creating a fair competition environment and promote overall social benefit[68] and proposed adding procedural justice to AML enforcement.[69]

61 See Jian Li (李剑), "Lun Meiguo Fanlongduan Fa Jiazhi Mubiao De Bianqian" (论美国反垄断法价值目标的变迁) [A Study on the Change of the Goals of U.S. Antitrust Law], *Journal of the Party School of CPC Zhengzhou Municipal Committee* 100 (2009): 73, 73–74.

62 See *Ibid*; also see Ping Cao and Yiliu Wang (曹平，王一流), "Zhuangui Shiqi Woguo Fanlongduan Fa De Shishi: Duoyuan Jiazhi Mubiao De Chongtu Yu Xuanze" (转轨时期我国反垄断法的实施：多元价值目标的冲突与选择) [The Enforcement of China's Antimonopoly Law in the Transitional Period: Conflicts and Choices of Multiple Goals], *Social Sciences in Guangxi* 186 (2010): 79.

63 Xiang Zeng and Yandong Qu (曾翔，曲衍东), "Lun Woguo 'Fanlongduan Fa' De Jiazhi Quxiang" (论我国《反垄断法》的价值取向) [A Study on the Goals of China's Anti-Monopoly Law], *Price: Theory & Practice* 378 (2015): 40, 42.

64 See Bing Chen (陈兵), "Fanlongduan Fa Shishi Yu Xiaofeizhe Baohu De Xietong Fazhan" (反垄断法实施与消费者保护的协同发展) [Synergistic Development of Antimonopoly Law Enforcement and Consumer Protection], *Law Science* 9 (2013): 82.

65 Weicai Dai (代伟才), "Lun Fanlongduan Fa De Jiazhi Quxiang" (论反垄断法的价值取向) [A Study mn the Values of Antimonopoly Law], *Journal of Shanxi Police College* 17 (2009): 39, 40–41.

66 Shiqiang Chen (陈世强), "'Fanlongduan Fa' Dui Xiaofeizhe Liyi Baohu De Jiazhi Fengxi" (《反垄断法》对消费者利益保护的价值分析) [Analysis of the Value of Antitrust Law in Protecting Consumer Interests], *Foreign Economic Relations & Trade* 189 (2010): 86, 87.

67 Xiaoming Zhou and Yunqiu Yan (周晓明，颜运秋), "Lun Fanlongduan Fa De Lunli Jichu" (论反垄断法的伦理基础) [On the Ethical Basis of Antitrust Law], *Journal of Southwest University of Political Science and Law* 16 (2014): 20, 21–25.

68 See Hongzhen Chen (陈红振), "Cong Gaotong Gongsi Shou Xingzheng Chufa An Kanwoguo Fanlongduan Fa De Jiazhi" (从高通公司受行政处罚案看我国反垄断法的价值) [The Value of China's Antimonopoly Law From the Case of Qualcomm's Administrative Punishment], *Knowledge Economy* 20 (2015): 37.

69 See Zhanwei Zhu (朱战威), "Cong Xiaolv Dao Gongzheng: Jiazhi Zhuanhuanxia Fanlongduan Fa Zhifa Chengxu Zhi Shanbian" (从效率到公正：价值转换下反垄断执法程序之嬗变) [From

5.2.1.3 The AML's goals in the digital era (2020–present)

By the 2020s, China's digital market has enjoyed almost three decades of prosperity and rapid growth. Anti-monopoly enforcement has converted from prudence and restraint to active regulation and then back to a normalised regulation, given the exponential increase of market power by digital giants. The AML's role in regulating the digital sector has become a hotly debated point. New goals such as 'innovation' and 'consumer privacy' are frequently mentioned alongside the antitrust goals that have been traditionally discussed. Discussions about the AML's goals during this period present the following traits.

5.2.1.3.1 A CLEARER SENSE THAT CHINA IS EXPLORING ITS OWN PATH

Professor Xiaoye Wang, in her latest article, introduced the New Brandeis movement that has prospered in the United States and questions its claims about the decentralisation of private power, abandoning the goal of consumer welfare, and the 'curse of bigness'.[70] She also reminded Chinese decision makers to be cautious about so-called global regulation trends[71] and criticised the rigorous regulatory model adopted by the European Union in the Digital Market Act (DMA).[72] Following the EU model, Wang said, could hinder growth and innovation in China's digital economy.[73]

Former SPC Justice Xiangjun Kong warned that China should not blindly follow the current trend of American and European antitrust enforcement in the digital sector, but should clearly realise the macroscopic goal of China's AML.[74] According to Kong, there are always two levels to antitrust enforcement: the macro level, including political and policy analysis and judgements, and the micro level, focusing on economic and legal technical approaches.[75] The macro goals determine the AML's direction, function, and application, especially when facing challenges and new issues brought by the digital economy; and those goals also guarantee that law enforcement remains in line with China's national targets for the development of the digital economy.[76]

Efficiency to Fairness: Transformation of Antitrust Enforcement Procedures Under Value Changes], *Journal of Anhui University (Philosophy and Social Sciences Edition)* 6 (2015): 111.

70 See Xiaoye Wang (王晓晔), "Fanlongduan Xinsichao Xin Bulan Daisi Zhuyi Pipan" (反垄断新思潮新布兰代斯主义批判) [A Critique of the New Antitrust Thought New Brandeis School], *Law Review* 249 (2025): 26.

71 *Ibid.*, at 38.

72 See Xiaoye Wang (王晓晔), "Woguo Pingtai Jingji Fanlongduan Jianguan 'Oumeng Moshi' Pipan" (我国平台经济反垄断监管"欧盟模式"批判) [A Critique of the "EU Model" of Antitrust Regulation in China's Platform Economy], *Law Review* 245 (2024): 11.

73 *Ibid.*, at 24.

74 Xiangjun Kong (孔祥俊), "Lun Hulianwang Pingtai Fanlongduan De Hongguan Dingwei—Jiyu Zhengzhi, Zhengce He Falü De Fenxi" (论互联网平台反垄断的宏观定位——基于政治、政策和法律的分析) [The Orientation of the Anti-Monopoly Law Concerning Internet Platform From a Macro-Perspective: An Analysis Based on Politic, Policy and Legislation], *Journal of Comparative Law* 2 (2021): 85.

75 *Ibid.*, at 86.

76 *Ibid.*, at 86.

In addition, some are exploring the AML's contemporary mission in the digital era, claiming that it should be responsible for achieving economic democracy.[77] Others argue, in the digital era, that the AML should treat 'privacy protection' as a direct goal of the AML and incorporate privacy into the system of anti-monopoly analysis.[78] However, others oppose that proposition, maintaining that the AML is not the proper (or major) instrument for protecting privacy since intensive competition itself requires fuller use of data.[79]

5.2.1.3.2 SHOULD 'ENCOURAGING INNOVATION' BE AN INDEPENDENT GOAL OF THE AML?

'Encouraging innovation' was added as an independent AML goal in the 2022 amendment, which reflects the State's purpose of strongly supporting the development of new economic forms: namely, the digital economy and internet industry. This revision, however, generated fierce debate.

Professor Jianzhong Shi, an expert on AML revision, said the reason for making 'encouraging innovation' a goal of the AML is that 'AML enforcement should be changed from focusing on static efficiency and price fluctuation to dynamic efficiency and encouraging innovation'.[80] Furthermore, the goal of 'encouraging innovation' is not just a declaratory slogan or a subordinate goal, such as the goal of 'protecting competition'; rather, it has a binding effect as an independent AML goal.[81]

Other supporters agree that making 'encouraging innovation' a goal of the AML not only promotes the digital economy, but also coincides with common practices in both domestic and foreign antitrust practice.[82] China's internet market has already

77 Lizhi Ning and Tao Gong (宁立志，龚涛), "Shuzi Jingji Beijingxia Fanlongduan Fa De Shidai Shimin" (数字经济背景下反垄断法的时代使命) [The Contemporary Mission of Antitrust Law in the Context of Digital Economy], *Wuhan University Journal (Philosophy & Social Science)* 77 (2024): 135, 135–37.

78 Dong Yang (杨东), "Lun Fanlongduan Fa De Chonggou: Yingdui Shuzi Jingji De Tiaozhan" (论反垄断法的重构：应对数字经济的挑战) [A Study on Restructuring the Antimonopoly Law: Solutions for Challenges of the Digital Economy], *China Legal Science* 3 (2020): 206, 213.

79 See Jian Li (李剑), "Hulianwang Fanlongduan Neng Cujing Shuju Yingsi Baohu Ma?" (互联网反垄断能促进数据隐私保护吗？) [Can the Antimonopoly Law Improve Data Privacy in the Internet Industry?], *Journal of Business Economics* 355 (2021): 85.

80 Jianzhong Shi, ed. (时建中主编), "'Zhonghua Renmin Gongheguo Fanlongduan Fa' Zhuanjia Xiugai Jianyigao Ji Xiangxi Shuoming" (《中华人民共和国反垄断法》专家修改建议稿及详细说明) [*Proposed Draft Revision of the Anti-Monopoly Law of the People's Republic of China by Experts and Detailed Explanations*] (ZhongGuo Zhengfa Daxue Chubanshe 2020) (China University of Political Science and Law Press, 2020), 4.

81 Maozhong Ding (丁茂中), "'Fanlongduan Fa' Guli Chuangxin Guifan De Shiyong Guize Jiqi Lifa Biaoda" (《反垄断法》鼓励创新规范的适用规则及其立法表达) [Rules of Application of the Provisions of Encouraging Innovation in the Antimonopoly Law and Legislative Expression], *Social Sciences Digest* 7 (2024): 118, 118–19.

82 Bing Chen and Qian Cheng (陈兵, 程前), "Hulianwang Jingji Fazhan Dui Fanlongduan Fa De Tiaoshi De Yingxiang Ji Yingdui" (互联网经济发展对反垄断法调适的影响及应对) [Impacts of the Development of Internet Economy on the Adjustment of Antimonopoly Act and Solutions], *Journal of Liaoning Normal University (Social Science Edition)* 43 (2020): 51, 52.

exhibited features of highly dynamic innovation—including a low threshold to market entry and a short cycle of technological updates—that push digital companies to stay alert to competition pressure and keep pursuing innovation. The market structure of China's internet sector already reflects, to a large extent, the nature of competitive monopoly.[83] In the internet market, the 'innovation factor' has a more significant factor than the 'price factor' does in traditional antitrust law.[84]

Some commentators go on to say that adding 'encouraging innovation' to the AML's goals paves the way for reorienting the anti-monopoly analytical paradigm from 'price-centric' to 'innovation-centric'.[85] By that logic, damage to innovation should be incorporated into the current theory of competition injury, and decision makers should give more consideration to arguments that claim innovation as a defence and give more weight to granting an exemption when companies assert they have improved innovation.[86]

Undoubtedly, innovation has already been factored into China's anti-monopoly practice. In *Qihu v. Tencent* in 2013, the SPC noticed that competition in the internet market focused more on quality, services, and innovation than price. Thus, the Court concluded that Tencent, despite having a market share of more than 90%, did not enjoy dominance since competition in the relevant market was dynamic and full of pressure, including pressure from technological innovation.[87] In the *Seagate Technology/Samsung*[88] merger review case, Seagate acquired Samsung's hard drive business and filed pre-merger notification in 2011 with MOFCOM, one of the former AML agencies before 2018. MOFCOM concluded that the merger had anti-competitive effects and that hindering 'innovation' was a major effect of restricting and eliminating competition. Thus, despite approving that merger, MOFCOM imposed restrictive conditions. MOFCOM required Seagate to promise to make an annual R&D investment of at least USD 800 million for the next three years in the field of innovation, at the same rate as in recent years, to ensure that more innovative products and solutions reach customers.[89]

83 *Ibid.*, at 54.

84 *Ibid.*, at 54.

85 Jia Yuan (袁嘉), "'Fanlongduan Fa' Zhongde Guli Chuangxin Mubiao Yu Fanlongduan Fenxi Fanshi Gexin" (《反垄断法》中的鼓励创新目标与反垄断分析范式革新) [Encouraging Innovation in The Antitrust Law and Paradigm Shift of Antitrust], *Journal of Nankai University (Philosophy, Literature and Social)* 5 (2023): 96, 99.

86 *Ibid.*, at 100–1.

87 Beijing Qihoo Technology Co. Ltd. v. Tencent Technology (Shenzhen) Co. Ltd. and Shenzheng Tencent Computer System Co. Ltd. (北京奇虎科技有限公司诉腾讯科技(深圳)有限公司、深圳市腾讯计算机系统有限公司滥用市场支配地位纠纷案), (2013) Min San Zong Zi Di 4 Hao [(2013) Sup. People's Ct. Final Decision No. 4] (China), Wolters Kluwer, at 21–27.

88 Mofcom Anti-Monopoly Bureau, "Guanyu Futiaojian Pizhun Xijie Keji Gongsi Shougou Sanxing Dianzi Youxian Gongsi Yingpan Qudongqi Yewu Fanlongduan Shencha Jueding De Gonggao" (关于附条件批准希捷科技公司收购三星电子有限公司硬盘驱动器业务反垄断审查决定的公告) [Announcement of Antitrust Review Decision on Conditional Approval of Seagate Technology's Acquisition of the Hard Disk Drive Business of Samsung Electronics Co.], Mofcom Announcement No. 90 of 2011, *mofcom.gov.cn*, December 12, 2011, http://fldj.mofcom.gov.cn/article/ztxx/201112/20111207874274.shtml

89 *Ibid.*

Therefore, the debate on this issue is focused not on whether 'encouraging innovation' should be considered when enforcing the AML, but on whether 'encouraging innovation' should be an independent AML goal on an equal footing with other goals.

Professor Xiaoye Wang, who is opposed to making 'encouraging innovation' an independent AML goal, argues that the current goal of 'improving efficiency' adequately covers the purpose of 'encouraging innovation', so it is not necessary to set them apart.[90] More importantly, if 'encouraging innovation' is an AML goal, rather than a benefit derived from the goal of 'protecting competition', which should take precedence when goals conflict with each other?[91] In order to encourage innovation, should the government protect large enterprises (considering innovation normally requires large investments and high risks) or implement certain industrial policies (such as granting subsidies to innovative companies)?[92] All those measures would grant certain undertakings competitive advantages and meanwhile injure free competition. Other scholars present similar concerns. Adding the goal of 'encouraging innovation' to Article 1 will confuse legal interpretations and complicate the pursuit of different goals.[93] In addition, the evaluation of innovation requires AML enforcers to foresee a given behaviour's future impact, which is inherently uncertain. That makes it difficult to set an objective, unified, and coherent analytical framework for such an evaluation.[94]

5.2.2 Ideas for a future research agenda

It is of particular value to explore the AML's goals in the context of the digital economy since they can guide law enforcement, interpret abstract and general legal texts, and shape the image of antitrust law in society, especially when the era is full of market changes and booming technology. More than a hundred years ago, Americans had 'a deep feeling of unrest' and fear of 'another kind of slavery' when tremendous wealth was aggregated in the hands of a few corporations, like Standard Oil.[95] Nowadays, similar fears seem to be staging a comeback, when people's daily lives rely heavily on products owned by a couple of digital tycoons, from Tencent Meeting and WeChat Work in workplaces to assisted driving of electric

90 Xiaoye Wang (王晓晔), "Woguo Fanlongduan Fa Weishenme Baohu Jingzheng" (我国反垄断法为什么保护竞争) [Why Should the Anti-Monopoly Law Protect Competition?], *Research on Rule of Law* 4 (2024): 3, 8.

91 *Ibid.*, at 8–9.

92 *Ibid.*, at 9.

93 Lei Wang (王磊), "Chuanxin Mubiao Zai 'Fanlongduan Fa' Shangde Dingwei Yu Shixian—Jianping 'Fanlongduan Fa (Xiuzheng Caoan)' Di 1 Tiao" (创新目标在《反垄断法》上的定位与实现——兼评《反垄断法（修正草案）》第1条) [Positioning and Realisation of Innovation Objectives in the Anti-Monopoly Law—Comment on Article 1 of the Anti-Monopoly Law (Draft Amendments)], *Journal of CUPL* 87 (2022): 173, 176.

94 Jian Li (李剑), "Fanlongduan Fa Chuangxin Mubiao De Tiaozhan" (反垄断法创新目标的挑战) [Challenges to the Goal of Innovation in Antitrust Law], *Competition Law and Policy Review* 10 (2024): 9, 12.

95 Standard Oil Co. v. United States, 221 U.S. 1, 83, 83–84 (1911).

vehicles and grocery shopping and delivery apps in daily life. Many are scared that their lives would be completely disrupted and brought to a standstill if these digital apps were to break down one day. People are always afraid of the unknown. Thus, we expect that clear and definitive statements about the AML's goals would give us a sense of security.

However, defining the AML's goals is no easy job. As notions of the 'curse of bigness' and placing more responsibility on gatekeepers are becoming more prevalent in the international antitrust community, China's digital sector is contributing 42.8% of GDP as of 2023.[96] While Chinese people live with the fear of digital giants, competition in the digital market has not been stifled and continues to surprise the public. DeepSeek, launched before the Chinese New Year in 2025, has disrupted the AI sector like a blue whale, as its icon shows. With an investment of less than USD 6 million, the company poses a substantial threat to its powerful rival ChatGPT, whose annual spending exceeds USD 5 billion.[97] Pin Duoduo (also known as Temu), a small C2B e-commerce platform, was founded in 2015, when Alibaba and JD.com already dominated the e-commerce market. According to traditional antitrust theory, Pin Duoduo should have had little chance to survive, let alone defeat its mighty rivals. But by attracting a large number of price-sensitive users who live in small cities and rural areas, Pin Duoduo not only survived, but became the second-largest e-commerce platform, exceeding JD.com in 2019.[98]

Such examples of 'ants trying to shake a big tree' are not uncommon in the digital era, so it is worth considering whether the fear of 'bigness' people had a century ago is similar to our fear today. In a speech presented at the Boao Forum for Asia Annual Conference in 2023, Vice Minister of Industry and Information Technology Jiangping Wang said that

> At the early stage of the digital economy, if there is no legal prohibition, it means freedom. When the situation is unclear, it is better to 'let the bullet fly for a while'. However, the digital economy has boundaries, too. When problems arise, government regulators need to keep up and promptly improve laws, regulations, and the regulatory system.[99]

96 CAICT, "Zhongguo Shuzi Jingji Fazhan Yanjiu Baogao (2024 Nian)" (中国数字经济发展研究报告(2024年.) [Research Report on the Development of China's Digital Economy (2024)], *www.caict.ac.cn*, August 27, 2024, http://www.caict.ac.cn/kxyj/qwfb/bps/202408/P020240830315324580655.pdf, at 3.

97 Eduardo Baptista, "Explainer-What Is DeepSeek and Why Is It Disrupting the AI Sector?" *Reuters*, January 27, 2025, https://money.usnews.com/investing/news/articles/2025-01-27/explainer-what-is-deepseek-and-why-is-it-disrupting-the-ai-sector

98 "Pinduoduo Cheng Zhongguo Dierda Dianshang" (拼多多成中国第二大电商) [Pinduoduo Becomes China's Second Largest E-Commerce Company], *tech.sina.com.cn*, March 14, 2019, https://tech.sina.com.cn/i/2019-03-14/doc-ihrfqzkc3848948.shtml

99 Zhao Sun and Liling Huang (孙朝，黄莉玲), "Gongxingbu Fubuzhang Jiangping Wang: Shuzi Jingji Fazhan Chuqi Ningyuan 'Rangzidan Feiyifei'" (工信部副部长王江平：数字经济发展初期宁愿"让子弹飞一飞") [Vice Minister of MIIT Jiangping Wang: "Let the Bullets Fly" in the Early Developing Stage of the Digital Economy], *news.qq.com*, March 3, 2023, https://news.qq.com/rain/a/20230329A08WFD00

Therefore, it may be wiser for China to explore its own path rather than to blindly join in the global antitrust crusade against digital companies. In the following pages, I present two preliminary ideas, but more research will be needed in the future to explore them in greater depth.

5.2.2.1 Making 'freedom for competition' a central goal of the AML

Although it is undeniable that the AML's goals, just like antitrust laws in other jurisdictions, are inevitably and sometimes significantly influenced by political factors and industrial policy, we should never abandon our determination to keep AML enforcement within the legal framework. The mission of making AML enforcement more legalised and professional largely depends on a definitive statement of the AML's chief (or supreme) goal. While goals like 'overall social benefit', 'economic democracy', or 'promoting the development of the socialist market economy' are no doubt worthy targets for the AML to pursue, I am dubious about making any of them the AML's supreme goal. It is all too easy for such goals to be mingled with political and non-legal purposes.

I agree with some scholars' advocacy[100] of making 'protecting freedom for competition' the central goal of the AML. China had a long period of planned economy, and administrative monopolies and a paternalistic regulatory model still hinder AML enforcement even today. Making the freedom for competition the AML's most important goal is of great value for China. Freedom for competition requires substantial freedom, including the freedom to let undertakings have opportunities to compete and chances for development, which could essentially cover protecting SMEs, as the goal of fairness requires. But freedom has deeper implication than fairness. We need not grant SMEs special competitive advantages that may cause other kinds of unfairness; rather, the freedom of competition can guarantee all companies have a chance to compete, leading to a dynamic market and economic efficiency. Additionally, the freedom for competition should include procedural freedom, which means that market players and consumers have the freedom and opportunity to defend themselves, supervise the public enforcers, and raise objections against AML enforcement decisions. That requires AML enforcement to be more transparent and pay more attention to procedural issues.

In a word, making the freedom for competition the AML's supreme goal requires that decision makers trust the market mechanism and exercise caution about governmental interference. The attitude of 'let[ing] the bullet fly for a while' demands China's regulators to be confident and courageous toward challenges and difficulties.

100 For example, Xiaoye Wang and Jian Li advocate in their papers that protecting freedom for competition should be the core goal of the AML. See Jian Li (李剑), "The Value in the Antitrust Law," note 57; see also Xiaoye Wang (王晓晔), "Why Should the Anti-Monopoly Law Protect Competition?," note 90.

5.2.2.2 Being alert to the trend of 'pan-antimonopoly'

As discussed in Section 5.2.1, some scholars suggest that 'protecting consumer welfare' or 'protecting privacy' be made goals of the AML. While such goals may sound 'absolutely right', they may run the risk of blurring the AML's goals. We should stay alert to the trend of 'pan-antimonopoly'[101] and refrain from placing too much expectations on the AML.

First of all, protecting consumer welfare should not be a direct goal of the AML. Consumer welfare is a controversial concept in competition law. It has even been labelled the most abused term in modern antitrust analysis.[102] Although competition laws in most jurisdictions listed consumer welfare as one of their goals, most did 'not specifically define consumer welfare and appear[ed] to have different economic understandings of the term'.[103] In the digital era, the discussion about the relationship between consumer welfare and personal privacy makes the problem even more complex.

How should we define the consumer? If the consumer refers to anyone who uses commercial goods, it could apply to everyone, from common people to monopolists.[104] Here, the concept of 'consumer welfare' is actually replaced by 'social welfare'. In other words, the terms 'consumer welfare' and 'social welfare' blend together. When economic efficiency has increased, suspicious behaviour may be justified even though the money (that is, surplus welfare) has merely been transferred from the hands of ordinary people to monopolists' pockets. That is, a company could justify a problematic behaviour by proving that more economic efficiency can be generated from collecting and using personal data, rather than leaving it to consumers.

Some academics claim the definition of consumer welfare should be narrowed to individuals who consume economic goods. For example, Judge Robert H. Bork defines consumer welfare as the 'maximization of consumer wealth or consumer want satisfaction'.[105] In contrast, Lawrence A. Sullivan and Warren S. Grimes think that consumer welfare should involve maintaining allocative efficiency, preventing wealth transfers, and preserving consumer choice.[106] However, these definitions may cause confusion as well, when the AML is enforced in the digital sector. In the

101 In "Antimonopoly Issues in Platform Economy," an online seminar held by the China University of Political Science and Law on February 5, 2021, scholars such as Prof. Ping Lin and Xianlin Wang stated that we should be cautious about the trend of 'pan-antimonopoly', which mistakenly treats antimonopoly law as a panacea to solve all problems in the market.

102 Joseph F. Brodley, "The Economic Goals of Antitrust: Efficiency, Consumer Welfare, and Technological Progress," *New York University Law Review* 62 (1987): 1020, 1032.

103 Maurice E. Stucke, "Reconsidering Antitrust's Goals," *Boston College Law Review* 53 (2012): 551, 571.

104 *Ibid.*, at 573.

105 Robert H. Bork, "Legislative Intent and the Policy of the Sherman Act," *The Journal of Law & Economics* 9 (1966): 7.

106 Lawrence A. Sullivan and Warren S. Grimes, *The Law of Antitrust: An Integrated Handbook* (West Academic Publishing, 2006), 12–16.

digital field, almost everyone enjoys daily convenience and welfare brought by the development of technology, and consumers only need to give away part of their personal information (or privacy). If we treat consumer's privacy as the cost and the benefits of using online apps as the revenue, cost and revenue are very different for each individual. Everyone has varying expectations about, reliance on, and preferences for new technology, as well as divergent attitudes about the value of their personal data. That is very different from how the prices of goods are determined through supply and demand in the traditional market. Therefore, subjective terms (such as 'wealth', 'satisfaction', and 'consumer choice') of an uncertain scope will make it more difficult for the enforcers of anti-monopoly laws to delineate the boundary between regulation and free competition.[107]

To sum up, the AML cannot solve all problems in the market. Protecting consumer welfare and consumer privacy should not be the AML's direct goals, although they may be protected in the pursuit of other goals, such as improving economic efficiency or protecting competition. Nevertheless, laws such as the Consumer Protection Law and the Personal Information Protection Law should be the major instruments for protecting those interests.

5.3 Conclusion

Anti-monopoly regulation of the digital market is a cutting-edge topic at the present stage, as controversies, uncertainty, and inconsistency pervade the international anti-monopoly field. Despite China being a nascent antitrust jurisdiction, the challenges and problems it faces are just as many, and just as complex, as those faced by advanced antitrust jurisdictions, especially given the scope and exponential growth of China's digital market. Whenever new issues pop up in the digital market, we must identify and cut the Gordian knots to move forward. With that in mind, I have put some of those key 'knots' on the future research agenda: Solving conflicts within the competition law system, clarifying the AML's relationship to other laws, and defining the chief goal of the AML may help us address tricky and specific problems. Although sound answers have yet to be found, answers to these issues can help China find a regulatory path of its own, a path distinct from that of Europe and the United States. In the digital age, China's approach may become a quiet but vital force to shake up the seemingly unbreakable global antitrust order that has formed over the past century in advanced antitrust regimes.

107 Jingmeng Cai (蔡婧萌), "Dianfu Yu Tiaozhan: Chaoji Pingtai Fanlongduan Guizhi Zhi Tantao" (颠覆与挑战：超级平台反垄断规制之探讨) [Revolution and Challenge: A Study on the Anti-monopoly Regulation Over Super Platforms], *Journal of CUPL* 6 (2022): 257, 261.

Index

Note: Page numbers in *italics* indicate figures, **bold** indicate tables in the text, and references following "n" refer notes.

FSC
www.fsc.org
MIX
Papier | Fördert
gute Waldnutzung
FSC® C083411

Kolibri 360 GmbH
Ferdinand-Jühlke-Straße 7
99095 Erfurt, Deutschland
produktsicherheit@kolibri360.de